LEAF HOUSE

LEAF HOUSE

Days of Remembering

A MEMOIR BY

Ruth Engelmann

1817

HARPER & ROW, PUBLISHERS, New York

Cambridge, Philadelphia, San Francisco, London
Mexico City, São Paulo, Sydney

Though I have changed the names of all persons and most places, *Leaf House* is a faithful recounting of the life I knew as I grew up.

FIRST EDITION

Designed by Lydia Link

Library of Congress Cataloging in Publication Data
Engelmann, Ruth.
  Leaf house.
    1. Engelmann, Ruth. 2. Revier (Wis.)—Social life
and customs. 3. Finnish Americans—Wisconsin—Revier—
Social life and customs. 4. Revier (Wis.)—Biography.
5. Finnish Americans—Wisconsin—Revier—Biography.
I. Title.
F589.R36E533   977.5°2[B]   80-8201
ISBN 0-06-011282-4   AACR2

82 83 84 85 86 10 9 8 7 6 5 4 3 2 1

TO

Hugh, John and Deborah

ACKNOWLEDGMENTS

I am deeply grateful to my editor, Ann Harris, for her invaluable criticism and her enduring patience. I am indebted to my parents, to my sister and to my brothers for sharing their recollections, to my husband for his aid and counsel and to my friend Iris Saunders for her secretarial assistance.

LEAF HOUSE

1

I WAS BORN ON A SNOWBOUND DAY in the small village of Revier, six miles northwest of Hadley, Wisconsin, seven miles northwest of Woodland, Michigan, and three hundred thirty miles northwest of Milwaukee. The distance to Lake Superior at its closest point was a pleasant three-mile ride.

The village is only a memory now. The loggers have left, the farmers have died, and the houses and barns, except for a few, have burned or crumbled to the ground. The scrub trees have grown back on the meadows and fields; the bears, wolves and skunks have returned. In another decade, perhaps two, all evidence of human labor expended on that rock-strewn earth will be obliterated.

At the busy time of my birth, however, there was a train stop, a post office in one of the farmhouses near the railroad tracks, a grade school, a population of seventy-five, give or take a few, a logging camp with a population all its own and an annual snowfall of two hundred inches. Usually the snowfall was above that, but no one kept count after the twenty-first of March, and the snow continued to fall until May. It still does—every year.

I had two names, one Finnish, Maria Ruutti Muurari, and the other English, Mary Ruth Morgan. The latter was legal, the former good for nothing outside our Finnish village. My father also had two names—one for the stiff-tongued English-speaking folk and one for the stiff-tongued Finnish. My brothers had two names as well and so did my sister. We all had other names too; good and bad nicknames in Finnish, and good and bad nicknames in English. Thus, in all, we had six names apiece.

But whatever anyone called us, we kept our English names foremost in our heads. My parents were pleased with the names they had chosen for us and insisted upon our using the proper form. Even Grandmother made an effort to pronounce our English names, though we forgave her when she forgot and called us Jussi or Kalle, Liisa or Maria, Etvartti or Olavi, and we forgave other Finnish-speaking people too. But we didn't forgive each other and we didn't forgive our classmates. We were English in name no matter how much we prattled in Finnish. So were our parents. Mother was Louise Katharine Harper Morgan. Father was John Paul Morgan. Before my mother was born, her father had changed his name to Harper so that his child would have the advantage of an English name. Though my father had to change his name himself, he was no less proud of it.

My parents say that I began to speak clearly and to walk confidently when I was nine months old and that until the age of six I was so earnest I was exactly like my maternal grandmother, who was seventy-five. I always felt that as a small child I was obedient, gentle and tearful; and that after I went to school, I became disobedient and belligerent and full of laughter. Was it true? I don't know. Mother and Father said that I was always an agreeable child, full of fun and laughter once I stopped being earnest. But they were loyal, as good parents always are.

Our home was in the wilderness—a rugged, lovely place. The house was surrounded by meadow, pasture and forest, and way beyond them were the hills, glacier-formed mounds which sheltered us from summer storms. They were green hills on a clear day in summer; purple when the clouds swept across the sky and cast their shadows on the land. They were white hills in springtime when the wild cherry and plum burst into bloom; red and gold in fall when the maples and birches changed color. And when the sky was low and the snow lay deep on the ground, they were the sad gray hills of winter. The hills of my childhood. Beyond them lay the oceans, the foreign lands, and the cities I wanted to see when I was old enough to leave my village.

From the south flowed the Montfer River, bordering our farm

on the east and north, and separating it from the alien soil of Michigan. The river shrank and grew with the seasons, from a muddy creek to a lake cutting across road and field and filling the night with its liquid sounds. Beside the river was our sauna, built of logs, and our barn, half log, half board; west of the barn stood the outbuildings and the house. To the north was the woodlot of scrub pine, cedar, wild cherry and plum, a few oaks and elms, and a whole stand of poplars full of ants. Beyond the woodlot was the Northfield, adjacent to the river.

Crops grew well there in the Northfield, for the rich black earth, protected by trees on the east and the west and by a steep hill across the river, was a natural hotbed. It was our clearing, cut out of the jungle, heated by the sun and moistened by the fogs rising from the Montfer—the Mississippi, the Amazon, the Nile of our childhood.

Coming from the shade of the woodlot to that tilled patch of ground sent a chill to the spine. What wild creature would leap and flee at the sight, the sound and the smell of a child? What wild bird would beat its frantic wings? Sometimes a crane rising out of the river; sometimes a deer fleeing across the field, rarely a bear or wolf. Nothing more. Never a tiger; never a lion. Of course not. But why not?

Back along the path through the woodlot, back to the safety of barn and sauna, back to the house.

Yes, the house.

To the south of it, past the sauna, along the winding river, ran the road through a pastureland of hazelnut and huckleberry, over the Soo Line railroad tracks and across a piece of land that was ours but wasn't quite, because Father had given it to a widow with four children. There our road ended and the township road began, stretching through the village of Revier for a mile and a half to the east and to the west. At the crossing of our road and the township road stood our mailbox, with JOHN P. MORGAN printed on its side. He was the father of us all—John, Carl, me, Elizabeth, Edward and, later on, Oliver and any other child who decided to live with us for a while.

Our house was intended to be a stable, strong enough to hold horses as big as elephants, to hold feed and harness and wagons. A stable needs no basement, no bathroom, no porches with rail-

3

ings, no dormers, and we had none. A stable could use running water, but we had a pump in the front yard, a sturdy pump which brought up the coldest, clearest, sweetest water in all the world, except in winter, when the water table fell out of reach. Then we had to melt the clean white snow which lay so deep in our yard that we could build igloos and snow caves in which we sat until we froze into polar bears and came out growling.

Grandmother planted flowers around the house. The pansies were as big as saucers and the roses like small cabbages, and once a sunflower grew taller than the house. We had a basswood tree, and under it a cooler box filled with sawdust in which barrels of ice-cold water from the well were buried. We had a fir tree full of chickadees, a lilac full of wrens, and a mile of clothesline for the birds to swing upon.

The steps leading to the covered porch were dotted with nails which I had pounded in when I was three. Bursting with stove wood, milk cans, water buckets, skis, sleds, skates, bits of rope and, sometimes in winter, a quarter of beef, the porch leaned away from the house a little. Still, it was a porch and whatever it held did not have to be in the kitchen, which was already as crowded as a ship ready to sail.

We had an enormous cookstove with a reservoir for hot water, a kitchen cabinet, a table large enough to seat twelve, another big storage cabinet, a woodbox, a cream separator, a worktable, a rocking chair to rock babies in, Grandmother's spinning wheel and Father's shoemaking machine, which stood under the higher section of the slanted staircase leading to the attic. Up there the older boys and Hank, the hired man, slept, and any other men or boys who needed a place to sleep. On the landing we kept our dirty clothes; under the landing, our boots and rubbers.

Behind the kitchen was the bedroom, filled with beds: a bed for my parents, a bed for Grandmother, a bed for my sister and me and small beds for my little brothers. Mother's sewing machine was there too, covered with a cloth, a table covered with flowering plants, an oleander tree which once had forty-one blossoms, two dressers, a long clothes rack and a box stove.

That was my home for eighteen years of my life and so I remember it. But before I had any memory of our place, the meadow was woodland; the Northfield a stand of virgin hardwood. After Father cleared the land, he built the barn and the outbuildings, but he never had the time nor the money to make the stable into a real house with separate rooms, with porches and railings and dormers, with bathrooms and running water.

When I stood on the nail-dotted steps and looked out across the meadow I could see the house of my godparents, the Kaaris, and beyond that, on a rise, the Revier School. The morning sun set its windows on fire and burned it down over and over, but it stands there still though it has been a house and not a school for three decades and more.

From the steps of our house I could see the purple hills where I was made. There in a tiny shack among the blooming cherry and plum, I was put together and later when the snow began to fall, I was brought down in a black satchel. My sister, an apple-cheeked, dark-haired angel of a child, came in a box with the midwife. The doctor had brought my two older brothers because at that time my parents were living in town. My younger brother, Edward, just came. One day he wasn't; the next day he was, a thin, blue scrap of flesh wrapped in a blanket and tucked into a shoe box. When he cried, his tongue quivered in the dark cavity of his mouth. My youngest brother came normally; I was eleven years old then.

I remember that black satchel, and even coming out of it, bald and sucking my toe. "You can't remember," said my older brothers.

"Yes, I can. I remember everything. I remember wearing my christening dress and crawling up the stairs and a big dog came out of the door."

They ran off laughing into the summer sunshine.

"That was Father's satchel," said Mother, "and you did suck your toe but you weren't bald."

Yet if I wasn't bald I could not have been far from it, for I remember the baldness as I remember the christening dress which, Mother said, I wore until I was two. I remember a fire close to the house; I remember rocking my sister in her cradle when her face was no bigger than my doll's. To reach the cradle, I had to sit on Grandmother's trunk which she had brought from Finland. I remember odd tatters of feeling. I remember sights, sounds and snatches of conversation.

5

"Close your eyes, Mary! Don't look. Walk forward slowly," says Carl.

I do, and fall into a tub of cold water.

Carl and I are sitting on the stairs. "Look, Mary." He has the Sears, Roebuck catalogue opened to the women's dresses. "These ladies are so high-toned they don't even go to the toilet."

"Why?"

"They've been to school," says Carl.

"You're crazy," says John. "Everyone goes to the toilet!"

John runs around in a circle. Around and around, sounding like a car going up a hill. He stalls, backs up and then turns to crank the motor. The car starts and he goes up, up, up the hill.

"Where are you going, Johnny?"

"To Lake Superior."

"Wait for me!" And I run after him.

I remember my sister at breast, dawdling, sucking, then turning away to smile at me with her milk-filled mouth. "Eat, baby. Halli's coming, and he'll eat it all." Halli was our neighbor's black romping dog.

Babies at breast, then on Father's knee, then beside Father. Mother suckled the babies; Father fed the children. Grandmother rocked the babies to sleep during the day; Father rocked the babies in the evening. Whoever came to the house held the children, sang to the children and played with the children.

I remember sitting beside Father in the horse-drawn buggy and riding across the field, and again in our first car, a Model T. A horse will stop; a car won't. Not when one is just learning to drive. The car goes up the green meadow and down until Matt Kaari, my godparents' son, runs over, jumps on the running board and pulls the brake.

I loved Matt. Matt was sixteen. He had big ears and a red face.

"He's too old for you," said my brothers.

"He is not."

I told Matt that I would marry him and after that he wouldn't come over to visit us. A few years later, he and his brother went to Russia to help all the poor people who were starving.

"He ran away from you," said Carl.

"Don't be foolish," said Grandmother to him and then to me.

Matt never came back; his brother did, but no one said anything about Matt, the boy I wanted to marry.

I remember Mother's porcelain mustard dish, sealed to a saucer. The cover has a cutout for the spoon. The spoon, the cover, the dish and the saucer are covered with forget-me-nots. I want the dish and I ask Mother if I might keep it. Then the cover drops, I try to catch it, then the spoon drops and then the whole dish. I see the slivers of porcelain on the floor. Afterward Mother rocks me and sings a song about the sunrise in a voice so high and clear and sweet my throat begins to ache.

I remember my sister sitting in the yard. The sheep comes over and butts her. I scream because I am afraid of the sheep, the chickens, the bees and even the flies. My sister is afraid of nothing. She has the sharpest teeth in the world and she bites. I run away when she bares her teeth, but John makes her close her mouth when she does that and Carl runs to get a spoon and sticks it into her mouth. "Bite, Elizabeth!"

Father is building something in town. Every evening we run to the gate near the sauna and jump in the car so we can ride the hundred feet to the house. Edward sits as close to Father as he can. Next to him sits Elizabeth. John, Carl and I ride in the back. I like to lean out of the car because I like the wind in my face. Once I fell out and Father didn't know. He drove over me. Father and Mother were so frightened that I didn't cry. My legs hurt, my stomach hurt, my back hurt, but I said nothing hurts because it wasn't Father's fault. It was mine. Sometimes Carl says, "She's leaning again!" Then I'm in trouble. I have to sit way back with my feet straight ahead of me. I can't feel the wind in my face and I can't see anything. "Would you rather fall under the car?" John asks.

Father brings Cracker Jacks in his lunchbox and sometimes he brings apples and oranges. Every day he has something different. Even a sandwich tastes good if it has been in Father's lunchbox all day long.

But the baldness. My sister lost her dark baby hair. Fine white hair grew in, just like mine, and we were two bald little girls. "Wash their heads with whiskey," someone said. Whiskey? On a child's head?

"Cow's urine makes the hair grow," said Uncle Eric.

"Cow's urine!" We don't want cow's urine even if we never have hair. Mother assures us that cow's urine will not go on our heads.

Everyone else has hair: John, a mat of reddish blond hair, Carl, heavy blond hair, and Edward, long yellow curls. Only Elizabeth and I have "poor" hair and people say, "Isn't it terrible? On girls especially."

"Look at Ingrid's hair."

"Look at Ethel's hair."

"Look at Helen's, Elvi's, Elsie's, Martha's, Taimi's hair!" Hair, hair, everywhere.

And Aunt Harper has a bushel of hair on the top of her head. When she took it down, it was down to her waist, down to her ankles, down to the floor and out the door, into the street, down the hill, into the valley.

"What's wrong with their hair?" asked Aunt Mandy, Cousin Otto's wife. "It's nice hair."

Nice Aunt Mandy, smelling of soap. She always brings sacks of clear soap, pink, yellow and green, for the sauna. It's good soap, but it hurts my face and hands and I can't stand it. Still, Aunt Mandy is soft and round and fat, and I like to lean on her. It's like leaning on a pillow.

Our hair grows and Mother braids it. It comes out of the braids, stands on end, and Mother combs it with water.

"If you cut it off, it'll grow in strong," says an uncle, and off comes the hair.

The hair grows in the same as before, but now no one worries. Now my aunt and uncle have a baby girl as bald as a snowball, and their older girl's hair has turned white and stands on end. I see a lot of white heads and no one thinks about hair anymore.

In the summer of 1920, in the middle of a busy haying season, I was baptized Maria Ruutti—Maria in honor of Maria Elisabet and Maria Fredriga, my maternal and paternal grandmothers, and Ruutti in honor of the Biblical Ruth, whose story my mother loved. Pastor Anderson, my step-grandfather, a self-proclaimed missionary in the Finnish Apostolic Lutheran Church, performed the deed with the help of a gold glass fruit bowl which later served the same purpose in the naming of my sister and my two younger brothers. Because they squirmed, kicked and protested their forced entry into the Christian community, I believed I could remember my own baptism as painful. But it had not been; my parents said I slept peacefully through the ceremony.

The glass bowl stood on a special shelf in the kitchen along with a porcelain clock with red roses framing the dial. Behind the two were the baptismal certificates, wrapped in brown paper, covered with a layer of dust which Mother blew off when she took down the rolls proclaiming our significance and individuality. Under the brown paper was a sheet of brittle tissue paper and under the tissue, the certificates tied with a white ribbon.

The preparation for the untying and unrolling of each document, two feet long and a foot wide, was a tedious process and hence seldom undertaken. First, Mother had to clear the kitchen table, wash it and then dry it with a clean towel. Then she had to wash her hands and dry them. Only then would she take down a roll at a time. She'd untie the ribbon, roll out the certificate, first one way and then the other to straighten it. One by one, she'd lay them on the table, flatten them with the palm of her hand and say at last, "There they are!"

There they were indeed! In all their rose-columned, angel-bottomed, Gothic-lettered glory.

Sometimes she'd take down the bowl too, wash and dry it and place it on the table. We touched its smooth inside. We stroked its rough rose-covered outside and wondered how it would feel to put one's head into it.

Then Mother read each of the documents, the eight godparents of each, and the twelve of mine. I had the bonus of four because Pastor Grandfather, Father's stepfather, thought it unseemly that I should have been allowed to go unbaptized until I was ready to talk, and Father replied by gathering together all the neighbors who were not harvesting hay. Mother said I'd have been christened earlier had the winter not come so soon after I was born and had Pastor Grandfather come to visit, but the storms had come and he had not.

After we had studied the certificates, Mother put them back behind the clock, which at that time was still running and striking the hours, the half hours and quarter hours. Many years later at the unholy hour of midnight, that clock began striking and would not stop. Soon we were all awake and waiting in the kitchen. We waited and watched while the mad porcelain clock banged away. No one ever bothered to wind it again, though I kept telling Father that the clock had probably "cured." I knew it hadn't, but I wanted another night of mindless laughter. For us, the heedless young, because Grandmother did not laugh. She was too old to find such a thing funny.

Besides, that rose-covered clock was Grandfather Harper's wedding gift—a young man's gift of love and roses. What unearthly meaning did that midnight gong convey to Grandmother? What did it say? Was Grandfather's lonely spirit moving through our house? Perhaps. We couldn't ask, because such matters were private. So we foolish children, awakened from sleep, laughed until our sides ached in the cold dark hours of winter.

Grandmother was an austere soul, not given to easy laughter in any case. Sometimes she smiled, a tentative, fleeting ghost of a smile, and then she was serious again. And she wanted us to be serious too.

"Speak Finnish," she'd say, "even if you speak only one word a day," and since we liked to talk, we had to speak Finnish to her, and to anyone who spoke Finnish to us.

Later on, if we complained about anyone, she told us to be more understanding. "There are many flowers in the garden of our Lord. Don't condemn others for being what they are." She never did; we could not. "Mind your own spirit," she'd say.

If we complained about work, her invariable answer was: man was not placed upon this earth to sit idle and useless. She had worked hard all her life and she hoped God would give her the strength to work until she died.

"Don't you ever get tired, Grandma?" I'd ask her.

"Yes, I get tired, but I'd rather feel tired than lazy."

She had never gone to school, but she had taught herself to read and read the Finnish newspapers regularly. She could not write, however, and this disability hurt her sense of dignity and human worth. When she was very young and her hands still nimble, she had not had the time; now they were stiff and would not bend to do her bidding. Thus, when we complained about schoolwork, she gave us no comfort. "Learning will never lead you astray," she'd tell us. And all through my years at home, as we sat doing our homework at the big table under the kerosene mantle lamp in the kitchen, there was Grandmother right beside us, carding the wool from her sheep, placing the soft rolls into paper boxes, spinning the rolls into yarn and then knitting it into stockings and mittens, and crocheting it into petticoats which scratched my legs all winter long.

It was Grandmother who filled our ears with the sound of the sea from her seaside village in Finland. It was she who told us of sailing ships, of lighthouses, storms and lost fishermen, and of lonely widows standing on the shore, their eyes fixed on the horizon. Her brother was always in the lighthouse; he kept the lights shining in the Finnish night, and brought to shore whatever was riding the waves and not below in the cold green water of the sea.

He had been a member of the Palace Guard for the Czar of Russia, and when he looked at us from the oval frame above Grandmother's bed, he *was* the Czar—or at least a general. Grandmother was proud of him, proud of his guarding the palace and keeping the lighthouse, and proud of his going away and coming back.

After Grandfather Harper died, Grandmother had wanted to go back to the seaside town she had left when she was forty years old, but my mother, fifteen, born in America and devoted to her cousins, didn't want to leave.

"Someday I'll go back," Grandmother would say to us.

I'd become excited by the mere thought of her going back to see the lighthouse, the stormy sea, her brothers and her sisters.

"Why don't you go right now, Grandma?" I'd ask. "Then you can come back. We'll save the wool from the sheep, and I'll water the flowers and feed the chickens." Feeding the chickens was the supreme sacrifice. I could not bear their squawking and flapping.

Grandmother said nothing, just sighed and went on with her spinning.

She loved the earth, the sky, and all living things. To her, the universe was one whole, unseparated into animate and inanimate, plant and animal. She tended the earth with loving care; she planted seeds by the phases of the moon; she watched the sky for its omens of storm. And when she worked with animals, she talked to them softly as if she were sharing secrets.

"They don't understand, Grandma," I'd say.

"They understand," she said.

11

They must have. The animals followed her sedate form from barn to house, from house to woodlot, from woodlot to sauna, first the cats, then her favored chickens, then the ducks, the dogs, and finally the wobble-kneed calves. She was like a queen followed by a long parade of her courtiers. And her plants responded too. Everything grew as nowhere else in the whole village: roses, pansies, Canterbury bells, gladioli, primroses, moss roses, asters and dahlias; and Finnish flowers, English flowers, Italian flowers, Polish flowers and Swedish flowers, all from neighboring enclaves of immigrants, to whom growing flowers was a way of bringing a feeling of home to the alien American soil.

Grandmother wore long gathered skirts with tight waistbands, and long-sleeved blouses buttoned in front, with rows of tucks on either side of the buttoning. When she went to church in wintertime, she put on a black wool serge dress, a long black plush coat and a thin black wool scarf; in summertime, a shining black poplin dress with a short matching coat, and a thin white scarf. She sewed her own clothes, including undergarments, always in the same pattern and always carefully.

I loved Grandmother as one loves a familiar rock, unyielding, durable and permanent. I could rest my frail body against hers, feel her solidity, her imperturbability, and give nothing at all, just rest as I might against a wall or mass of stone. She'd say nothing; she'd go on spinning or carding her wool or making her quilts.

But in the evening when it was time for bed, I'd whisper into her white shell of an ear, "Grandmother, I want to go to bed," and she'd set aside her work, come with me, and we'd lie on her big soft quilt-covered bed, and she'd tell me stories about working by the light of the midnight sun, of the Laplanders and the reindeer, of gypsies riding their horses through her town, of name days and saint's days, and of the waves which sang her to sleep when she was a girl no bigger than I.

I never saw her grieve or weep, and I never heard her voice raised in anger, but I saw her pride. She was aware of her appearance, of her good hearing and eyesight, and she had a right to be. We children were deaf when we were out at play, and showed every sign of becoming as nearsighted as the bats which swooped at the clouds of mosquitoes at night. She was conscious of her straight back and her strength; at eighty-five, she would still, with one swift swing of an ax, chop in two a block of hardwood. With the same ease she would lift a hundred-pound sack of grain and empty it into the storage bin, hoe a field or turn the earth with her shovel.

One could not help her without implying that she was weak. Sometimes when she had a bad cold, Mother insisted that she stay indoors. Yet after a day or two of rest, Grandmother had had enough coddling; she'd put on her coat and scarf, and go out to chop an armload of stove wood.

She had come to America in the middle years of her life, after she had raised her family of siblings, left motherless when Grandmother herself was still a young girl. When they were grown, she worked for years as a housekeeper on a large estate, and only then, at the pleading of a younger sister, did she decide to leave Finland. They came to Woodland, Michigan, where she met Grandfather, eleven years younger than she and much softer and easier in his ways. And then at forty-six, she gave birth to my mother.

Grandmother was thoughtful, humane, and kind in an unsentimental way, but to idealize her is to do her an injustice. She was totally ignorant of the modern world, its politics as well as its science and medicine. She used exotic medications to cure her ailments; she rubbed a strange potion on the babies' legs and ribs to prevent rickets. She prepared the newly freshened cows some special concoction of hot water, coffee, liniment, molasses and black pepper. Once out of curiosity I tasted the brew, and I didn't envy the cow. After drinking a bucket full to the brim, she could not possibly feel anything at the back end because her front end would be on fire.

Grandmother was superstitious. The bark of a dog, the hoot of an owl, the howl of a wolf in the forest on a winter night, had deep and subtle meanings to her, meanings lost to us. And when we asked her about them, she'd say, "They're just old-time tales," quietly, almost sadly, as if she no longer totally believed in them either but had nothing to put in their place. Then she'd go on with her spinning and we with our studies—in English, which Grandmother never learned well enough to let herself speak when we were present.

When we listened to Grandmother, we could not say for certain if we were Finnish children in America or Finnish children in Finland. The ocean disappeared and the lands merged. It was Father who placed us squarely where we were. He always spoke English to us, and brought the expanding outside American world with him when he talked about the railroads and factories, the shops and the stores where he had worked to make a living. And he talked of hauling timber with teams of horses, and he talked of the mines.

When I was young, I thought of the holes going down, down, down into the very middle of the earth. There the men hunched in the caves and looked for iron with their carbide lamps. I remember the smell of carbide, because Uncle Eric worked in the mine. His hands were red with iron dust and his face was whitish. "A miner never sees the sun," someone said, but I don't know who it was. All we knew was that Father wouldn't go there. Not our father. Mother would never allow it, nor would Grandmother.

"In the iron mines, there were always accidents," Father said. "When a man was killed, he was brought to the surface and the rest went on with their work. The shifts were long, ten and twelve hours, one day shift, one night shift. Who knows how many died down there? There were so many, and the men kept coming by the boatload from Europe, and down into the iron mines."

My father's father lived through several accidents, and then at the age of twenty-five—when he was the father of two, my father and Aunt Taimi, and of Aunt Tilta, still unborn—he became ill and died four days later. Other men died too, all of typhoid fever from the drinking water down in the mine. Not long after, Grandfather's brother became ill too; he could no longer breathe the close air underground. He died of silicosis and pneumonia. So did my mother's father and his brother. All of them, still in their teens and early twenties, had come to Woodland, Michigan, in the 1880's to work in the iron mines.

"There wasn't a family who didn't lose someone, and in some the losses were doubled and tripled," Mother said. "If it wasn't a cave-in, it was some other accident. And if that didn't take the men, disease did."

Though the work was much safer now, the mine whistle was still a call of death. When the whistles didn't stop there was a major disaster below, and when the dead were brought up, the whistles blew again, one long wail of grief. I thought I remembered the church bells ringing too, filling the air with their dirge, but my brothers say they remember only the whistles. It may be that the bells were silent and the sound was in my head, for we all feared the mines. There was no way we could forget; the old men we knew coughed and struggled for breath; they were stooped and bent before their time. Still, they had earned enough to pay for their rock-strewn farms, and compared to the others they were lucky.

Father was born in 1891, in the small house his father had rented and then bought just before he died. For six years his mother ran a boardinghouse for miners; she was a midwife too and a bonesetter, skilled in both trades, for she had been well trained in Finland when she was a girl. "She set human bones and animal bones, even horses' legs," Mother said. "People say she was better than the doctors." She may well have been; doctors there seemed to have little interest in setting bones properly, particularly the bones of immigrants.

Being the oldest child, Father had responsibilities early. He had learned English from the English-speaking miners and to his delight, he could often translate for his mother, who spoke her own variant of Finnish-English. Once when he was five, his mother sent him to the grocer to ask for "motness stew."

Father doubted the sense of it. "There's no such thing as 'motness stew.' "

"There is," his mother insisted. "Just ask for two pounds 'motness stew.' "

"It's wrong," he said, but he went to the store. He waited and waited, listening to the women as they asked for meat, eggs and other groceries. Finally a woman came in and inquired about mutton. "For roast or stew?" asked the grocer.

"Mutton for stew," said the woman.

There was his mother's "motness stew." He waited until the woman was finished ordering and then said loudly, as if he'd intended to do so right along, "I want two pounds of mutton for stew."

Father said he liked going to school, though the teachers were often too handy with the ruler. One day it was his turn; he was in the first grade and had fallen asleep at his desk. His teacher hit him on the head with the metal-edged ruler; Father woke up, went to the cloakroom, picked up his cap and went home, and told his

15

mother that if that's the way people are treated in school, he wasn't going there again. The next day he had the measles. When he recovered, he was ready to go back, he said, because he wanted to read more than he feared the ruler.

A few years later, his mother married the preacher who christened me, a man so imbued with the thought of going to heaven that he was hardly aware of the ground he walked upon. He was strict and Father, having grown up rather freely, must have had a difficult time with his stepfather, whose understanding of the bright and questioning young was always limited. Grandmother, an independent and determined woman, defended her son, but God's will, as defined by the preacher, prevailed in the household.

After several years, the family moved to a farm in Marengo, Wisconsin. Father said he could pick wild raspberries in the thickets there, sometimes twenty-five quarts a day, and at ten cents a quart he made more money than a grown man working a ten-hour shift. But, he said, he was always happy when school began, because study was easy for him. His stepfather, however, had no use for learning outside of the Bible; at thirteen, Father's school days were over. His stepfather found him a job at a brick mill, where he worked a ten-hour day for one dollar, out of which he received a small allowance. The next year he worked on the railroad and made a dollar fifty a day, and again he got an allowance, which he saved so he could buy a .22 rifle. When he had enough saved, his stepfather took the money. Since God had no guns in heaven, man needed none on earth.

At sixteen, Father left home to work in a country store. His hours were long, from seven in the morning until eight in the evening, but he earned room and board plus thirty dollars a month. He was now a man; he could spend his money as he wished. He bought himself a suit of clothes, a shotgun from Montgomery Ward for $3.98, and a horse-drawn mower for his mother so that she would not need to do the haying by hand. His stepfather refused to use the mower, however. God did not approve of machines because they induced laziness. Angered by his stepfather's rigidity and worried about his mother, who now had a new family of two young boys, Father quit his job at the store and came back to the farm to help his mother with the haying.

When the haying was done, he had to find a way of leaving

again. What should he do and where should he go? Then he read an advertisement about railroading, and learning through correspondence courses. All one needed to do was to apply and send a money order. First, however, he'd change his name from Muurari to Morgan. After that, he'd surely succeed. He passed the course and was offered a job as a boilermaker's helper for the Illinois Central Railroad. He was seventeen and Freeport, Illinois, an exciting place to see. For two years he worked and waited to get the job of brakeman which he had been promised if he worked hard. Finally he discovered that he would have to wait until he was twenty-one. He was now nineteen. Two years was too long for him to wait. He quit his job and found a better one at a buggy factory.

In the two years he worked there, he saved $650—a fortune. He bought $250 worth of oil stock and loaned $400 to his father's old friend Karl Harper. "I sure felt rich the day I sent in those money orders," Father would say. But not more than two months later, the buggy factory went out of business. Father was left with a handful of useless oil stock and a loan which wasn't due. He was penniless again and the furniture factory moving in wasn't opening until fall. Since he hadn't been home for years, he decided to go back for the summer to help his stepfather build another barn.

It was the summer of 1914, the summer he met Mother. "It wasn't until August that I discovered she was Karl's niece," Father told us. "If I hadn't lent Karl the money, I'd have stayed in Freeport and never met her."

Early that spring, Grandmother and Mother had come from Woodland to Marengo to care for Grandmother's sister, who died soon after. They stayed on to tend to her family, and Mother and Father had the summer for courtship. It must have been a lovely time, for the summers are glorious in the northern areas bordering Lake Superior. The colors are brilliant compared to the white-gray landscape of winter; the sun is hot, yet there is always a briskness by evening when the wind shifts to the lake. But the earth stays warm; the fields give off their heady odors of clover, alfalfa and timothy; the woodlands their fragrance of cedar, pine and fir. And the sky, glowing in starlight, goes on and on.

By the end of the summer my parents made their plans to be married in spring. Father's family approved of Mother. "She was so lovely," Aunt Taimi told us, "she was like an angel come to earth, and I couldn't understand what she saw in my brother, who was so ordinary." That was sisterly prejudice; Mother was beautiful by any standard, but Father was handsome as well, and to an eighteen-year-old country girl, he must have seemed urbane and sophisticated.

Father went back to Freeport to work in the factory for the winter months. In May 1915, he came to Woodland to marry Mother. "My plans were to go back to Freeport, because I was doing well there, but I started clerking in a small furniture store in Woodland and worked part time in the new co-op store." That is what Father said, but there is more to the story. Mother had promised Grandfather on his deathbed that she would never leave her aging mother as long as she lived, and Mother didn't. Father stayed with the two of them. A short time later, the J. C. Penney Company opened a new store and Father found a full-time job there, and soon became the assistant manager.

I have often looked at my parents' wedding photograph and have compared it to others, so dated in time and placed in locale. Theirs is an unusual study, unposed and casual, unlike any I have seen. Father is dark-haired, Mother fair. They are seated at a table and leaning forward a little as if to see the world they have no reason to doubt. This wide-eyed stance gives the photograph a poignant quality, forever a symbol of youth unhardened and unprepared for life. When I was a child, that picture always touched me with its beauty, softness and tenderness, and when my parents were having trouble, I tried to bring back the mood of that innocent time, as if by reviving it I could infuse our lives with its special grace.

"I love that picture too," Mother would say, holding her head to one side as she held the photograph away from her.

Compared to Father's life, Mother's had been easy. She was the only child of middle-aged parents who were fond of children, and she was the youngest of a group of cousins who considered her a part of their own families. Still, it was no pampered life, for my grandfather moved to the country after his health began to fail, built a two-room log cabin, and it is there that Mother grew up, in a place surrounded by forest.

Her father was able to clear enough land to support a cow; to have a potato field, a garden and a small grainfield. There must have been work enough for all of them, but Mother remembered it as a happy time. Much of the work was shared with neighbors, and thus planting and harvest were social events, with work and pleasure combined.

Mother walked two miles through the woods to the country school. That too was pleasurable; she was a good student. Moreover, the teachers made an effort to include the immigrant parents in the activities of the school. There were programs and picnics that became community affairs to which everyone came, to hear the children recite their poems and sing their songs in the alien English tongue. Mother remembered these events as joyful, as if reality had not touched her at all, as if she and everyone around her were held within a charmed circle of love, understanding and goodwill.

She finished grade school and planned to go to high school, but her father was now mortally ill. She stayed home to help her mother care for him in his final days, and a few months later he died. "I lost my best friend," she always said, and wept still, years after, when she told us the sad story of her father's death.

Grandmother sold the farm and bought a house in Woodland. Mother found a job in a dime store and then in a doctor's office. Recognizing her brightness, the doctor wanted to train her to be a nurse, but Mother had little interest in a career, for the town offered the diversion of movies, ice cream parlors, pretty clothes, parties and lonely young men newly arrived from Finland. Her life again was touched by magic.

From Grandmother's point of view, Father was an ideal husband. He was six years older than Mother, had many skills, was hardworking, and he was Finnish. Moreover, my two grandmothers got along; they were both sturdy, independent women practiced in managing children, husbands, households and horses.

My brother John was born a year after my parents were married, and Carl a year after John. Carl's birth was difficult, and the doctor less competent than the Finnish midwives, who brought to their tasks a knowledge of cleanliness and a respect for sobriety. The doctor brought neither: he was drunk and careless. Mother developed puerperal fever and nearly lost her life. Yet convinced that he had done his best, she credited him for saving her life. Perhaps she was right; he did all he could to correct his original bungling.

By this time Father was ill with stomach ulcers. "Fully clothed, I weighed a hundred and seventeen pounds," he said later. The doctor who had tended to Mother now advised Father to get out in the country, where the air was good. Perhaps the man was drunk again, for any sober man would conclude that with an ailing wife, two small children and a mother-in-law to support, a sick man could hardly do better on the frontier than in a small town, no matter how fresh the air might be and how much a man breathed of it.

Long years later, Father told me that he hadn't been certain of the doctor's good sense, and that he had wanted to go back to Freeport, where he could attend night school again. In time, his health would have improved, but Mother was too frail and needed Grandmother's aid in caring for the babies. Besides, it was then that Alex, Grandmother's nephew, was threatened by foreclosure of his eighty-six acres of virgin timberland in Revier. Grandmother wanted to help him, to sell her Woodland house and buy the land. There Father could be out in the country air and would recover. "What could I say?" Father asked. "Grandmother couldn't have lived alone in the wilderness."

Father and Mother rode out with a horse and buggy, down the big road, then north along the narrow mud road which became even narrower as it came to Revier. Along the way, they saw houses, yards blooming with phlox and hollyhocks, fresh green gardens, yellow fields and trees along the roadside. "The colored leaves were blowing over us. It was so beautiful it caught my breath," Mother told us. And lovely it must have been: Mother in her hat and wedding suit and Father in his, dressed like city people out to inspect the land they wished to own.

And there it was. Trees everywhere, the river gurgling in its path, and the birds twittering in the branches. Who could have denied the beauty of it? Moreover, the timber was valuable and the soil better than anywhere around Woodland.

With the option to live in it until the following summer, Grandmother sold her house and bought Alex's land. Father's pioneering days began at once; he quit his job at Penney's and he and Alex started to clear the land. There, on a small plot, they built the house which Father wanted to use as a stable as soon as he had enough time and money to build a house. Then in the full bloom of summer, he brought his family to their new home.

My godmother Kaari told me that when she heard that they were coming, she went to the new house with her welcoming gifts of cake and cream and bread. When she saw Mother, still a young girl, holding one baby in her arms and another by the hand, and Father a frail boy so thin the wind could blow him away, she began to weep. She and her husband were older by ten years at least, and had been one of the first frontier families there. "Oh, you poor children, you too have come to this awful place." And she told me she knew they didn't understand, because they laughed and said it was so beautiful there in the forest. My older brother, puzzled by the scene, asked why the lady was crying. "They must have thought I was foolish," Mrs. Kaari said, and wept again.

When Mother remembered that eventful day, she would say, "I knew that if my father had been alive, he'd have been happy to see us there, because we were back on the land again and in the wilderness that he always loved."

And Father would look at her and smile. "Yes," he'd say. "It was a wilderness all right."

Father and Alex cut the trees around the house; the first fall and winter they cut two hundred cords of wood and hauled it to town with their team of horses. During the bright days of summer, Father worked as a carpenter in town, and during the long evenings and on the weekends farmed our land. That became the pattern: woodcutting and hauling in winter, building and farming in summer.

In a few years there was enough cleared land to support a cow. Anxious to begin with good stock, Father borrowed a hundred dollars and bought a purebred Holstein with udders so large her teats almost touched the ground. She was a gentle beast with enormous eyes, a star-shaped marking in the middle of her forehead, and black spots all over her shining white hide. We called her Beauty, a name even Grandmother could say without making it sound like something else than our cow. Unfortunately, Beauty was a careless eater; when she wandered into the clover patch, she gorged herself and began to bloat. Mother saw her standing in the field, her sleek sides round with gas.

I was four then, old enough to be sent on errands. Mother wrote a letter to Father, who was working in a town nearby, and sent me to my godparents' house, where the trains stopped to pick up the farmers' milk cans, drop off the mailbags and take the outgoing mail sack hanging on the post near the tracks.

I ran with the letter, and Mrs. Kaari placed it in the bag just before the train came whistling and hooting to its stop. For a moment, the monster stood at the road crossing, puffed steam from above and below, and then rumbled away hooting and wailing into the forest. Mrs. Kaari took the incoming mailbag, brought it into the kitchen and showed me how she sorted the mail into the boxes behind the counter.

Then I told her about our Beauty, and she cried, really cried, with tears coming down her cheeks. I patted her arm, and she gave me a cinnamon roll with raisins on top. "Father will cure Beauty," I said. "He'll come home as soon as he gets the letter."

Father did come, but Beauty died anyway. He said he had just paid the last payment on her. Still, she was our cow even if she was dead.

Not long after, Father's mother wrote us that she had two cows she didn't want and Father could have them if he came for them. The next day Father took the train to Marengo, forty miles away, and was gone for two days because he had to walk with the cows all the way back to Revier. Now we had two cows in place of Beauty!

Father had to make hay, gather it and put it in the loft above the barn. When the frost came he dug out the potatoes and hauled them into the cellar. And when the cold winds began to blow down the snow, Father harnessed his team of horses, hitched them to the big logging sled and went to work at the lumber camp, which had beds full of lice and cookstoves as big as our kitchen. He'd write us a letter telling us the day he'd come back. Mother made cakes and I frosted them green and red and blue, awful uncakelike colors which turned my stomach, but I had insisted that Mother buy the coloring pills from the Watkins' salesman, who had one eye blue and one eye brown.

It was always dark when Father came home on those winter nights. We waited for him to say "Whoa" to the horses, and then when he was stamping his feet outside, we'd open the door. His cap and his coat were covered with snow and his face was red from the cold. He always brought in box after box of good things: wooden boxes of dried figs, peaches and apricots, apples and pears; he brought jars of olives, and Brazil nuts and walnuts, and pails of peppermint candies. Once he brought my sister and me Dutch dolls with golden hair, and for the boys wind-up cars a foot long. He brought us skates, and Mother said, "Mary's only five!" And when I was six, I got a pair of fur-trimmed boots so grand I couldn't wear them in the snow.

In summer he bought tickets to the circus in Woodland Park so we could see tigers and elephants and angry lions jumping through hoops of flame, and clowns more foolish than we could ever be. My yellow straw hat fell off and went down through the bleachers to the floor of the tent, and then Father had to get the hat. I cried because I was sure he'd never find his way back to us. Later that summer, we went on a picnic and that same hat flew off into the river. Mother said, "Let it go. It's too small anyway." Father jumped in, however, and swam after the racing hat. I began to weep, not for the loss of the hat but for the loss of Father, who'd float away to Lake Superior and never return to us no matter how long we waited. A few minutes later, he came out dripping water and laughing. "There," he said, and put the hat on my head.

"She always cries," Carl said.

"She cries more than the baby," said John.

"She won't cry all her life," Mother said.

How did she know? Perhaps I would. How could I stop myself? I tried to laugh so that the cries inside me wouldn't get out, but they did.

"My head is wet," I wailed, though that was not the reason. I could still see Father floating away from us.

Once Mother and I went to see the doctor. Afterward Father took us to a restaurant and ordered soup for us. When the waitress came, he asked for oyster crackers, which we threw into the soup. The crackers grew and grew like water lilies until they covered the whole surface.

One evening we all went to see a movie made in Finland, but all I remember of it was one scene of an old woman holding a coffee grinder in her lap and turning the handle just the way Grandmother did in our kitchen. Everyone said the movie was certainly like Finland.

23

Father always liked to spend money to amuse us; Mother always liked to budget and save. The arguments were friendly, but underneath were all the things they didn't speak about—subjects I felt they couldn't have agreed on even if they had argued all year. We knew what Mother had wanted; she had it beneath her feet and around her, the wilderness world her father had loved. We children did too. How could we not love it? It was our world, and we had seen no other.

But Father's wanting was hidden. He'd listen to the talk around him and say nothing at all. Sometimes he'd smile and his eyes would look away, far beyond our village and the hills around it. When I was young, I'd climb into his lap, which smelled of cows and horses and the outdoors, and I'd say to myself, "Father, I'll go with you wherever you go," but I knew I couldn't, because I was too little. Later we saw his dream to escape come alive within us, and realized he had nurtured it with all the means he had. Mother could say it cost too much; Grandmother could say we were foolish. Father didn't hear them.

In time, I think, Grandmother began to understand why Father had to give us more than he could afford, because she didn't complain anymore. "It's the one pleasure he has, Louise," she told Mother, "and it's not the worst a man could have."

Her life with us wasn't easy. Having invested all she owned in the purchase of Alex's land, she was penniless and dependent, but she was the co-owner as well and worked long hours beside Mother. They baked, cooked and sewed for us; they canned quantities of food for the winter. The care of the newborn was Grandmother's by choice; she was unhurried and tender. She could rock a baby for an hour and not tire of it.

Mother told us that in those early years they had so much work to do they were never finished at the end of the day. Father labored from morning to night and was always behind in his chores. Sometimes they were so tired and weary of endless effort, she and Father would wade out to the middle of the Montfer behind the sauna, sit on the large gray rock and watch the water as it tumbled down the stream, broke on the hard face of the stone, parted and then flowed on around the base.

Where Grandmother found peace when she was too tired, I don't know. Perhaps in her garden with her flowers, for I often saw her sitting there alone. Once when I joined her she told me that she was thinking of Grandfather, who had loved roses best of all.

She had his picture hanging above her bed, and when she looked at him, she had a soft and gentle expression on her face, as if she were rocking one of the children to sleep. Though Grandfather had died long before our time, we knew him as the opposite of Grandmother's brother, the general, the keeper of the palace and the lighthouse. We were aware that the brother had had his feet on the ground and that Grandfather hadn't. He had been a singer and a poet, Mother always told us. "We were alike," she'd say proudly.

And Grandmother would look at Mother and say, "Yes, God bless him, he was a bit flighty too."

Sometimes Mother could get past remembering how much like her father she really was and go on to recalling his goodness until Grandmother too was caught in the memory of it. Then we were sorry that Grandfather wasn't alive to tell us stories and to stuff pennies into our pockets, and sad that he was under the gravestone which looked like a truncated steeple of St. Paul's Lutheran Church set on an oblong of grass and flowers. It was there that Grandmother knelt on Decoration Day, dug the earth around the stone and planted a miniature garden. And once when we were there, all the church bells in Woodland began to ring. Grandmother listened until they stopped and then said into the silent air, "Your grandfather had a voice as clear as a bell ringing to the skies. Like your mother's."

I remember Mother singing to herself or hailing the men from the field and the cattle from the pasture. All over the farm we could hear her and even to the neighbors', that high "Yoo-oo" echoing all the way to the forest, to the hills and back again.

She loved to read to us—poems and psalms and fables and fairy tales which lifted me out of that place and out of that time, and made me ask over and over, "What if this happened? Then what?" It was she who made us conscious of status, for she had different ways of saying things—one for the family and neighbors, one for the minister, one for the doctor and the teacher.

We, the people of Revier, had a unique position. We were pioneers; we were opening the land and building new lives; we were brave and courageous. Father was special, because he had become a pioneer in order to restore his health. Otherwise, bright as he was, he could have done anything he wanted to do.

"There's nothing wrong with being a farmer or a worker," said Grandmother, and then added, "if that's what one wants to be."

"Well," said Mother, "I think it's good to be special." Maybe that's why she never seemed to care when Father could find no work.

"Isn't that nice," she'd say. "Father doesn't have to go away." It didn't occur to us that money would be scarcer than ever; Father was home. And somehow she could make sitting at the table, drinking a cup of coffee and eating a homemade biscuit, a celebration of the wonderful news that Father's job was over.

In fall, when school was ready to open, all the mothers said they were happy at the prospect of having the children gone all day. "My goodness!" Mother would say. "Don't they miss their children? Why, the house is so empty and lonely, I don't know what to do with myself for a week."

But if the house was empty to her when we were gone, it was a tomb for us when she wasn't there. "Where's Mother?" was our first question. She had to be there. For us, for Father, for anyone who stayed at our house. And when on occasion she planned to be gone for a day, we'd ask, "Who'll take care of us?"

"For heaven's sake! A houseful of people and you ask, 'Who's going to care for us?' Well, you'll just have to get along somehow!" she'd answer, exasperated with the whole foolish houseful of us.

Of course we got along. That's not what we meant. We meant that we wanted her, our mother, to be with us, so we could see her standing at the stove or at the table or just sitting in the rocker with the baby and singing about heaven and God, birds and flowers, sunrises and "Skip to me, Lou, my darling." That is what we meant by her caring for us.

We knew other children lied to their parents. We could not lie to ours. Our parents were different.

Was our family really like that? Were we such loving children and my parents such loving adults? I cannot tell. I do know we children quarreled; my brothers teased and badgered each other; and we provoked them because they were older and could not strike us. Then to return the favor, they played jokes on us, awful jokes which we could never match, not if we planned for a week, a month, a year. Our voices grew louder and louder. "My heavens," Mother would say. "The roof will fly off!"

Lost in his newspaper, not caring at all whether or not the roof flew to the heavens, Father read on.

"John! Can't you hear anything?" Mother would ask.

"All right, children," he would say finally. "Fight gently, if you must, and shout softly." Then he went back to his *Daily News*.

When we had done something truly stupid—broken a window, thrown eggs or beets or tomatoes at one another, or trampled a bed of seedlings—Father would ask, "Was that really necessary?" Since we knew it hadn't been, we had to conclude that we had been thoughtless. In her turn, Mother could give us a glance which would wither a whole forest, and then we knew we had really misbehaved. But the glance was only a glance; it did not mean that we were out of favor for long.

We were proud of our parents. In Revier, all the children envied us because we had books, games and toys; parents who spoke English and understood how it was to grow up alien; parents who trusted us. We were poor, but we did not feel poor; compared to the other children in our village we felt privileged.

Moreover, my parents were generous. The unspoken law of their lives was: we are not poor as long as we have something to share. At times, they shared more than was prudent, but what is prudent and what is not among the impoverished, cut off from all aid save that which they can give each other? Who knows? Eventually the giving and the taking balance.

Sometimes the giving did seem to be headed in one direction only. It was so in the case of Mother's cousin Otto. He and Alex, who had helped Father clear our land, were the sons of Grandmother's sister. She had died when the boys were small, and though Grandmother did her best to shield them, they were still subject to the drunken rages of their father. When Otto was three, his father, drunk beyond reason, kicked the three-year-old boy, broke his hip and crippled him for life.

He was a bright lad, Mother said, and though he had no schooling beyond the eighth grade, he managed to teach himself bookkeeping. When he was still quite young he found a job with the Federal Land Bank. Apparently he liked such high life as Woodland had to offer, and his bookkeeping became something less than accurate. When he could not account for a thousand-dollar discrepancy, he was charged with embezzlement.

My parents mortgaged their farm, paid the thousand dollars and trusted that Otto would pay back the money. For two years he sat in a federal prison; when he returned, he married Aunt Mandy, a widow with two children, bought a house in Woodland and forgot about the thousand dollars.

Not entirely, of course. They visited us. Otto brought us books and candy; his wife sewed my sister and me two dresses and brought soap for the sauna; her daughter brought us striped hair ribbons and fixed our hair with a curling iron she heated on the cookstove. And Otto never forgot Grandmother on her birthday, at Christmas, at Easter and on Mother's Day, though he forgot about Father taking the mortgage on our place. Father paid, never said a word, and he never got enough money together to fix up the house the way he had wanted to.

We liked Otto. There was something jaunty about his bobbing gait; he played games, which his older brother Alex, dreamy and speculative, never did. He hid peppermint drops in Mother's silver chest above the clothes rack, and told us about prison life, solitary confinement and eating bread and water. We thought it all heady stuff, for who else had a relative who'd been in a federal prison? No one we knew.

Meanwhile Alex thought aloud about Theosophy, which both he and Aunt Mandy espoused. No doubt she had initiated him into its mysteries, which addled him more than ever, but Alex was ripe for addling all his life. Had he had more education, he might have become a philosopher of sorts and probably could have made a living at piling one assumption upon the next. As it was, he made a living cutting trees, and spent his free time inventing more or less useful gadgets. When he wasn't inventing, he thought about the world and the hereafter, and talked to us about it whether we listened or not.

Aunt Mandy was older than Otto, good for him apparently because he never strayed again, but I thought her too matronly for such a young and handsome man. Still, I liked her, and I believe she had a special fondness for me. She said I had an old soul. No one disputed it in her presence, though Grandmother, staunch St.

Paul's Finnish Lutheran Church member that she was, could not have cared much for Aunt Mandy's contention that my soul had reached a prodigiously elevated state and was very likely on its last trip to earth. There could be spirits, yes, and there were signs and portents, but souls didn't hop in and out of people. But Mandy thought souls did, and that I was on my last earthly visit.

I wasn't worried about the age of my soul. What did worry me was my resemblance to Grandmother. Everyone said I was "another Grandmother." How could that have happened? How could a little girl look like an old woman?

I don't know how, but I did. Not long ago I thumbed through the family album of photographs, and there I am in a faded snapshot of the family, a miniature Grandmother standing in front of the full-sized Grandmother—one five and the other seventy-five! At that time, however, I refused to believe it, because Grandmother had wrinkles on her face and liver spots on her hands and I was neither wrinkled nor spotted. She was good and kind. Perhaps it would be nice to be like her, but even if my soul was a million years old, the rest of me was not much older than my little brother, Edward.

Yet whether I could admit it or not, the look of strain was imprinted on my face. Perhaps it was the eczematous rash which developed soon after my birth and did not cure until I left home and the farm animals. My face, neck, arms, legs and back were always itching, exuding and scaling, and sometimes for weeks on end I was bandaged like a mummy. I wheezed with asthma from fall to spring, from spring to fall; my frequent colds turned to bronchitis and then to pneumonia. And the food I ate apparently refused to digest, for I was always anemic, always drinking liver tonic, and all to no avail.

The winter I was five, my kidneys rebelled. For some unknown reason, my godparents' son, Taisto Kaari, died of uremic poisoning at the same time. We had often played together and we were both given to exploring. We may have eaten any number of poisons common around a farm or we may both have had some bacterial infection. In any case, he died, and I lay dying of kidney disease or refusing to die of it all winter long.

The icicles formed on the eaves and reached down to the windows; the snow came down in white furry mittens and settled into drifts. How still it was there in the cold! Then my brothers stomped in with their snow-covered jackets and leather-top boots. In a moment, the room was full of the outdoors. Later Father bought me bananas, a hat and a pair of skis. Mother brought her work into the bedroom; my sister played beside me on the bed; Edward toddled about on his still uncertain legs.

Every day the snow came down; every night the frost painted leaves on the windowpanes. And every morning Mr. Kaari, my godfather, picked up the urine sample, which he took away in a mustard jar so the doctor could test the contents.

Pastor Grandfather came, looked at me, and said I would die before I was ten. After that he could say that the sun rose in the east and I wouldn't believe him. Neither did our Grandmother Anderson, who came with him and brought me flannel, cinnamon hearts inside a glass horse, and a pink celluloid boat. She said that as soon as it was summer, I'd be running all over the field, and that I'd live to be a hundred years old.

Such a hazardous beginning has its advantages. I learned to overlook discomfort and to recognize the difference between minor and major illness. I knew that when I was lying on a glass slab, cold as ice, when I saw gnomes climbing over my feet and then back down again, I was really ill. The bed was there; I could feel it. I might even hear some faint sounds from the kitchen, but I was on the slab of glass and the gnomes scuttled over my feet; if I moved I would fall off and no one could save me. I'd lie still, watch the gnomes at their silent play, and concentrate on staying on the treacherous glass.

And then one day I woke up; the glass was gone, the gnomes were gone, and I was in my own bed. The sun shone through the window and turned everything to gold and red and orange. Though I wasn't well, I was no longer sick. I could remember how it had been in summer when I was able to run across the field with my brothers; how once when I was very young, I followed a black cat into a log, and when I got back to the house Grandmother took off all my clothes and buried them, because the cat was a skunk. I remembered that on one bright summer day I stood under the ironwood tree which Father had left standing in the field all by itself, because the tree was so old, so large, that it must have stood there hundreds of years, and as I stood there I felt almost as the tree must feel, straight and tall enough to touch the inside of the sky. I was wearing a white pile coat which Mrs. Wiita had given to me, a coat which was too small for her daughter and too big on me, only I would grow. It was a lovely coat, as soft as a kitten.

I stood under the tree with the meadowlark singing his song to me and no one else. Then he stopped singing; I felt something land on my shoulder. When I turned my head I could see the black and green excrement spread into the cat-fur of my coat.

"That was last spring," Mother said, "when you were four."

It was the spring when the river backed into the ravine and filled it with shining, rippling water which waited to take our boats away if we weren't careful, under the culvert, into the wild, roaring river, and away to the sea, where they would grow into big ships large enough to bring people from Finland to America. Later, when the river went down, my sister and I made mud pies on the river-bank and frosted them with lime from the storage bin in the barn where Father kept Paris green, which we could not use. John and Carl tasted our pies, and said if we couldn't make better pies, we could give them to the chickens.

I remembered the Christmastime before the last, when Father put us all, even Grandmother, into the horse-drawn sled, covered us with quilts, and drove across the fields to Revier School, where John and Carl had to recite poems. When we walked into the school, my sister, not quite two, began to cry. "But this isn't the sauna," she said, tears running down her cheeks, and I knew she must have thought of the warm, damp smell of cedar and Aunt Mandy's soap.

Mother said it was a pity that the only place Elizabeth knew about was the sauna, but it really wasn't a pity, because in summertime everyone came with their bundles of clean clothes, bags of sweet rolls, pans of cake and sometimes soda pop, so that we could all eat after we had gone to the sauna. Sometimes our yard was full of cars; people said we had more sauna visitors than anyone in Revier. But we had more aunts and uncles, more cousins, more people who were nearly uncles and aunts, and more people who came because we liked them. Of course we had more visitors!

Mother came into the bedroom. "Are you better, Mary?"

"Yes, I'm better." As long as I could remember I was better. In

31

no time at all, I'd be able to run to the barn to see the cats and to climb up into the hayloft. I could feel the prickly dry hay as I wallowed in it, feel the sudden tightness in my chest, and then the wheezing. But I could not stay away.

One day before I even realized, I was well enough to sit on the steps outside. Mother wrapped a quilt around me, and I sat watching the chickadees playing in the fir tree. The snowdrifts were melting into rivulets, running in streams around the house. The sun was blinding on the snow-covered fields; beyond them stood the black leafless trees, and way beyond, my purple hills and the little hut where I was made.

Then I was completely well. We were on a train going to Marengo to see our cousins, our pastor grandfather, our uncles and our aunts, and most of all our grandmother, Father's mother, who was dead.

When we went into the house, I knew I had been there before, because I remembered the square cut into the kitchen floor. Grandmother had pulled on the metal ring and the square had come up. Then she said, "Don't fall in," and went down the wooden stairs herself and disappeared until all I could see of her was the white edge of her long apron. Afterward we had raspberries from a Mason jar and hot rice porridge. I knew the living room too, with its white fluffy curtains and big green fern. The room was more crowded now because the furniture had been pushed to one side; on the other side were the dark coffin, the wreaths, and chairs on which some of the uncles and aunts were sitting.

First, Father took my brothers by the hand and led them to the coffin; then he asked me if I too wanted to see Grandmother Anderson. I said I did, so he picked me up, held me tight, and we walked over. It was strange to see Grandmother lying down, because I had always seen her walking or sitting or standing. Besides, her face was rosy, as if she had just come in from the sauna. "Is she really dead?" I asked Father.

"Yes, she's dead."

Mother was crying, but Father just looked sad and serious.

Then the undertaker closed the lid and some men carried the coffin into the hearse drawn by a team of black horses. My pastor grandfather, our aunts and uncles, a few of the older second cousins, Mother and Father and my older brothers went with her.

32

The rest of us, the younger ones, stayed behind in the still and empty house. Someone, I don't know who it was, someone young, stayed with us. We sat in a row on a bed and pretended we were birds. Whoever it was peeled orange after orange, sectioned them and placed slices into our open mouths.

Grandmother Anderson was only fifty-seven when she died, too able and spirited, too unready and unprepared. For years she had been bothered by gallstones, or so the doctor said, and finally he decided to operate, a hazardous decision in those days in the small-town hospital. He was very sorry; he even wept. So people said.

Later, whenever Father talked about his mother, she came to life and was as full of laughter as before, even if we could not go to her ruffle-curtained house to eat raspberries. Our grandmother had said she felt that they had been sisters, they had thought so much alike.

Yes, but not quite. Father's mother had a sense of the absurd; when she discovered foolishness in someone, especially in her husband, she never hid her discoveries. For instance, Pastor Grandfather deplored progress; any gadget, tool or machine not mentioned in the Bible was patently sinful. On the other hand, Grandmother liked new ways, especially if they eased her burden of work. Thus the Model T was God's gift to mankind. She bought one and enjoyed riding around beside her two sons, Albert and Roy. Grandfather disapproved, but would consent to ride if the need was great and the car running.

One Sunday he was to preach at the country church, several miles away. Grandmother climbed into the car and urged him to ride too. It was hot and dusty out, and sin or no sin, there was no need for him to walk. Grandfather refused because the devilish thing wouldn't start anyhow, and he'd be in church long before they ever got there. He left and Grandmother sat.

Roy cranked and cranked. At last the engine sputtered, coughed and then began to roar and shake. "Good!" said Grandmother Anderson. "You've just got to coax them along a little. Some horses are no better." And away they went.

It wasn't long before they came upon Pastor Grandfather trudging along the road. Roy was about to stop. "No, keep going," said Grandmother. "He probably likes to walk." And they drove on, leaving the poor preacher behind in a cloud of Marengo dust. They came to the church, went inside and sat down to wait for their Sunday sermon.

Father loved that story, and we did too, for it brought Grandmother Anderson into our house again. Right afterward, Mother always said that Grandmother had lived through so many sorrows that she had learned to laugh even when her heart was aching. She had been widowed at twenty-three, when my father was two and a half; she had had three children to support and a brother-in-law who was ill and needed care. After her own brother had died, there had been no one left to help her except Father, who was still young. Wasn't that tragic? Mother would ask, and give Father a pat of sympathy for the loss of the only parent he could remember.

Now Pastor Grandfather was left to practice his feeble cooking skills on Uncle Roy, Uncle Albert and Big Hank, the hired man. Everyone called him big though he wasn't. He was just strong; strong and clumsy. When he wanted to, he could do the work of two men, but only if his path was clear; if it wasn't, he could be the most stumble-footed creature on earth. Yet he wouldn't admit that his feet had a way of tangling with each other. Someone else was always to blame.

Grandmother Anderson had always treated him as she would an ill-tempered child. Sometimes he grew tired of her bossing, left the farm, went to the lumber camp, and when he got fed up with work there he'd come back. Grandmother accepted him, and they got along. But Hank didn't care much for Pastor Grandfather and Grandfather didn't care for Hank. Both of them were a bit lazy and both liked to preach; Hank was an atheist but he knew the Bible almost as well as Grandfather, who was determined to convert him.

When Grandmother was alive she undoubtedly kept the two of them from arguing day and night, but when she died, who was to stop them? They wouldn't listen to Uncle Albert; he got tired of trying and went to California. Uncle Roy certainly couldn't stop them, because they thought he was a little strange. Finally Hank left, came to our house and said he couldn't stand the cooking at the Andersons' now that Grandmother was gone. And there he stayed, in our crowded house. Sometimes Father said that Hank was useless, but Mother said he was like a child and had to be with us because he had no other family. Our place had to be his home.

Now and then he'd become angry with one of us. He would grumble and then leave in a great huff and stay away, usually until the seeding or the harvesting was over. When I saw him coming, walking slowly across the field and bending under the packsack on his back, I'd run to meet him.

"Did you bring the sausage again?" I'd ask.

Then he'd pull out of his dirty mackinaw pocket the sausage wrapped in brown paper, give it to me and let me carry it to the house. "Was it nice at the lumber camp? What did you eat? Were there lice in the beds?" And on and on. When we got to the house, Hank just walked in as if he hadn't been gone a month.

The two of us sat down at the kitchen table. I'd watch him take out his pocket knife, clean it on his dirty overalls and then cut the skin on the ring of bologna. Carefully, ever so carefully, he'd slice the meat into the thinnest of thin slices. We'd eat, slice after slice. When I had enough, he'd wrap the sausage in the paper and stuff the package into his mackinaw pocket and wipe the knife on his overalls. That was his homecoming ceremony, his offering of peace, repeated over and over. He was back in the family and back at our table.

But as we grew older, he became less comprehending, especially of the boys. Away from us, he was always fiercely loyal; no children were as good as we nor as bright. No children were as diligent; none so courteous to older people. Soon no other family would put up with him. Even the lumbermen grew tired of him, for though he was a strong and able worker, he was too easily injured, never forgot the injury, and never held his tongue. At last no one would hire him.

Father couldn't afford to pay him much. Hank was thrifty, however, and usually had money on hand to buy small gifts during the Christmas season and, winter or summer, bags of pink peppermints for us and a bottle of whiskey for himself. When Mother objected to his drinking, he became irritable and sarcastic, but eventually he stopped bringing his bottle into the house. Then he'd tell anyone who would listen to him, "There's one good thing about the Morgans. They don't allow booze around the place."

He told stories of his boyhood in Finland, of his father dying when Hank, the eldest, was only seven, of his having no shoes to wear and about warming his feet in newly dropped cow dung. He said that when he was six his mother washed his hair with soap which went into his eyes. Never again would he use soap, he vowed, and he never did. His pillowcases were always brown no matter how Mother boiled them, but no amount of urging would convince Hank that he ought to use soap. If it stings the eyes, he'd tell us, just think of what it does to the skin!

Hank had never gone to school, save to confirmation school at the village church, where he learned to read and write. When he read Finnish fables to us, he bellowed so loudly no one else could think, but to my mind, his reading was dramatic and the best way to read fables, especially Finnish ones. He taught me the Finnish alphabet before I went to school, listened to me read simple sentences and corrected me if I didn't sound out every letter. And whenever Pastor Grandfather came, Hank recited verses from the Bible, just as he read the fables, in a voice you could hear outside the house.

Sometimes he carved dolls out of stove wood, primitive legless stumps almost as tall as we, and played checkers and dominoes with us. He grew his own tobacco, dried it, chopped it up and then rolled his own cigarettes, so strong that no one in all of Revier would touch them. And sometimes, for no reason at all, he went on strike and did nothing but predict disaster for the whole world.

Yet despite his childish ways, he was a decent and private man. Had he been otherwise, neither Mother nor Father nor Grandmother would have tolerated him. Reticence was their shared trait and propriety a means by which they protected themselves from intrusion. They all taught us to shield ourselves and them. A whisper, a glance, a shake of the head, was enough to inform us that we were about to breach another's right to privacy. As reserved as we, Big Hank belonged in our family.

And whose will prevailed in our house? For years we thought that Father's did, because Mother always said that his word was the final one. For a long time, however, it was Grandmother who decided which animal would be kept and which sold, where fields ought to be planted and what would grow well. It was she who provided the practical guidance in the house. She knew how to use the coarse home-milled flour, the new milk after a cow's calving and the wool from the sheep; she had the skill to make quilts, to use leaves and berries to dye materials, and to preserve our summer's harvest for the winter. Mother learned what she wished to learn. The quilting, the carding and spinning, and the preparation of dyes remained in Grandmother's keeping. Eventually Father managed the fields, but never without consulting Grandmother.

The barn and what it held was contested ground. Mother couldn't bear to sell an animal; she would have kept them all. Father wanted to experiment but couldn't trust his own judgment. He always asked Grandmother to make the decision. Hence Mother felt subordinate and sought ways to prove that she was. Perhaps the effort added drama to her life and made it more tolerable. Yet it was she who had determined the conditions of her and Father's life together. She and Grandmother had decided where they would live. Having acquiesced to the arrangement, Father had the choice of working at anything which would bring in money to support us.

The three of them were our parents; they had equal say in what we children could do and not do. Their differences on other matters disturbed us sometimes; Mother and Father could have had a more perfect union. But on the whole, there was peace in our house and an unstated love and affection among us all. And though our days could have been easier and less driven, we wouldn't have had a richer life anywhere.

Beyond the family, it was the seasons which ruled, structured and ordered our lives, gave them substance and meaning. In winter, we waited for spring, waited for the last mounds of rotted snow to crumble away. Only then would the bloodroots come out of the ground and make great splashes of white under the leafless trees. After them came the May flowers, fragile white blossoms veined in red which wilted long before we could bring them home; and the hardy yellow adder's-tongues, the violets and trilliums, and over every waterlogged bog in our village, a whole sea of buttercups. Near the ravine where the water spilled from the river, the blue flags bent in the wind but never broke.

One day the sun burned the spring clouds out of its path and every spring flower shriveled in its sunlit bed. But the forget-me-nots hid in the dank places of the pasture; the wintergreen, bunch-berry and columbine bloomed along the forest path. All at once, the world was awash with green, all shades of green. Then the timothy, the clover, the oats and the barley, each glistening its own green, spread over the fields. At the fairgrounds in Woodland the Revolutionary War broke out again, and the next day all the strawberries along the sandy banks of the railroad ripened at once.

When Father mowed down the green hay, raked it into heaps, there in the naked field we caught a young sandpiper, held it in our cupped hands and felt its heart pulsing against our own. We found a baby rabbit, kept him, fed him clover, milk, bread and carrots, and when we put our noses on the screen of his cage, he stood up on his hind feet.

Then the green faded on the meadows; the daisies, asters and devil's paintbrushes bloomed along the hillsides. A blue haze hung over the hills; the morning and evening skies burned red. Before we could begin to count the days until Christmas, birds filled the autumn sky. Gathering and hoarding, we prepared for the snow.

And one day the soft, wind-driven flakes began to fall, shutting us off from the hills, the neighbors, sometimes even the sauna and the barn. The snowbound winter had come, and Christmas, lasting for months. The Christ child lay in the manger, felt the prickly hay on his baby skin and saw the star right through the roof just as we saw Santa Claus riding the sky in his bell-trimmed sled.

Christ grew up and rose from his grave. Everything around us melted in reverence: the snowy roofs, the white bushes, our igloos and caves and our icy paths. The river filled beyond its banks, crossed into Michigan, crossed our road and cut us off. We were shipwrecked; we were alone on our island.

And all the while we asked the eternal questions of childhood. Who am I? From where did I come? Where am I going? How shall I get there? The adults around us answered the best way they knew, in ways consistent with what they were themselves. Grandmother's answers were not Hank's, nor Hank's answers the same as Pastor Grandfather's. We had a choice. My parents bridged the gap of generations and the gap between different worlds. Yet even they offered us a choice; Father yearned for places beyond Revier and Mother claimed it as her home.

Our world was full of choices, though as children we saw them only as threads in the rough fabric of our daily lives. As we grew we questioned every alternative, rejected, accepted and finally absorbed each in some measure. And we began to see the harsh unyielding facts of our lives, facts which were no more amenable to change than were the rocks in our fields.

"If we didn't have any cows, no one would have to work," I said to John. And suddenly I saw an empty barn and flowers blooming all around it. We had no cows, no horses, no pig and no sheep to trample down this barnyard garden. Once more our lives became a fairy tale of endless pleasure. Mother would never have to say that she was too tired to move.

"Don't be silly," he said. "All farmers have cows."

Not wishing to shatter that lovely world of my childhood, the world I wished to hold and keep, Mother said, "Wouldn't that be nice, Mary?" And being young, she dreamed on with me. "I was just like you when I was your age. I saw flowers everywhere." And then I could see her, light as an angel, skipping over the meadows of her childhood.

2

IT WAS LATE AUGUST NOW. The sun was as hot as our oven. Wherever we looked, inside or outside the house, the heat rose in shimmering waves. We pumped cold water; we washed our faces and soaked our feet. "Sit in the shade," said Mother, but it was hot there too. The chirp of the katydids in the lilacs made us drowsy. The chickens with their drooping wings, the dogs with their lolling tongues, and the loose dust in the air made us even warmer. We went inside. Mother's breads were rising on the table. Pans and pans of them, as if she were about to supply all of Revier with her golden loaves.

"It was never this hot in Finland," I said as if I'd been there as Grandmother had and knew how cool it was even if one baked bread on a summer's day. Now almost six, I felt that I had lived forever.

"It was hot there too," said Grandmother, and told us about baking breads of different kinds and then hanging them on a pole near the ceiling, where they were out of the way but ready for eating all winter long.

"Let's make grate bread," I said.

"Mary!" said Mother, looking at me, knowing the reason for my suggestion. "It's hot, so let's make it worse. Honestly!"

Grandmother had returned to her Finnish village, to grate bread and salted herring taken to the fields and eaten during the work hours. "If you roll it thin, Louise, it'll bake at the same temperature as the other breads. That's what we used to do."

Mother divided the remaining dough, made balls of it, rolled them flat and then placed them on grates. Grandmother pricked holes into the flat surfaces. "Let me do it," I said. She gave me the fork and I tried to copy her even motion, but the holes were unequally spaced, some deep, some shallow.

"All right," said Mother, ending the impalement of her grate breads. "That's enough holes for six loaves." She placed the breads in the oven, glanced at the clock and ran to fetch the potatoes and onions from the field.

"Grandmother," I said, not quite knowing how to move her back once more to Finland. We always came between her and her memories. Then I saw the church in the big town which she always said was exactly six kilometers from her place of work. "Were there bells in the town church?"

"Yes, there were bells and an organ. I'd walk the six kilometers just to hear them."

"And the Czar went there too," I said, hoping that perhaps just once she had seen him in his royal robes, a golden crown on his head and his beautiful Czarina in gold and velvet walking beside him. The bells ringing. The organ rattling the windows.

"No," said Grandmother. "He had to stay in his palace and be a father to his people. My brother saw him many times and said he was a good man. But then the revolution came and the Czar and all his family were killed."

"Did he eat salt herring?" asked Elizabeth. She liked the small salted fish and could eat them right out of the barrel, but I couldn't. Mine had to be soaked in water and tasted like nothing.

"I don't think he ate herring. He had to eat finer things," said Grandmother. "Foods from France and England."

It was time for our own supper of potatoes, creamed onions, herring and grate bread as crisp and golden as any bread the Czar might have eaten if he hadn't been forced to eat finer things— whatever they were.

After we had finished our supper, Elizabeth and I cleared the table, dried the dishes for Grandmother and hung the towels on the clothesline outside. Mother and Father went to the barn to milk the cows and the boys to feed the chickens, ducks and rabbits. The only ones who had nothing to do were Big Hank and Edward —Big Hank because he had to sit outside and Edward because he always forgot to feed his cat.

41

When we were done with our work, Elizabeth and I went to sit on the steps and Grandmother left us to gather the eggs. Hank was sitting on the bench he had made for himself and Edward was chasing a moth which had invaded our front yard.

"Big Hank, was the Czar really a good man?" I asked.

"The Czar was a vulture feeding on his own people," said Hank.

"Did you ever see him, Big Hank?" asked Elizabeth.

"No."

"Then how do you know he was a vulture?" I asked.

"I know," said Hank. "The Czar was a king and all kings are vultures."

When Mother came back from the barn and Father brought the milk, we went inside to watch him run the separator. He poured the milk into the big metal bowl on top and began to turn the crank. The machine whined and complained and then its two silvery spouts began to pour out skim milk from one and cream from the other, into separate pails. Finally the last drops of cream and milk fell into the pails. Mother emptied them into clean cans, which Father took to the cooler box under the basswood tree.

Now we had to take apart the separator piece by piece, wash the disks and spouts, wash the pails and cans which had been used in the barn and then dry them with fresh towels. I said it was too much work and Mother said wouldn't it be awful if we sold sour milk, and then we reassembled the machine, rinsed out the towels, and hung them on the line to wave in the breeze with the others.

We all stayed outside to watch the moon rise red and fiery above the outline of the trees. We could hear the soft ring of cowbells in the pasture, the rattle of a car down Revier Road, the cry of a hawk and then nothing.

"Two more weeks of freedom," said Carl.

"I can hardly wait," I said. "All my life I've wanted to go to school."

The boys sighed as if I had much to learn, but they wouldn't tell me what it was.

Later, when the house had cooled, Mother, Elizabeth and I went back indoors to prepare for bed. Sleep was already claiming us and slowing our movements as we washed, brushed our teeth and combed our hair.

"What is a vulture?" Elizabeth asked as we climbed into bed.

"I think it's a bird."

She yawned. "Would you like to live in a palace?"

"Yes," I said. "I'd give anything."

Elizabeth was quiet. For a moment I thought how it would be to have a palace as large as the Czar's and then I too fell asleep.

The two weeks passed. "Pray hard, Mother," said Carl on the first day of school. Mother was standing on the stairs and waved to us as we walked into the green field still glistening with dew. No morning had seemed brighter; no day more promising.

"You'll have to keep up with us, Mary," said John.

"I will," I said as I scrambled after them. I could see the Revier School, its windows blazing and walls shining in the rising sun.

And then we were there.

Our one-room schoolhouse, made of white clapboard, stood in an acre of crabgrass, pigweed, dandelion and devil's paintbrush. In fall, we tramped them down; in early summer after school was out, they all came back again as strong as ever. The stairs leading to the door were high, with a sturdy railing to keep us from toppling to the ground, and the landing had a railing too; on it we pounded the chalk erasers every afternoon.

At eight-thirty each morning and at one each afternoon, our teacher stood on that landing and rang the bell—a big, wood-handled bell which called us from the schoolyard below, the swamp across the road, or the hill on the west side of the school. Five minutes after she had set the echoes flying and frightened the birds off their branches, we had to be inside and at our desks.

In the entranceway of our school was a door opening into the basement stairwell, and that door, for obvious reasons of safety, was to be closed tight at all times. But often the door was ajar, thus providing a hazard to education. When the teacher went downstairs to the toilet or to feed the furnace or to fetch supplies for the schoolroom above, the older boys piled the broom, the mop, the doormat, the wastepaper basket and sometimes their coats against that door. Then we all waited to hear her step upon the stairs, the turn of the knob and then the clatter as everything fell upon her, slid past and down to the basement.

Opposite the opening to the stairwell was another, which led into the boys' cloakroom, and straight ahead from the main entrance was the schoolroom itself, drafty from the wind which blew in beneath the outside door. At the west corner of the schoolroom was a long, narrow cloakroom for the girls. At one end of it was a high window, on the other, a floor-to-ceiling bookshelf, with old books on the top shelves, colored paper, paste and scissors on the middle shelves, and pegboards on the bottom shelf.

The schoolroom had five rows of desks, ranging from small to large, bolted firmly to the hardwood floor. Along the east and west walls were high windows which the teacher opened with a long stick when we needed air. We had no light other than that which came in from the windows, and if we had need for more, we never thought of it.

The teacher's desk stood beside the large floor register which was directly above the furnace. Behind the desk was a roll-up map of the world and a wall of blackboard, and to the right, a library shelf which the librarian from the Hadley Public Schools replenished each fall. At the back of the room, next to another door leading to the boys' cloakroom, we had a water fountain, filled each morning by one of the boys, who carried the water from the pump in the schoolyard. Beside the fountain stood a washstand with a metal basin, and above it, a large bulb of bright green liquid soap.

The ceiling was high in our schoolroom, and the air should have been as sweet as the outdoors, but the odor of Lysol, floor polish and chalk dust buried the freshness. And sometimes on quiet winter days, coal smoke drifted up from the register.

"I smell smoke!" someone said.

The teacher looked down into the great maw of the furnace and then, to save us all, rushed down to rattle its metal insides and ran back up the stairway to open all the windows and the big outside door. All the big boys hurried out to see if the smoke was now coming out of the chimney, and if there was none, they shouted, "No smoke yet!" Then the teacher had to go down to shake up the furnace once more.

We would crowd around the register, watch the top of the burner turn livid, feel the hot air rising, feel our hair standing on end and our skirts billowing away from our legs, and all the while the cold air streaming in through the door and windows bit at our skin.

"You've got goose pimples!"

"You're all purple!"

"You're blue!"

"Feel my hands."

Everyone was freezing. Even the teacher, wrapped in her thick sweater.

When our mittens were wet we placed them on the register, and if we didn't turn them, they baked brown as biscuits. When we were bored, we dropped a pencil into the red mouth of the furnace, or a small eraser, or best of all an Eversharp, a pencil made of metal, enameled and ready to flare like a torch. So keen, so pungent was the odor of burning paint, I could smell the first hint of it long before the teacher said, "Who dropped an Eversharp into the register?" She said it so indignantly she turned red. Then she pounded the desk with her ruler and hated all of us, one row after another, while the awful stench rose from the register.

I can hear her still, hear the blackboard erasers banging on the railing, hear the bell ringing, see the sun streaming in through the windows and see every one of the seats. I remember where I sat every year of my eight years at the Revier School, the Harvard of all one-room grade schools—better than Range School, River Bend School, Roosevelt School, any other school anywhere. It didn't matter at all who the teacher was, what she did or did not do, whether she ran in circles or stood on her head; it was the school itself that mattered: the boards, windows, desks, the clothes hooks in the closets and every stench that rose from the register.

There were twenty-two of us, varying in age from six to sixteen. During the first year, we learned to read and speak English if we had not learned before. During the second, we learned to read better, to add and subtract, and to memorize poems even when they made no sense. After that, the third and fourth grades, the fifth and sixth, and the seventh and eighth were grouped in twos, each having classes in arithmetic, reading, writing, history, geography, and in the last, human physiology, civics and agriculture, where we learned that the animals we had in our village resembled no beast bearing a special title. Ours were scrubs.

We all sang together every morning, pledged the flag, had our ears, nails and teeth checked by a health inspector we elected anew each week. If the teacher had received samples in the mail, tiny tubes of toothpaste or midget jars of Vicks or dwarf boxes of

45

Unguentine, she passed them out. Some children ate the contents right off, not because they were hungry but because there was nothing else to do with them, and the containers, once empty, could be used to hold something.

Once a week we drew pictures. My oldest brother drew brushfires. He could draw one in less time than anyone could believe possible. In one minute. He timed himself. He never tried drawing anything else, just those same crooked lines in the middle of the paper, a splash of red, of orange, of yellow, and some gray smeared over for smoke. One could see the fire, even smell it. And in one minute, John was back at his reading, oblivious of the rest of us, who were busy with our trees, houses, rivers and barns, or depending on the time of year, pasting pumpkins and Pilgrims, Santa Clauses and sleds, and tulips and Easter eggs on the lower panes of the high windows.

Once a year, the county supervisor came to see if we were being taught properly. In our eyes, she was in an advanced state of dotage, but we looked forward to her visit because the teacher had to go to the back of the room while the supervisor stood in front and demonstrated how we were to be taught.

"Boys and girls," she would announce, as if we did not know what we were. "Boys and girls, today we shall study the sounds of the letter *a.*" And we did. Then she wrote something on the blackboard. The chalk scratched up and down, up and down. "Now, what does the chalk say?"

"Squeak, squeak," someone said in a high voice resembling the chalk's scratching.

"No, children." She shook her head vigorously. "The chalk says, 'The Little Red Hen found a grain of wheat.' " She paused. "Now, where do you think she found it?"

"In the manure pile," someone whispered.

"No," said the supervisor. "It was on the ground! Wasn't the Little Red Hen clever?"

"Yes!" we all shouted.

Then she listened to the teacher ask us questions about nouns, verbs, modifiers, nerve cells and the longest rivers in the world. Most of the time we knew, and that was our doing. Sometimes we didn't know, and that was fine because our ignorance was the teacher's fault.

46

"I don't believe that's quite right. Does anyone know?"

And then we waved our arms frantically, twisting our wrists and snapping our fingers while the teacher glared and the county supervisor of education smiled. In short, it was a day of utter nonsense, matched only by one other: the day a herd of cows came into the schoolyard and mooed beneath the windows. The big boys chased away the cows, but the herder, a dim-witted fellow from a neighboring town, stayed behind to cackle, neigh and moo into the coal chute for the rest of the day.

We waited for the county nurse too. She came once a year to pronounce our eyes, ears, tonsils and teeth good or bad, to weigh us, measure us, and to place a thermometer inside our mouths. She wrote down her findings on a card, and urged each child to report to his parents the exact state of his health. Once I told my mother that my temperature was eighty-eight degrees. What other children said, I don't know, but surely the reports could not have been any more accurate, for we were less concerned with exactness than with the competitive scramble the nurse's visit provided. To own three cavities was better than to own none at all; bad tonsils were better than good ones; bad vision was better than normal vision. Some mark of distinction, whatever it was, was better than none. We had something. We could talk about it, compare it and be certain to keep it intact without suffering the pain of improvement. I would have given a week's supply of paste and colored paper for one bad tonsil, but I had nothing. In fact, I had less than anyone else; I was small and underweight. I did have eczema, but everyone knew I had it, and no one wanted it.

My first teacher, Miss Anastasia Malone, was an old lady with red corkscrew curls, long dresses belted in the back, and thin legs fastened to large oxfords. She had grown up in Boston, she said, but why she had wandered so far from her original habitat she did not say. She lived with the Salmi family, occupied their big bedroom, ate her meals off the tray which Mrs. Salmi brought in to her each morning and evening, used a chamber pot instead of the outhouse, and once she returned from school, remained in seclusion until the next morning.

On Friday evenings, Toivo, the fourteen-year-old Salmi boy, brought her to the bus stop on U.S. 2, where she caught the evening bus and rode into Hadley. On Sunday evenings, he fetched her again. What we knew of the private life of Miss Malone we learned from him.

Toivo was a handsome lad, a favorite of Miss Malone's. She said he was brave and no doubt her rides to and from the bus were hazardous, for the township road was rarely cleared of snow and Toivo, enjoying the chance to drive the horse, to shout at him, to stand in the cutter and to smack the air with the reins, made the three-mile journey as eventful as he knew how. The sleigh rocked and teetered and sometimes tossed Miss Malone into a snowdrift. Covered with Mrs. Salmi's blankets and bundled against the cold, she was helpless until Toivo retrieved her, saved her from freezing into one lump of blankets, red corkscrew hair, fur hat, fur collar, fur cuffs and fur-trimmed boots. In turn, he was paying himself for suffering a whole long miserable week of emptying Miss Malone's chamber pot, and of listening to her remarkable theories of education.

She said childhood was a time for play, not for exercising the brain. Thus she taught us as little as possible, gave us all the same examinations and had us recite together in order to finish quickly such work as she deemed of some use to us. After that, the older children went outside, skated in the swamp, built a ski jump over the neighbor's fence, jumped over it, and had hour-long snowball fights. We younger children stood on our desks and watched the activities outside, stuck pegs into pegboards and ate peanuts which Miss Malone brought us from Hadley.

When parents complained that we younger children weren't learning anything, she said, "Their brains are still soft. They need to play." When the farmers complained that the boys were running wild and ruining the fences, she said, "They're still young. They need to play. Can't you farmers remember how it was when you were young?" They did and were angrier than ever.

My first and last reader in the first grade was "The Little Red Hen." We never got beyond it, for Miss Anastasia Malone was devoted to that foolish tale. We drew pictures of the hen. We wrote stories about the hen. We dramatized the life story of the hen.

Beside me in the first grade were two other children—Anna, a white-haired, pink-faced girl, a head taller than I, and Arthur, a dark-haired boy. Anna and I were natural rivals. She could read simple sentences, she could add numbers, and she was obedient beyond my comprehension. But I could write anything I wanted to write and that made me superior. Though Arthur had none of our skills, he made up for it by being prettier than we were.

At first Anna and Arthur took turns being the hen, but soon he was raised to permanent henhood; Anna became the cat and I the pig. Miss Malone recruited the rest of the cast from the upper grades. Every day, week after week and month after month.

I had thought that we would learn more about the kings and queens in Mother's fairy tales and more about the big ships which brought the people we knew across the seas. I had hoped I could write stories of my own and poems which made me shiver when I read them. Now I had to think about a chicken not even as clever as the ones in our own chicken coop. How could Arthur willingly play the part of such a stupid creature?

But what else could he do? It wasn't his fault that Miss Malone laid the honor upon him. She liked him as she liked all the boys. That was her one redeeming grace. If they were obedient, she loved them for it. If they were coltish, she encouraged them and then excused them. In return, the boys laughed at her and played pranks on her, but her doll's blue eyes enlarged by her glasses saw no evil. Less given to stumbling and jumping around, the girls missed her line of vision entirely.

But my being a girl did not justify her casting nor explain it. There was something else. I was unpleasing to the eye and that offended her. She did not realize that beneath the bandages which covered my hands and arms and sometimes my neck was a child no different than another, a child who was unbandaged and well, a child who did not wheeze nor cough nor find running or climbing the steep stairs too painful to bear. This was the child I was and at home was encouraged to believe I was.

Miss Malone did not see that child. She saw another, bandaged and wheezing, who contaminated her idyllic world of childhood and possibly to her mind the physical world as well. This child I too had to accept, but I could not. And when the other children teased me about my wheezing and tugged at my bandages, Miss Malone became deaf and blind.

When my brothers were with me, they defended me. So did Toivo Salmi. But when they were out of the schoolroom, I was left to fight my own battles. One day when the sun was bright and the dry heat shimmered above the register, my arms under the layers of bandages began to itch. I squirmed and rubbed my arms. One of the oldest girls at Revier, Elvi Koivunen, began to mimic every move I made. She whispered to her friends, all of them old enough to be out of our school and on to more productive tasks. Now they all began to squirm. Because I was near the washstand, I threw the water-filled basin at them, and hurled the scrub brush, the metal basket and the package of towels as well. The splashing cold water and the flying towels were as soothing as autumn leaves falling into the Montfer.

"Look what she did!" screamed Elvi to Miss Malone, sitting at her desk.

"I saw her," said Miss Malone. "Into the cloakroom, Mary." She followed me and closed the door tight. I sat on the cold floor and became a prisoner, a lost czarina, a sea-tossed sailor. When I could no longer stand the boredom of being alone, I climbed the stepladder to reach the top shelf of the bookcase and there I found a book, its cover faded and its pages yellowed. I brought it down and began to read the names in the table of contents. Letter by letter. Longfellow. Wordsworth. Tennyson. I knew the names! Mother had read me poems which they had written. Now, as I studied the print, familiar words and then whole sentences formed in my head.

Again and again I went into the cloakroom to pay for my misdeeds and to enjoy my imprisonment. Finally I won daily punishment. The narrow coat-filled place with its one shelf of discarded literature, history and geography books became my private schoolroom. One day Miss Malone found me asleep. I had an old geography book in my lap. "What are you doing?" she asked.

"Reading."

"Out!" said Miss Malone, as if reading were the ultimate crime a child could commit in the cloakroom of her school.

I became a pig once more.

Now Miss Malone had to find a more suitable punishment for me, her "worst pupil." Her punishment could not have been better directed at my ailment. She would ask me to hold out my bandaged hand, palm up, and then she would bring down the ruler. After the first time, I drew back my hand just at the last moment, and the ruler broke as it hit the edge of my desk. She lost many rulers, for she could not bring herself to grasp my bandaged hand so that I couldn't withdraw it. I was untouchable except with a ruler.

After Christmas, I could no longer walk to school. I tried using skis, but the snow was heavy and the wind too strong. Even if John and Carl held my arms and tugged me over the fields, I still began to wheeze. Sometimes in the afternoon when the weather was unusually bad, the Kaaris called me in as we walked through their yard, kept me overnight, and then in the morning Mr. Kaari swept the snow off his sleigh and pulled me to school. Sometimes when Father didn't go to the logging camp or into our own woods to make logs, he would hitch the horses to the big logging sled and we'd climb on. Sitting scarved and mittened, covered with quilts, I couldn't tell where we were going. The runners squeaked on the icy snow, the sled swayed over the drifts, and if the school hadn't been where it was, we might have journeyed forever across the fields, the oceans, to Lapland and beyond. But the school stopped us and then I had to get out, to breathe the sharp winter air, go up the long stairs and see Miss Anastasia Malone, her curls in place, her belt streaming behind her, and "The Little Red Hen" written up on the blackboard.

Soon after, I became ill with bronchitis and after that I had one bout after another. I stayed home. Miss Malone sent a copy of "The Little Red Hen" and I taught my sister to read it. She could read it back to front, front to back, upside down or right side up. She was much better than I. For me, because I had a fever, the words jumped around on the page and if I didn't hold them down with my finger they'd fly clear off.

In fall when I had first gone to school, I had worn my new dress and my new shoes. I had a pencil box all my own, a box of new Crayolas and a big tablet with a picture of a little blond girl going to school. She was a lovely girl, and so was I on that day. I'd learn everything there was to know and I'd write stories of animals and small wee men who lived under mushrooms and came to play on my bed when I was sick.

But long before Christmas, I knew there was nothing to be learned in school; the only good in the long day was the going and the coming back. Then the sky was full of birds flying away for winter; there was smoke in the hills and frost in the puddles, and sometimes, way back in the forest, a train calling to another—the only sound in the universe.

I was happy to stay home now. Hank bellowed his Finnish tales to me; Mother read to me; Grandmother told me how it was in Finland; Father brought me good things to eat and watched me eat them; and the neighbors brought salves and medications which did no harm.

When I could sit up, I told stories about bears and wolves and wildcats. Sometimes I placed the bears under our bed and after they were there awhile, I began to believe that they were indeed there waiting for us. Elizabeth would go into the bedroom, stoop over and say, "Come out, bears!" And Edward, so tiny a bear could swallow him in one gulp, crawled underneath and made terrible bearlike sounds. I wanted to save them, to help them, to get them back to the safety of the kitchen, and yet I was too frightened to move. "Come back!" I'd scream, frantic with fear.

"There's nothing there," Elizabeth would say calmly, coming back to reassure me.

"I growled at him," Edward said, running in to demonstrate how he had growled at the bear.

On weekends, we would watch Carl's skiers. During the Christmas holidays, he had whittled these small figures out of wood, had painted them red and blue and yellow, and had pounded babbitt metal into their skis. Afterward he made a miniature ski hill outside the kitchen window, and now we could see him send his skiers flying down. The red one was the best; he flew down the hill, over the jump and down the icy path. He never wavered, never fell. But in the evenings when the lamp was burning, the boys read their books and did their lessons, which my parents corrected since Miss Malone had no interest in their work. John read the newspapers and magazines and sometimes Grandmother had him read her Finnish paper aloud so she too would learn something as she sat at her spinning wheel.

In school everyone was bored, Carl said. One day he came home and said that he had had to be the chicken. "Now I know that the lady belongs in the crazy house," he said. And John thought that they'd all be there before the year was done. Every other day he came home with a bloody nose. The big boys beat up the younger ones, ate their lunches at noon and ripped their clothes, but Miss Malone was as blind as always.

Then one day, John and Carl stumbled home across the drifted fields. Tony Koivunen had beaten them with his ski and had threatened to kill them if they said anything at home. But they didn't need to complain. We could all see that their faces were bleeding and swollen, their backs and legs welted.

"That must end!" said Grandmother. "If you don't go to see those parents, I will. And if I see Tony, I'll give him a beating."

I could see her in her long black skirt and pile coat. She'd float right over the banks along our road. And when she saw Tony, she would beat him.

Big Hank insisted that he was the man to teach Tony a lesson, but Father decided that he and Mother would go right after milking. He washed John's and Carl's cuts and cleaned them with alcohol. Mother filled rubber hot-water bags with snow, asked my brothers to lie down on the bed and put the cold bags on their faces. "How can I talk?" mumbled Carl, and Grandmother told him that for once he could be quiet.

After the chores, Father and Mother got into their good coats, lighted the kerosene lantern and went out into the frozen night. John was sure they wouldn't be able to talk to Tony because he'd hide as soon as he heard them coming.

We waited for an hour and then another. Grandmother made us hot milk and toast; we ate and waited some more. At last Mother and Father came home.

Tony hadn't been anywhere in sight, but Father thought he was within earshot. Mr. Koivunen had blamed Miss Malone for all the troubles and wanted to go to the school board, but knew that he couldn't speak English well enough.

"And what did you say, Father?" asked Carl.

"I told him that Miss Malone hadn't beaten you boys and that Tony had." Father picked up his *Daily News*. "I don't think he'll do it again."

John and Carl stayed home for the rest of the week, and on Saturday Tony came over with a pair of boots he wanted Father to fix for him. "Behaving yourself these days, Tony?" Father asked as coolly as he would of a stranger who wasn't welcome in our house.

"Yup. Pa's going to the school board. Wants to know if you'd go with him." He didn't look at Father or us. He stared at the floor.

"Is that so?"

"Yup. He don't like Miss Malone."

Father fixed the boots on his shoemaker's machine, cut the threads and looked at all the seams to see if they had tears. Then he gave the boots to Tony and said, "Tell your father that I'm going to the meeting and I'll pick him up."

That's what Father did. Later he told us that Revier School would be better the next year, but it was months away and I didn't need to think about going to school at all. I could listen to Mother's stories and songs, play with Elizabeth and Edward and practice writing. Mother always found new words she thought I would like to print into the notebook she had bought for me. Mississippi. Minnesota. Manitoba. She didn't know why, but some words sounded better than others. They sang all by themselves.

And Father said that even the sun was brighter now that I was feeling well. He drew pictures for me. Cats, owls, dogs, geese and ducks. He showed me how to make squares from triangles, helped me saw a board into pieces, and used his plane to shave curls off wood. When he found a pail with a hole in the bottom, he took out the soldering iron, opened the lid on the stove, put in the iron, and when it was red hot, he took it out and melted the solder with it. Most of the solder stayed over the hole but small silver balls always got away and raced each other around the rim of the pail.

Sometimes when Father brought home the rabbits he had trapped, Elizabeth, Edward and I would watch him peel off the soft fur. Underneath, the bodies looked like small people rather than rabbits, and when I thought of that I couldn't eat the meat. But the fur was lovely and after stretching the skins, Father placed a pattern on the leather side, cut it with his big scissors and stitched the pieces on the shoemaker's machine. One after another, mittens and moccasins, small ones and big ones.

And on clear days when it would've been pleasant to walk to school, I would take out books from the cupboard with the heavy glass doors. I'd look at the pictures—pictures of battlefields, of cannons blasting away, horses rearing up, and arms and legs flying everywhere. There were men in blue uniforms, gray uniforms, red ones and khaki, but no matter what the men wore, they bled red when the cannons fired. "That's how it was in wars," Mother said, and told me to put the books away because they belonged to Father.

Then there was a big brown one which Father called his "Dream House Book." It had thick shiny pages with photographs of houses on one side and line drawings on the other. All kinds of houses—big ones with columns in front of them and smaller ones with dormer windows. Houses with balconies and porches. Houses with none. When I asked Father which house he liked best, he showed me the last photograph. "There's a good house, Mary. It has a library," he said, and pointed to a square on the line drawing. The place was lovely, larger than any I had ever seen, and certainly a perfect dream house. But Mother said she didn't have a dream house because she liked the one we had.

There were other books, with pictures of fruits and flowers, and one having "Feeding the Family—Rose" printed on its light green cover, and on the first page, a picture of a lady with hair piled high on the top of her head; she had on a pinch-waisted gauzy dress and the little girl standing beside her had long yellow hair. I thought that the girl looked like me and the woman like Mother, and that the book was about feeding a family rose, someone frail, someone who needed special feeding to survive.

We had no rose in our family, but if we ever got one, Mother and I would read this book, find out what to cook and how to cook it. Then everyone in Revier would say, "Now look at that Family Rose!" If anyone wanted to know how we fed our rose, we would tell them. We could teach them, but we'd never ask them to read "The Little Red Hen."

The snow melted away at last and the school year was over. Miss Anastasia Malone was having a picnic to celebrate the end of the long winter. I wanted to go because Aunt Mandy had made me a dress of black and gray material. The dress had no sleeves, only a ruffle, and a red ribbon hanging down from a rosette pinned to the shoulder. I liked the dress, though Carl said it made me look like a ghost and John said it didn't make me look like anything and Mother said it wasn't a picnic dress. Still, I wanted to wear it, to say good-bye to Miss Malone and to carry the cake she had asked Mother to make.

I asked Mother to make a five-layer cake with jelly between the layers and white meringue frosting on top. She said a layer cake was hard to eat outside, but I thought no other kind of cake would go with a dress as pretty as mine. She didn't argue. She made the cake and together we frosted it the evening before the outing.

That night while we were all asleep, the snow came back, six inches of it, covering the green grass and the buds on the trees. "There won't be a picnic," everyone said. But I knew there would be one, knew that Miss Malone would have a picnic even if there were six feet of new snow, if the Revier School were covered with snow; even if no one came, she would have a picnic. And I would go to it, I'd wear my new dress and carry my five-layer cake even if the bottom of the box dragged in the snow.

Mother said I could wear my Christmas dress, that it would be perfect on a snowy spring day.

"The snow will melt," I said. I could see it disappearing, the patches of green growing until every field was green as far as the school and beyond.

"She's stupid," Carl said.

Then we had a long argument over my being stupid. First I said that I wasn't, and finally I said I didn't care if I was.

While we were arguing, Mother bandaged my arms and helped me put on the gray dress.

"Now she looks like a mummy," said Carl.

John shrugged. "What difference does it make? It's just a picnic."

I remember standing in the snow, my coat off and the high winter boots almost touching the hem of my dress. The cake was on a table under a tree nearby, the boys were playing ball as if there were no snow at all, and Miss Malone was pouring lemonade. Had a volcano erupted in the pasture, she would have ordered Mr. Wiita to put up the sawhorses and the planks for the table and she would have behaved as if that was just the place to have a celebration. She had promised us a picnic and we would have a picnic. "One cannot tell lies to children," she would have said.

After we had eaten, we went back to the school. She gave us our report cards. Everyone passed, she said, except one. I did not. I failed in reading, writing, arithmetic and drawing. I even failed in deportment. According to my yellow report card, I hadn't learned a thing. I accepted the judgment. Either one learns or one doesn't. I hadn't, so there was nothing to be done.

At the end of May, when the school year was over, the summer ahead was a lifetime of sun, river water, dusty roads, birdsong, and flowers bursting into bloom in Grandmother's garden, in the pasture and in the hidden places of the forest. School would never begin again, for we had won our freedom.

On the first day of our liberation, we woke up early, hurried to the barn to watch the milking and to feed the cats the foam from the milk pails. We had white, long-haired cats with blue eyes, black ones with tiger eyes, calico cats, and one scrawny gray cat, the mother of every cat we had, short-haired or long. She was always lying on her side in the hay while the kittens tugged at her belly and the other big cats lapped at the foamy milk with their efficient tongues.

Or we watched the chicks, a hundred of them, sometimes two hundred fluffy balls of darting yellow with frail pink legs and beady eyes. They drank pink water, beautiful to look at but dangerous for us to drink though it kept the chicks from getting fatal diarrhea. If they caught it, they would go about with their rears inflamed and the feathers stuck together. In a few days they would die and we'd find them stretched out, the fluff on their bodies matted.

Every year when the postman brought the warm, peeping, brown boxes with nickel-sized holes all over the sides, we gathered around to see the living mass of yellow inside each box. When I was six—the year of "The Little Red Hen"—we found one chick with an injured eye. Father took her out because the others would peck her to death, and then having had the experience of pecking at one of their members, would choose another to peck to death.

I adopted that one-eyed chick, fed her, cared for her and kept her in a shoe box. When she was lonely, she made a sorrowful peeping sound, but when I talked to her, she began to eat and move about in the businesslike, self-important way that chicks have. Father said I shouldn't become too fond of my pet, for no matter what I did, the infection from the injured eye would spread to the brain. But I was determined to love my one-eyed chick, to keep her alive and to raise her to one-eyed chickenhood. No one could persuade me to stop willing health into her. "She'll live," I'd say. "She eats and she's growing."

One morning when I looked into the shoe box, my chick was huddled in a corner. Her yellow down was faded and matted together, and her body shrunken to half its size as if it had been

57

crushed by a weight. I knew at once that she was dead. No angels sang for her as they had for Grandmother when she slept into a dream of heaven. My chick was gone forever.

That was the first real death in my life, a death which was irrevocable, leaving me nothing at all—only an empty, smelly shoe box and a remembrance of holding a frail, warm living thing in my hand, a creature which could have grown, could have followed me around and maybe even become a very special being not limited by her birth as a chicken. Perhaps she could have become a queen —a queen of all the animals. Then I could have made a crown for her. But she was gone and never again would there be another like her.

After lunch, I asked Mother to give me an empty match box. I colored it red, and covered the bottom of it with flannel, placed the chick on it, covered her with cotton wool and closed the box. Then Carl dug a hole under the lilac and I placed the box inside the hole. John preached a sermon; we sang Christmas songs, the most holy songs we knew, and then we packed the dirt over the box.

I adopted other ailing young, loved them, tried to keep them alive, but they died too, always suddenly. I no longer grieved. They were dead and we had to look for boxes in which to bury them, had to plan funerals and sing songs. After we put a fence around our cemetery, we no longer had funerals, because we couldn't remain sad enough. We'd begin to fool around, say all sorts of crazy things just to make each other laugh, and though it seemed awful to be laughing, we couldn't stop.

Later on, I thought the animals weren't really dead, but had moved to a log cabin deep in the forest where the calves, pigs and ducks had gone, all the kittens and puppies, all the animals who suddenly disappeared and never returned. Who had built that cabin long ago when I was very young, I don't remember, but it may have been one of the larger calves, who wanted to have a place for all the animals leaving the farm. There they cooked and ate, swept the floor and kept the curtains clean. The only one who wasn't there was the one-eyed chick.

3

EVERY YEAR WE CELEBRATED the arrival of summer just as the Finns had celebrated in Finland, or so Grandmother said. We began our preparations early. Big Hank called this the Time of the Great Anger, and maybe it was for the adults, though not for us. For us it was a time of excitement, with every last shred of order gone and forgotten, lost in the summer sun, lost among the quilts on the clothesline, the tables, chairs, cupboards, mattresses, bedsteads and picture frames, all in the yard. Everything that was inside the house was now outside the house, all except the big black kitchen stove and the big square heater in the bedroom. But even they stood useless for their pipes were outside, and someone was scraping out the winter's soot from the insides, making them clean once more. And now when we went into the house, our footsteps were the footsteps of giants; our voices shouted back at us from the end wall of the house; and when we looked at the windows, they stared back at us as if they were blind.

Father set up an old stove in the yard. John and Carl fired the stove, threw everything useless into it, and once I threw in Edward's shoe, which wasn't useless because it was newly bought at Penney's, but I didn't know that. Mother put a kettle on the stove and a big pot of coffee. Father brought summer sausage from the store in town, great loaves of bread white as cotton, brown bags of lemons, white bags of sugared doughnuts and bunches of bananas.

Mother, Father, Otto and Aunt Mandy and anyone who wanted to join us came, pasted wallpaper, scrubbed woodwork, washed windows, pounded quilts and rugs, and hung curtains on the stretchers leaning against the west side of the house, where the afternoon sun would bleach the cotton lace. Alex mixed the paint for the floor. We watched while he poured linseed oil, turpentine and pigments from small cans into big gallon cans, and then stirred and poured until the paint was smooth. Then he stopped for coffee. While we waited, he talked about his car or his saw rig or his new invention which would revolutionize the whole world but wouldn't change religion one bit because religion had to do with souls, which never changed at all.

"Aren't you ready, Alex?" we'd ask, once, twice, three times. He looked at us, placed his empty coffee cup on the ground, picked up his big brush, and we all went inside to watch him cover the floor, inch by inch, just the way the floodwater did when it licked its path up the banks of the river. Part of the floor had to be saved for the next day so that the mattresses, quilts and clothes could be brought in before the evening dew fell on them. On the following day we finished the painting, which gave us a new floor, a glistening blue or gray or brown.

Now everything seemed nicer inside than out. The tables and chairs sat at ever crazier angles. There was nothing left to burn in the stove. Our insides, afloat in lemonade, would take no more. At last Father and Hank fetched planks from the garage, covered the stairs and made pathways in the house. Everything that had been carried outside was carried inside; the curtains went up, the black stovepipes smelling of paint, and the pictures in the oval frames. The Time of the Great Anger was over.

Father hitched old Maud to a sledge and went into the woodlot to look for young maples. By afternoon, he had enough to build the midsummer leaf house. He dug postholes in the yard on the east side of the house, stuck the maples into the holes and we stamped the ground tight around the trunks. By late afternoon, the leaf house was done—three sides of maple trees and one side of our house, the benches made of sawhorses and planks, and the old wobbly kitchen table braced against the wall—all ready for us. We said it was the most beautiful leaf house we had ever had, but we always said that, every year. And every year, on the Eve of Midsummer, Hank heated the sauna, and just as night was falling we went there with our clean nightclothes wrapped in a towel.

Afterward, as I climbed into my bed smelling of the outdoors and saw in the dim light of the kerosene lamp the red roses climbing on the new wallpaper, and heard the flutter of the maple leaves in the leaf house outside, separated from us by only a wall, I felt at peace and wondered then if I would always feel so, even when I was grown or even next year when I'd be one year older.

For a whole week, sometimes until the Fourth of July, we children lived in the leaf house. Mother cooked supper outside so that our real house would stay cool for the night, but early in the morning when I was still not quite awake, I could hear the muffled sound of her pounding the cardamom seed, of slapping the cake dough with a big wooden spoon, and I knew she had heated the big stove to bake sweet biscuits and lemon cake.

Then it was the Fourth. We woke up early. Elizabeth and I put on our good dresses, the boys their white shirts and school pants, and Father took us to Hadley to see the parade, to hear the trumpets and bugles and drums, to watch the floats ride by and to catch the balloons, flags, gum and candy which the people on the floats threw down to the children on the sidewalk on Iron Street. I clung to my sister, to Edward and to Father, but John and Carl scrambled into the crowd, leaped for anything flying over their heads and sometimes jumped into the street to pick up what had fallen there.

I feared for their lives. They'd get lost in the crowd and we'd never find them. They'd fall in front of a horse or a truck or a car. They would die, so heedless they were.

But the floats went by and finally the last. People began moving away. Only Father waited still, kept looking up the street, up to the corner from where all the floats had come. I hoped that at least one more red, white and blue paper-covered float would come down the street, but the float never came. The last was always the last.

"Where do we go now?" Father would ask.

"To the creamery!" we shouted as if Father had gone deaf.

"Where's the creamery? I never heard of a creamery," said Father.

"It's over there," Elizabeth told him. "You can go down that street!"

"Maybe it's over there," said Father, pointing toward Woodland, where the creamery wasn't.

By this time we had found our car. The boys were there too, their pockets full, their white shirts ballooning from their trousers and their faces red from running up and down tavern-lined Iron Street. "Look what I got!" And we all looked at the sticks of Wrigley's in their wrappers, bars of Hershey's and flags too small to be of use, too big to be intriguing.

We climbed into the car, Elizabeth and Edward in the front with Father; John, Carl and I in the back. In a moment, we were at the Hadley County Creamery and its big picture of the brick of Neapolitan, with the neat slice cut out of it and placed in the center of a plate. Father left us, and soon came back carrying a bucket full of ice and a smaller circular container all but buried in the cold blue squares, triangles, slivers and chips of ice. A whole gallon of maple nut ice cream!

"Now we've got to hurry," Father said, and as he started the car we all bounced against each other.

"Look at the dust," someone said. And there was always dust, a big red cloud of it as we drove out of the creamery yard and to the grocery store. Father got out, went in, and came out, this time with a whole crate of bottles. All the way home, the boys read the labels: ginger ale, root beer, strawberry soda, cherry, cream, orange and lemon. They tried to decide how the bottles could be shared, to remember who wanted what in just what order, and argued because halfway through the second round, all the bottles would be open and fizzing away into the Fourth of July sunshine. "It won't work! You can't have all of them open!"

"I don't care. I want cherry." It had the same color as the water which the little chicks drank, day after day.

"Don't you ever take anything else?" asked Carl.

"If she wants cherry, let her have it," John said. "We're all having what we want."

We rode home along the highway, then the rutted township road going through Revier, past all the farms, and finally past the Salmis', the last before our mailbox and our own road. No one was celebrating. Everyone was home doing ordinary daily things. Only we were flying about with a whole gallon of maple nut ice cream and a crate of soda.

As soon as we were in the yard, the boys ran in to fetch their firecrackers. Big fat ones, long thin ones, round ones, blue ones, red ones and white ones, firecrackers that shook the windows and firecrackers that smoked, fizzled and did nothing else. Elizabeth and I had firecrackers too—very small ones which Father lighted for us, only I didn't want them and would give them to my sister or even to Edward, who would stand watching solemnly as Father put the match to the paper fuses, and then when the crackle was to come, dropped the whole package, covered his ears and closed his eyes.

We always had wieners on the Fourth—the kind which came in a long sausage with tiny waists along the length of it. Maybe they were special wieners made by the Italian butcher in town or maybe they were ordinary wieners before their downfall. Whatever they were, they were a part of our Fourth, just like the floats, the soda pop and the ice cream.

If there was a carnival in town, we went to it in the afternoon, but if there wasn't we stayed home, ate ice cream, drank soda pop and watched the boys blow up their firecrackers—whole boxes of them, but never enough. Still, no afternoon was ever longer. We couldn't go into the barn or play on the riverside or even run around too much, because we had on our best clothes, and we wouldn't put on our play clothes because it was the Fourth of July. We had to wait for the evening to come so we could all climb back into the car and ride to the county park to watch the fireworks.

Father was fascinated by the rockets, by every loud bang and every blazing streak of color above our heads. "Look at that!" he'd say, and then, "Gee," with a shake of his head as the colors fell down along the sides of the night sky. We ate popcorn, shrieked, exclaimed and clapped with everyone else, but no matter how loudly I shrieked with the rest, I was frightened by the noise, the crush of people, the boys darting away from the car, and the thought of cannons blazing somewhere. All the while Elizabeth sat on the hood of the car and Edward on Father's shoulder. They feared nothing. The sky could have fallen over us and they would have accepted it as part of the celebration.

Afterward, riding home in the damp and quiet night, I felt that the whole world had fallen asleep at last and that only we were stirring about and preparing to wake it up again, because for us the

Fourth wasn't over. We would have our own fireworks once we were home. First, we had to burn our sparklers, for each of us had a box and they had to be used on that day and no later. The boys lighted theirs, waved them in the air, and ran around in circles like fireflies gone wild. Elizabeth, Edward and I stood on the steps and Father lighted ours. One after another they burned, firing their harmless sparks at us as we watched the light eating its way to the end of the dead gray covering on the stick.

Then Father set off his own explosives, rockets which zoomed into the sky and broke into stars with trailing tails, and Roman candles with showers of sparks and balls of fire, and best of all, Japanese balloons which floated blazing across the fields. Finally he set off the blast of dynamite somewhere deep in the darkness behind the barn. The sound rocked the stable, the barn, the house, the hills and the earth beneath our feet. Dizzy with the sound of it, we came into the house, the varicolored lights of the evening still in our eyes and our legs numb with fatigue.

"Who wants ice cream? It'll spoil if we don't eat it."

Half asleep, we drank the rest of the melting ice cream and then stumbled into our dark and silent beds.

Someone was always sick the day after. Mother said the celebration certainly wasn't worth the sacrifice. Grandmother said that it was foolish to blow half the county into the sky. In Finland, she said, people had not been so witless. Big Hank, who did not think the Fourth was worth celebrating, said that if the children wanted the hands from the wall clock, they must have those too.

Father said nothing. We knew it didn't matter what the others said. Our Fourth would always be the same—red, white and blue, one loud crash after another, maple nut ice cream, popcorn, and cherry pop if you wanted it.

The next day the mowing began. Field after field of clover, alfalfa and timothy came down before the blade of the mower. Mother, Father, Hank and John raked and spread the hay over and over, and finally pitched it into the hay wagon, which the horses pulled into the barnyard. The hay had to be lifted with a fork into the loft. The operation was a drama of life and death or so I thought, for if the fork attached to ropes running into pulleys broke away, the man below in the hay wagon was doomed. If the ropes became enmeshed in the high reaches of the loft, a man risked his life in unloosening the snarls. If the rope broke at the moment the fork released its load in the loft, the fork trailing its tail of frayed rope would sink its pointed teeth into the man below.

We watched speechless as Big Hank loaded the fork and yelled "Gohet" to John, who drove the horse harnessed to the ropes on the ground. Slowly the load rose, reached the track and then disappeared into the dark loft.

Day after day, wagonload after wagonload came in from the field, into the barnyard. Everyone was tired—"too tired to think straight," Mother said. Even we smaller children were tired of carrying sacks of lunch, thermos bottles of coffee, and jars of cold drinks to the people working in the field, and when they stopped working we sat with them under the shade of a hay wagon while they drank water from blue Mason jars and cold home brew which tasted almost like root beer, and we drank root beer which tasted almost like home brew.

Once we fed the dregs from the beer keg to the chickens because neither the cats nor the dogs would touch it. The chickens wobbled about and tried to crow like roosters but they couldn't. Carl said they were drunk, and if we wanted to, we could get drunk too, but the dregs tasted too awful, more like yeast gone bad than like beer. So we pretended we were drunk and wobbled around just as the chickens were wobbling. Then we pretended we were blind, then deaf, and last that we were dying of some terrible disease.

John said we did nothing while he worked in the field. It was true. He did work in the field, and all we did was bring food and drink to the workers, scrape pots and pans, wash dishes, pump up water for the horses, and try to keep ourselves amused while the grownups were gone.

But if the weather turned rainy, there was nothing to do for any of us. Nothing but worry. We could look out at the soggy landscape, the drooping branches of the lilacs and the waterlogged rose blossoms hanging from their stems. We could watch the yard turn into one puddle of red mud. We could fret with the adults and wait. We learned to hope, accustomed ourselves to seeing good omens everywhere. A break in the clouds. A shift in the wind. A change in the feel of the air. I was the first to see a clear sky in a mass of clouds so heavy it could pour down rain for three days. I could see a streak of sunlight where there was none. I could wish the hay as crisp as bread crust though the rain kept coming down, wish the rotting piles into sweet-smelling mounds and wish the Sahara onto our front yard. I could wish anything, only nothing came of it.

Still somehow, year after year, the hay did get into the loft. Sometimes there was so much hay the loft would hold no more and the men had to make stacks, huge ones like pyramids. And somehow no one fell off the hay wagon; the fork did not come crashing down; the hay did dry and did not begin to rot, or to heat up and burn the whole barn down.

Someone got a thistle in his finger, the finger turned red and Mother had to prepare a plaster. Sometimes dust flew about and lodged in an eye. Then Mother had to turn the lid back and take out the offending specks before they injured the eyeball. John always had a sunburn; Father always had a rash and had to be dusted down with baby powder. Carl always had swollen glands from drinking the water straight from the pump. And sometimes I turned white in the hot sun and had chills which rattled my teeth. Then I had to sit in the shade. Grandmother mixed a solution of vinegar and water, dipped cloths into it, wrung them out and put them on my throbbing head. After a day or two, I was well again. I could feel sorry for the horses who had to pull the wagon, for the cows who had to eat the hay with thistles in it, with mouse nests and bird nests and the dust from the field.

Grandmother said that nests weren't edible, but the thistles didn't hurt the cows. As for pulling the hay wagon, who would do it if not the horses? After they were done working, they could rest in the pasture. People could never rest. They had to go on thinking, not just about themselves but about animals too. So if you begin to worry about one, you have to worry about both. I did. Life just wasn't easy for animals and it wasn't easy for people.

Soon afterward, the grain turned yellow. When the wind blew across the fields, the stalks bent and rose in long golden waves. It was at that time that the combine needed to come, to cut down the grain and to bundle it into sheaves. But sometimes the combine did not come. The rain came first. The stalks bent and fell to the ground. Then the field appeared matted and patched. The man who operated the combine said it would be hard to get the grain or it would be nearly useless to try. Somehow I had the feeling it was our fault that the grain was lying down on the ground instead of waving in the wind. But the rains came without permission, at night often, and when we woke up the damage was done. How were we to stop the rain? Still, I felt that maybe we might have done something to save the man the trouble of cutting a matted grainfield.

After the grain dried, the threshing machine came rattling down our narrow road. For a whole day the barnyard and the house resembled disturbed anthills. No one walked; everyone ran. In the barnyard, everyone shouted; in the kitchen, everything steamed, boiled and sputtered. Everything edible in the woods, the fields and the gardens had to be cooked for the threshing crew, the final arbiters of cooking skills in the community.

The children in the neighborhood followed the arbiters and joined in the competitive game.

"My mother made an angel food cake plus a bushel of doughnuts."

"My mother made three kinds of pies!"

"My mother put six eggs in her cake."

All the while the threshing machine rattled, shook, and filled sack after sack of oats, barley and wheat. The chaff flew in clouds over everything. And once Mr. Lahti, who owned the thresher, began to argue with his son, Robert. The son hit his father on the jaw. Then they wrestled and the older man fell to the ground. The son held him there, though he was smaller than his father.

Mother had come to call the men to dinner. When she saw the fight, she began to weep and to wipe her eyes with her apron. No doubt it was sad to see a father and his son pounding each other as if they were strangers, sad in Mother's estimation, though not in anyone else's because somehow the father had forfeited his special status. How he had done it, I don't remember.

When they were standing up again, someone said they should shake hands and forgive each other. Perhaps Mother said it, muffling it through her apron. But they wouldn't shake hands. They just stood there, one beside the other, united by nothing save their anger. It was then that I noticed the boy's harelip.

The whole crew went inside to have dinner. Mr. Wiita said our yield was better than his. Mr. Lahti said nothing at all; Robert talked and talked, but I couldn't understand him. The words didn't come out; they disappeared into the corners of his head and all that emerged was a garble ranging from high to low.

After the threshing was done and all the grain was in the bins, the threshing crew in cars and Mr. Lahti on the tractor pulling the threshing machine rattled down our road like a noisy funeral procession.

"Well, that's done," Father said as he came in.

Mother said nothing. She was clearing away the left-over food.

"We had a good harvest."

Mother wouldn't answer him. She just closed the cupboard door much harder than she ought to have. The glass on the door cracked. She looked at the door and then sat down at the table and began to weep. "What on earth will people say?"

"The Lahtis have fought before," Father said.

"They were drunk!"

"Perhaps they had a drink earlier," said Father, "but they weren't drunk. They were angry when they got here and for all I know, they're still angry. I can't help them."

"People will say that we gave them liquor," Mother said, wiping her eyes.

"People have better things to talk about," said Grandmother.

No one in Revier ever mentioned the fight between the harelip Robert and his father. Maybe they felt sorry for him because they couldn't understand his garble. I wondered how he felt, and if he thought of himself as flawed. He was only one of many who had some fault glaring enough for us all to see. There was the Watkins' salesman, with one eye blue and the other brown. There was a young woman who had one arm which stopped at the elbow, with no hand on it, only three fingers small as a child's. Then there was Mrs. Lahti, who had a glass eye, a much darker blue than her real one. I always wondered if the lid came over the glass when she fell asleep or if the glass eye just stared into the dark and never got any rest. Mother said it wouldn't matter because a glass eye doesn't need to relax since it doesn't feel anything.

Otto had his bobbing gait, which didn't really seem like a flaw after one got to know him. In many ways it made him appear more jolly and carefree. Another man, Mulari, had the same kind of walk—side to side, like the pendulum on our clock. He had other problems too; one leg was badly twisted and his eyes were crossed.

And that was a pity because his eyes were as green and bright as those of our long-haired cat.

And we had a crazy woman living nearby. When she came to visit, she raved, her eyes rolling in her head and her hands twitching. If Father was home, he told her to sit on the well cover and to tell him about her calves, which she loved though they were the skinniest, scrawniest calves in Revier. Soon she was quiet, almost like everyone else, except that her eyes rolled and darted about, not really looking at anything but flying over us, the house and everything around it. When Mother called and said that the coffee was ready, we all went inside to watch, though there was nothing to watch except that the crazy woman seemed normal or nearly so.

Toivo Salmi's older brother had a scarred face and was crippled besides. He had been burned as a baby, so badly burned that no one thought he would live, but he did and now his right arm was bent at the elbow as though he had been born with a sling. His twisted fingers were always blue as if he had just come in from the cold, even on the hottest days, but I thought that he was very handsome, at least as handsome as Toivo, whose chief joy in life had been to pester Miss Anastasia Malone. The older brother really looked more like his sister, Ann, who was by far the most beautiful creature I had ever seen. Excepting Mother, who had golden hair and looked like a princess.

Ann was so beautiful a rich young man from Milwaukee fell in love with her one summer, and though his family said she was too poor for him and at first refused to even see her, once they did see her they consented to the marriage immediately, and invited the young couple to live with them in their mansion on the shore of Lake Michigan. All she had to do there was to sit in the garden, talk to her husband, Glenn, watch the sailboats float by on the surface of the blue lake, and when dinner was called, find a suitable dress among the hundred which hung in her closet.

One day when the lake was as smooth as glass, Glenn went to the yacht club to join the regatta. Who would have thought that the lake would turn gray and choppy? Who would have dreamed on that sunny morning that the sailboats belonged in the harbor? No one. The boats went out like great sea birds with white wings flapping hard and fierce in order to gain the lead. Glenn did as he always did, and flew far ahead of the rest. And there when he was alone the great wave came. His boat overturned and threw him into the dark churning water.

People said that Ann was left with nothing but her beautiful face. Some said that she was even lovelier than before; some said she looked like an angel in mourning; some even said that she would never marry again. Yet she did and she was happier than she had ever been, because her new husband was poor, just as she was. They would work together and get ahead. But before they had a chance to buy a house or even new furniture, she became with child. For some reason everyone found this news sad, as if Ann should have been spared the fate of ordinary girls who marry and have babies. Perhaps the feeling was a premonition of the fate which was to befall her; perhaps it was only a wish that Ann might escape the common lot. She did in a sense, for she died in child-birth and her grieving husband committed suicide. That was the story of beautiful Ann.

Her story ended that year when I was six. During the lull between the harvesting of grain and the beginning of school, the long telegram came to the Salmi house when Elizabeth and I were there sitting at the table and eating currants. Toivo read the telegram and translated the difficult parts for his parents.

Mr. Salmi said that if he were to go to the funeral in Milwaukee, he would need a new suit because the old one wasn't good enough for city wear. Mrs. Salmi was sure that no one would look at his clothes. It was then that we learned that Ann was her stepdaughter, for Mr. Salmi had been married before. I don't think Mrs. Salmi would have bought herself a new dress even if Ann had been her daughter, but to Mr. Salmi clothes were important. They declared to the world that he honored the memory of his daughter now and as long as he lived, and honored the memory of the man who had chosen to be her husband and then to die with her.

Why would anyone choose to die? I wouldn't. Not immediately, anyway. I'd wait. I asked Toivo if he'd wait. "Sure," he said. "Fifty years! After that you might as well wait for the end."

The next morning on his way to work, Father drove Mr. Salmi to the railroad station in Hadley. Mother went along as far as River Bend, where she got out and began collecting money from every house along the road. Not that she could collect enough to pay for the new suit and the long train ride to Milwaukee, nor even that a gift would ease the burden of sorrow at the Salmi house. Mother just wanted to show the family that everyone was sorry.

Having had a good response on the first day, Mother went out again on the next. This time she went to Michigan, on the other side of the Montfer. Many people knew the Salmis there and surely they should hear about Ann. How else would they learn of her death? Many of the people didn't get the *Daily News;* some didn't get the Finnish paper. And even if they got both, how could we be sure the news would be in the papers?

While Mother was gone, we children stayed at home with Grandmother. Elizabeth and I dusted, set the table, cleared the table, and then set it once again. We picked raspberries, now dry and dust-laden and almost useless, but Grandmother washed and cooked them anyway. We amused Edward by looking for toads which we couldn't find and for turtles which we could see but couldn't catch because they were swimming, noses in the air, as if they were taunting us to wade into the middle of the Montfer. We didn't. We caught minnows instead and asked Grandmother if they could be made into fish stew. She said they couldn't. In fact, she wouldn't eat a salmon if it were in the Montfer. She wouldn't eat anything from the river. It was just an extension of the Hadley sewer system.

Five times Edward asked when Mother was coming home. Then another five times. Carl took him for a ride in his wagon when we fetched the mail from the box. John read a story to him. We ate a whole bottle of sweet pickles with him, but he said they were too sour. We offered him milk and he said that was sour. We offered him sugar; that too was sour. Everything was sour. Then Elizabeth began to fret. "I wish my mother would come home," she said.

"And I wish you kids would stop whining," said John. "If she goes out to get some fresh air, what's the difference?" He was ten and could tell when our whining was within the bounds of reason.

The difference was that Mother wasn't home as she usually was and Grandmother was cross for being left with us. And as soon as Father came home from work and asked, "Is Louise home yet?" Grandmother wanted to know if there wasn't enough work at our house.

"There should be, but I suppose she'll work all the harder to-morrow," replied Father.

"Not if she wears herself down running all over the township."

But we knew Mother wouldn't be worn down. She'd scrub the house from back to front and all the while she'd be telling us stories about the people she had seen, all the problems they were having, and how important it was to be a good Christian. Even a two-hour trip with someone who needed a translator at a doctor's office gave Mother a whole afternoon of story material. Everyone was always in Hadley when Mother happened to go there. Two days of misery seemed a small price to pay for all the entertainment we'd derive from her collecting for the Salmis.

Carl was standing at the door so he could tell us when Mother emerged from the clump of trees in the pasture. "Here she comes," he shouted, and Elizabeth, Edward and I ran to the door to watch her.

As soon as she walked in, happy and restored, Grandmother asked her the question which had been bothering her all afternoon. "Where do you think your responsibilities are?"

"I'm not a slave," Mother said cheerfully.

"None of us are free, Louise," said Grandmother, looking about for her egg basket. "It's good to help the neighbors, but our own household has to come first." She left to gather the eggs.

Mother wanted to know if we had misbehaved and we assured her that we hadn't, but Edward had whined all day and we hadn't been able to stop him.

"Grandmother gets tired and it's no wonder," Father said, and got himself and Mother a cup of coffee from the pot on the stove. "Not that the Salmis can't use the money. I know they need it."

Mother didn't say anything in return, but I could tell by the look on her face that we wouldn't hear any stories about her adventures. She would keep them all to herself. Maybe she was angry with Father or with us or Grandmother. Perhaps she was sorry that she had tried to be a good Christian. But whatever she felt, I knew that the lonely day would go on until we lost it in our sleep.

Father was right. Not only had Mr. Salmi had to pay for a train ticket, a new suit, and lodging and meals; he had had to pay half of the funeral expenses. Ann and her husband hadn't had any money and his family didn't have much either because they were farmers.

"That's how it is with people like us who try to start a new life on the land," Mother said, and she wiped her eyes on the hem of her apron.

The summer passed. My cousins living in town came to visit, stood in their long white stockings and patent leather shoes and stared at us in our overalls. We took them into the barn to show them the new kittens we had and then it was we who seemed in place, as free as the cats to leap, to hang and dangle. And the uncles came with their wives and Great-Aunt Harper with her piles of hair. The friends of my parents came too and brought their children. At first we never had anything to say but after a while we did, and still I often wanted to go inside "to help my mother." That is what I said, and did too, just like a grownup, the women would say, as I cut the cake and set the table. Soon they weren't thinking of me at all but about Hilda whose baby had come five months after her marriage, about Frank who drank too much and his wife who didn't because she was a Christian, and about Andrew who kept changing cars, getting bigger ones each time and none of them any good at all. The minister wasn't just right either or his wife wasn't, or his children; something was always wrong with ministers.

Mother said one shouldn't look at what ministers do but hear what they say, and Grandmother said ministers were human beings. No one could say she was wrong. They were human beings. Because Grandmother said they were, because she was old and rarely said much, people listened to her. Before I could really tell what had happened, everyone was talking about flowers, vegetables, berry picking and canning.

We spent days on end walking to the Salmi house, and back again with Rachel and Reino, the two young children in the family. We ate bowls of fresh peas which their mother shelled and cooked, currants off the bushes, strawberries from the field and great sugar-covered molasses cookies straight from the black oven. We sat at the kitchen table, listened to Mrs. Salmi talk about God as if he were one of the neighbors, and drank our afternoon coffee. When Edward's cup was empty, he would bang it on the table and say, "More!" Mr. Salmi filled the cup and offered him a cookie. "No, thank you," he'd answer, and open the brown paper sack in which he carried two pieces of rusk—always two pieces. "I carry my own lunch."

This scene was enacted every day because he was Mr. Salmi's favorite. Fragile, blue-eyed and golden-haired, Edward was the opposite of the Salmis' robust, dark-haired offspring. Mr. Salmi would lift Edward to the ceiling and say that he weighed less than a feather. Back on the floor again, Edward stood stern and unyielding. "I'm a big man," he'd say. He may have weighed twenty-five pounds; there was nothing at all to him but the thought of his own bigness and competence.

Before going home, we watched Mr. Salmi hammering out horseshoes, pickaxes and chisels in his blacksmith shop near the road. Finally, tired of the noise, we walked back home along the dusty road, then through the pasture where the bushes hung over the road, and along the cool river, then past the sauna and to the house, different from any other, more cheerful and alive, a place where we could laugh or cry or tease or joke and still remain just what we thought ourselves to be.

At last it was time for the county fair. We went there to see it —all of it—from the monstrous bulls who could break loose and come charging through the fairgrounds, to the baby rabbits who did nothing more than twitch their noses; from jars of pickles to cakes a foot high; from tablecloths to hand-loomed rugs; from the daintiest violets to the tallest cornstalks. All of them were there at the fairgrounds, draped in dust and stench—the stench of cows, chickens, wieners cooking in steam kettles, and popcorn, all stinking clear down to the road while the Ferris wheel turned in the air, the merry-go-round horses went up and down, and the roller coaster carried its screaming passengers along a dizzying course.

Women gossiped near the flower stalls; men shot at targets to win Kewpie dolls with feather hats or pillows with "Welcome to Woodland" on one side and a lake scene on the other. John and Carl ran off to spend the money they had earned by picking potato bugs; Elizabeth sat on a horse on the merry-go-round; Edward sat on Father's arm; and I held Mother's or Grandmother's hand and waited for the worst to happen—for the bulls to charge, the boys to get lost, and Elizabeth to remain forever on the wild-eyed horse which went up and down. The sun beat down on my head and burned down to my dust-covered feet.

"I want to go home!"

Eventually we did. We found the boys, we got Elizabeth off her horse, we all stayed together no matter how many people there were, and we all came home.

After the fair was gone, we went to Woodland to buy lunch

buckets, pants, shirts, sweaters, shoes and, best of all, pencils, tablets and crayons. Each tablet had its pack of clean paper, each pencil its gold lettering and red eraser, and each box of crayons sixteen different colors, including one which I had to see right then at the store: a red but no ordinary red, a color belonging to some higher order—a deep, luminous fuchsia which I used to color houses and barns.

At least I would have crayons, I thought to myself. Even if I sat forever in the first grade and never progressed from one row of seats to the next at Revier School, I could make my drawings. Someday when people would come to visit the school, they'd see me and say, "Well, there's Mary Morgan still sitting in the first row and coloring barns."

And I wouldn't care because Mother would say, "What's wrong with the first row? She can write beautiful words there just as well as anywhere." And Father would say, "She has the finest red barns in Revier."

But it wasn't so much what anyone said. It was what I said to myself. "Dumb Mary." That's what made me want to cry, only I wouldn't let the tears come out. I kept them inside and held on to my new box of Crayolas.

4

THE SUNDAY BEFORE SCHOOL BEGAN was always as long as two days glued together. This time I wished that the drowsy day would last forever. The goldenrod was as yellow as our bowl of churned butter after Mother had stirred in "just a drop or two" of orange coloring from a bottle which stained our fingers. "Don't play with the bottle," someone usually said, but I did and Grandmother asked me if I had ears. Far beyond in the hills, the morning mist hung like the gossamer webs which stretched from bush to bush in our woodlot. The Montfer was low and the water dark as ink; the rocks had turned green with moss and stood above the waterline; giant dragonflies landed on the stones and rose again to fly once around the sauna. There the daisies bloomed as if summer were not over, but it was.

"If we went to Finland, Grandmother, no one would know how old I am," I said, but Grandmother was too busy with her wool to leave, to go anywhere except into the woodlot or to her garden. Everyone was too busy gathering and hoarding to take me away from school and its dangers. Everyone except Mother, who wanted to braid my hair so I would look ladylike in the morning. I said I didn't want her to, but she braided a red ribbon into my hair and then asked me if I didn't feel better, and though I said I did, I didn't. I felt worse.

As the day dragged its heels, Elizabeth and I picked flowers, played with the cats, caught minnows and drank lemonade under the lilac bush. "I wish I were going too," she said, as if her ability to read my "Little Red Hen" would save me.

"It wouldn't help, Elizabeth."

"It might."

We were miserable together. And then, as if we weren't unhappy enough, my classmate Anna, her sister and her parents came to talk about the school, the school board and the teacher, and to be as excited as they always were about school affairs. Before she had even tumbled out of their car, Anna said, "I'm in the second grade," as if I didn't know. Having passed the first grade, where else could she be?

"I know," I said. "Do you want to look for copper snakes?"

She didn't and her sister didn't. They had Revier School firmly anchored inside their heads. "I'm so anxious to go," said Anna, "I can hardly wait."

"How about crabs? Would you like to look for some? Or cocoons?"

Nothing interested them except Revier School. And what could I say about it? Elizabeth and I left them to look for copper snakes, cocoons, butterflies—anything to be away from another reminder of rulers breaking against the edge of my desk. Later Mother complained that I hadn't been polite, but I told her that Anna and her sister hadn't been much better. "It's not polite to talk about school just before we have to go there."

Mother was sure that Anna had thought that I was as eager as she. But I knew that wasn't true. Anna had passed and I hadn't and that's what she was telling me, as if it were something worth printing in the *Daily News.*

"Come on, Mary," Father said. "Let's go put some new shoes on old Maud. She's starting to limp a bit."

I followed him to the stable. He took down his heavy leather apron and took out the files, clippers, the hammer and nails from his toolbox under the window. We arranged the tools on a bench outside and Father led Maud into the light. I handed him one tool after another. Every time he pounded in a nail or clipped a hoof, I winced, but Maud stood steady. Then he told me about winter shoes which had spikes that kept the horse from slipping on ice. "They're really good when you're going up a hill with a load of timber."

77

I remembered Revier School again and asked Father if he had ever worried about school and he admitted that he had and would now if he were going. "Somehow one always does, Mary. But you're bright and you'll be all right."

We finished the shoeing, gave Maud some oats and water and then walked her to the pasture. "There's a star, Mary," Father said. There it was, shining in the sky as wide as the whole world.

Then it was Monday. We set out on a clear and sunny day, for it was always clear on the first day of school. It was only later that the weather turned bad and, hunched like animals, we trudged one after another over the sodden fields. It was later that the sky pressed down upon us, came at us in gray streams from all directions, and was bent on absorbing us as it absorbed the fences, fields and woodland, all into a single mass. But now the sun was with us and the three of us, John, Carl and I, dressed in splendid school clothes, arrived dry and unmuddied to find Miss Aho behind the desk, not Miss Anastasia Malone!

Miss Aho was a Finnish girl who had gone away to school for two years and had come back to teach us whatever it was that she had learned. She was blond and blue-eyed; she had flower-petal skin, slender hands and a dress which smelled of roses or violets or lilies of the valley or maybe all three. For some reason, no one whispered; no one asked foolish questions; we just sat until she called upon us.

She passed out the readers and again, as if a whole year had not gone by, as if we hadn't done all that could possibly be done with a reader, there it was, "The Little Red Hen." I told Miss Aho that I had not learned to read the story, that I probably never could, but that I had learned to write instead. She said that I should write her a story and I did. After I had used up two pages of my tablet, she said I should stop. When she read the story, she said it was very good except that I used "on" for "no" and "no" for "on," but that wasn't a real mistake.

The mistake may not have been a real one, but even I could see that my mouse story was no better than the hen story. The only difference was that the mouse didn't expect a whole loaf of bread out of one grain of wheat. All he did was hunt for cheese and he never found it because Miss Aho told me to stop. "You're now in second grade," she said, and she gave me a seat with the others who had passed.

What else Miss Aho did I don't remember, for what happened outside school was more important than what happened inside. The big boys chased the big girls but never the little ones; the big girls used lipstick and had great secrets. They often said, "I'll pay you back," to the big boys, but I couldn't see what the boys had done or how the girls would pay back. It was a foolish game, I decided, a game I'd never play.

Only when something extraordinary occurred did school life take on the aspects of reality which existed elsewhere. When the Kaaris' house began to burn and to puff out smoke from all the windows, the big boys ran there, even John and Carl, to help put out the fire. From the schoolyard we could see them dragging out tables, chairs, beds and cupboards, and carrying buckets of water, but the fire burned on, licking the sides of the house and then the roof until the bare bones of the house were visible. Finally even they burned and collapsed. By this time the mill was on fire and the barn too. The smoke rose in great clouds into the sky as if the Kaaris' yard were the brewing kettle of all the storms in the universe.

That afternoon when we went home from school, I saw the small fires still burning and eating up the last boards of the place I had known as long as I could remember—the high stairs to the mill, the stables, the post office, and the kitchen always smelling of raisins and cinnamon biscuits. All of it was gone in one afternoon. Only the sauna was left, and there on the doorstep sat Mrs. Kaari, weeping into her apron and mourning at the graveside of their house and barn and mill.

For years after they had all moved away, whenever I thought of the place, I saw everything there as it had been—the girls, Laima and Olga, in their candy-striped blazers, Oscar telling me to stop twisting my handkerchief made out of a salt sack and pinned to my dress, and Mr. Kaari reading his newspaper. Across the fields I saw it all, but when I looked out, there was nothing, just empty air filling the space between earth and sky. No sheep to frighten me, no horses for Olga to chase so that I could walk home in safety, no windows turning red in the morning light. Nothing. And I associated all this emptiness with the deaths that came soon after the fire, as if it in its fury had also consumed Mrs. Ojala and Mrs. Wiita.

Thus Eino Ojala was motherless at six and Liina Wiita, who had owned my cat-fur coat long before I did, more bewildered than she had ever been. Because their lives changed, ours did too. Their loneliness spread to us and to all the children, for while our mothers helped the bereaved of Revier, our homes were disordered and cold. Our meals were late; our days longer than usual. And despite all the help, the Ojalas and the Wiitas were left motherless and the Kaaris homeless. "That's how it is," Mother said. "One can only do so much and no more."

"I'm glad you found that out," said Grandmother. She complained. She was seventy-seven and Edward only three. There were grown children at the Wiitas' and Ojalas' and the Kaaris'. What were they doing?

Mother said that had it not been for the Kaaris, who had taken me to see Dr. Malowski when I became ill with kidney disease, I might have died. When Father had to work and couldn't get to Hadley, they had brought me medicines and had come to see me every day all winter long. And when I was born, Aili Wiita, Liina's older sister, had come daily for a whole month, and when Edward was born, the oldest Ojala daughter had come to help.

"And we paid them, Louise," said Grandmother.

"But who would help us in Revier if we didn't help each other?" asked Mother. And she talked of Mrs. Ojala and Mrs. Wiita, both older than she, women who had raised their large broods except for the youngest children, women who had suffered and been burdened to their deaths. I listened to the loveliness of Mother's voice, the conviction in it, and the beauty of the language she always used to express her sorrow.

"Burdened?" asked Grandmother. "I don't know who was more burdened there—the husbands, the wives or the children."

I remembered Mother helping Mrs. Wiita write her order for a new hat and coat from the Sears' sale catalogue, and then Liina wearing the older coat, and Elvi Koivunen the still older one. Grandmother had said that Mrs. Wiita's coats were everywhere in Revier and Mrs. Ojala's curtains too, because she had needed new ones every year.

Now, as if we hadn't had enough deaths in Revier, another death came to us in the headlines of the *Daily News.* DEBS DIES! It was printed in letters so large I could read the headlines from the door, halfway across the room. Father said we were the losers, because a workingman like Debs who knew how to organize and got people to support him was a far better man than those who had placed him in prison to wither.

I wondered why he had withered. Otto hadn't. He always talked of his prison stay as if he had enjoyed it. Perhaps he felt good because Father paid his debt and he didn't have to worry about it anymore. "Did Mr. Debs have a lot of debts?" I asked.

"Not that I know," said Father. "He wasn't poor."

But he must have been and since no one could pay his debts, he withered. Now his family had nothing but debts and worries. "No one can ever settle down because the banker is always at the door," Mr. Kaari had said when he sold half of his herd to pay the bank.

Mother was right. One had to do something when a person died. Collect money, bring food or stay with the family. One always did something. But what could we do for the Debs family? We didn't even know them. Grandmother wouldn't approve of our collecting money for them. I could save the headline and paste it on a piece of construction paper. Tell every pupil in school. "Who's Debs?" they asked. Tell Miss Aho. She said he was just a socialist. I might as well have remained silent. That's what Carl said. "It's not as if one of the neighbors had died."

Gradually our lives became more stable. We did our chores at the usual times; we ate our meals without haste; we did our lessons in the evening. One night the frost came, killed the potato stocks, turned them dark green and pungent. Out of school in the dank late afternoon, we rode on the wagon full of dusty sacks of potatoes and left behind us a whole field of opened furrows with potatoes like rocks rising out of the earth. Sometimes the men found potatoes with round heads and round feet, and potatoes which were bent, and potatoes which looked as if they had wanted to become gourds. In the next field, the pumpkins sat on the hard ground and the pale green cabbages as big as baskets waited beside them.

And later, when Miss Aho left us to attend the two-day teachers' convention, Father, Mother, Elizabeth and I went to visit the

Kaaris in town. We had not seen their rented home before and now there it was, narrow-windowed, crowded between two houses just like itself. As we opened the front door, we looked straight up the stairway to the second floor and into a bedroom at the head of the stair. All the plants which the Kaaris had salvaged from the fire were sitting on the living room floor and they were colorful and healthy though the place was damp and cold.

Near the kitchen was a bedroom and next to it a bathroom with a broken tub which Mrs. Kaari had filled with books and papers because she could find no other use for it. And as we sat listening to the coffee boil, she told us that the girls worked at Kresge's after school and on Saturdays, and that she was a maid for two days a week. Only Mr. Kaari had not found work. She asked us about all the children, and about Liina and Eino, who had visited them every day in Revier. As we talked, I had the feeling she hadn't accepted this new and shattered life and that she was waiting to become accustomed to it.

As we were driving home, the snow began to fall, first lazily, floating down and hanging in the air, and then faster. There was a loneliness even in the dancing flakes; too many lives had been altered in Revier; too much had happened to us all. And now the dead and frozen ground was turning white. The muffling sounds of winter were in the air.

Then it was Thanksgiving. At school, the turkeys went up on the windows and the Pilgrims with tall hats and buckled shoes. At home, we peeled pumpkins and cracked the hazelnuts which the boys had picked from the wild bushes in the pasture. Mother made pies, cranberry sauce from the cranberries Father had found in the bog, and wild black currant jam. She made rutabaga porridge, mashed potatoes, pork roast and chicken. Father opened jars of her pickled beets and apples, and corn and yellow cucumber pickles with turmeric. We turned into Pilgrims and gave thanks that the harvest was in.

But long before we became Pilgrims, Carl began drawing Santa Clauses, fat ones with long arms bent like hoops. John said the arms were too long and too bent. Carl said Santa Clauses always had long arms. If they hadn't, they could never carry all the packages, the packages would fall into the snow, the reindeer would stamp on them, and no one would find them until spring.

John tried drawing a Santa Claus. His was long and thin, with short useless arms. "That's no Santa Claus," said Carl.

"Well, it's at least a man," said John.

We had to choose, but to choose was to applaud one and not the other, and if I had to choose between them, I would have had to choose John. He didn't feed me Vicks salve with sugar when I was blindfolded nor whack me on the head with a stick to find out if my head was hollow. He never made me smell kerosene to make me vomit and he never told me that I wheezed when I knew I did. He sometimes said he wished I weren't so ugly, and asked Mother why he couldn't have a sister who wasn't, but he didn't make me vomit for being ugly. Carl did. He said he didn't intend to. He just didn't want me hanging on to him all the time.

But it was Santa Clauses we were choosing, and we chose Carl's fat hoop-armed symbol of a child's Christmas. John threw his into the stove, stamped out and slammed the door as he went. Mother made him come back and go out without banging the door, but if I'd been Mother I'd have let him bang all the doors in Revier and go in and out several times to bang them some more.

So Carl drew his Santas, made us lie down on the beds and then came ho-hoing in Mother's red coat. He stuffed prunes and dried pears into our mouths, told us there were bells in the sky, bells we heard night after night as the hoop-armed Santa Claus flew from North Pole to South Pole over and over.

John said there was no Santa Claus at all, just a star over Bethlehem and three kings on camels thumping on desert sand. They looked like tall buildings swaying in the night and over them the angels sang.

Then we looked for the star in the eastern sky. "There it is!" someone said, and I saw it move and saw angels flying across our own sky.

"Those are clouds," John said. "Bethlehem is thousands of miles away."

"Someday I'll get a camel and I'll go there," I said.

But before we could do anything the boys had to sell Christmas seals to save people from tuberculosis. Every night they went out to tramp up and down the road. While they were gone, other children came to our house to sell seals, and Mother bought some from each one. Whoever sold the most was the winner of the seal sale at Revier School, but being winner was not as important as getting the leading part in the Christmas play or drawing the teacher's name from the box and buying her handkerchiefs neatly folded into triangles with the embroidery showing. We weren't to tell anyone whose name we drew because the last day, the day of the Christmas program, was to be one of excitement and surprise.

Usually it was. Someone always forgot half his lines. Someone always sang too high or too low. Sometimes the first graders cried because they were too frightened to get up in front of all the parents. Once a little girl began reciting her poem as soon as she rose from her seat. When she got to the register, her hair flew up into the air. Then she turned around, walked back to her desk, and just finished her verse as she sat down again. A moment later she burst into tears and had to be led out to the cloakroom.

Our school tree was always tall and spare, as if it had suffered long years of want and hunger. No matter how many paper chains we hung on it, no matter how many paper bells, Santa Clauses, wreaths and trumpets, the tree was not a Christmas tree but an ordinary tree decked with pasted paper. And yet, when we got our presents and each of us our brown paper sack of candy from the teacher, I felt that the real and holy Christmas was near. That Christmas could only be at home.

But before that, we had our Sunday school program at the Salmi house. There was a special amateur flavor to this effort because no one really knew how a service for children should be arranged or what belonged in it, but everyone was determined to have one in order to remind us that Christmas was about Jesus and not about toy cars, dolls and checkerboards.

We drew names, exchanged presents and received a brown sack of candy. It was this part of Mrs. Salmi's program that increased the enrollment to at least fifteen just before the holidays. The other part—the recitations in Finnish, Mr. Salmi's mumbling over his Finnish Bible tracts straight from Helsinki, and sometimes a sermon given by one of the self-ordained preachers—we could tolerate by watching the Salmis' calico cat clean herself in front of the crackling kitchen stove, the steam rise from the teakettle and the pendulum swing in the big wall clock. When the babble ended, we sang Finnish hymns and bellowed in order to hear ourselves above the organ.

After Mrs. Salmi recited the blessing, the program was over. Mr. Salmi gave us our presents and our brown sacks of candy. We went into the bedroom to fool about until the mothers had the table set out with cakes and cookies, and until the coffee in the big enamel-ware pot boiled over, hissing and spattering on the stove. Then it was time for us to line up, to heap our plates and to eat what God had graciously placed before us.

It wasn't church, it wasn't school, and it wasn't home either. It was just Mrs. Salmi's kitchen with the organ in the corner, hymn-books piled on tables and benches, and Bible tracts everywhere. There was less warmth than in our kitchen and less laughter; there was more of God, more of dying and more of preparing for it—even at Christmas.

The preparation for our own long and holy Christmas began even before Carl's Santa Clauses. Before Thanksgiving probably, for already then there were attic corners into which Mother said we could not go because Christmas secrets nestled there behind the boxes of tinsel, bells, and red and golden balls. And there were the secrets between ourselves, between ourselves and the adults, and between the adults themselves. Secrets everywhere.

While we whispered and wondered, the whole house began to change, not inside out as during the Time of the Great Anger, but outside in, as if all the Christmases from Finland and Woodland and Hadley were streaming in day after day.

First, Grandmother had to make the headcheese, which filled the house with the smell of bay leaves and peppercorns. When she was finished, Mother stored the pans covered with wax paper and cloth on a shelf in the porch. Then Grandmother made dark molasses bread just as she had in Finland. She started the dough in the evening so the yeast would have a chance to grow and it always did, filling the whole big stoneware bowl. She poured different kinds of flours into the mixture, dark ones, light ones and coarse ones. In the afternoon when we came home from school, we could smell the fennel, caraway and anise long before we got to the door. There were the loaves cooling on the table—ten loaves, fifteen loaves, all as brown as nuts. When they were cold, Mother wrapped them in wax paper and stored them in a copper boiler in the porch.

Next Mother made the sweet cardamom loaves and the baked

cheese which squeaked when we ate it. Those too went into boilers in the porch. Father brought smoked salmon and a keg of pickled herring—two more items for the porch. The porch was filling up.

Father brought home a box of kumquats, which certainly wouldn't keep until Christmas. We ate them right away. A box of chocolate-covered cherries, which were really meant for Christmas, but we could get another box. We ate the chocolates too.

Now the preparations began in earnest. Every curtain had to be washed; every window polished. Grandmother's Christmas cactus was now in full bloom and had to have a special place so everyone could see it. The floor had to be scrubbed wall to wall, and every spider chased from her web.

"When will we get the tree?" we asked.

"It's too early," Father said.

"No, it's not." We knew that he had picked out the tree long before, but he wouldn't tell us which tree it was. The pasture and the woodlot had pines, firs and spruce by the dozen, but which one would it be? One day when we were all at home, while we were still wiping away the last speck of unwanted dust, when everything sparkled and gleamed, Father said, "It's time for the tree!" The time was always the day before Christmas Eve. The day was always clear; the air was always calm. Father put on his high-top boots and his sheepskin coat, his fur cap and his leather mittens. We watched him through the window. Now he was near the woodshed. Now he had the ax. Now he was heading back into the woodlot.

"I know which tree it is," said Carl.

"How do you know?" asked John.

They argued. John said it would be a pine; Carl said it would be a spruce. We waited and waited. Then we saw Father coming out of the woodlot. "There he is!"

"It's a spruce," said Carl. But it wasn't. It was a fir, straight, tall and full. The boys scurried up the attic stair to fetch the stand.

"It's in front," called Mother.

The boys came down, both holding the stand though one could have easily carried it. Father chopped bits off the trunk and then wedged it into the stand. "Where will it go this year?"

"Next to the separator!" The tree always stood next to the separator, but Father always asked the same question. The boys tramped upstairs again. Down came the boxes of tinsel, the boxes of balls and bells and icicles, the candleholders and the angel for the top. Down came the big red paper bell for the door and the Santa Clauses for the windows.

"First we'll have coffee," said Mother. "Who wants cardamom biscuits?" We all did. We sat around the table. As the frozen branches loosened and lifted themselves in the warmth of our kitchen, the smell of fir spread through the house. "It's the most beautiful tree we've ever had," she said, as she had last year and the year before and the year before that. We always spoke the same words during our holy Christmas.

We began to trim the tree, all of us except Big Hank, who said he had never had a tree and didn't care if he hadn't. But if we placed a ball too close to another, he said, "Too close!" Or if the ball was too far from its neighbor, he called, "Too far!" If the tinsel draped too much in one spot, he said, "Too low!" He never moved from his chair while we were trimming the tree because, he said, "A tree that isn't trimmed right is worse than no tree."

After we had hung all the balls and bells we had, Grandmother fetched her special glass bell, a gift from Grandfather Harper on their first Christmas together, a bell so delicate, so fragile, that she kept it wrapped in tissue paper and sealed in its own box which hid all year in her dresser drawer. Now she gave the shining, green-and-red-veined glass trinket with its delicate tongue to Father, who hung it precisely where she wished it to be, on a branch high above our heads. Ringing with the slightest motion, the bell stayed through all the days of Christmas, and when we were quiet we heard the pure sound of heaven singing to us.

Mother and Father clamped on the candleholders with their candles, pink, white, green, yellow and luminous red. As the sun fell down below the trees, Father lighted the candles one by one, and then we watched them as we ate molasses bread, pickled herring and baked cheese, saw the small flames twist and turn in the currents of air, flicker, shrink and grow again. Grandmother said we had to eat our rice with blueberry sauce; Father said it was time to do the chores; Mother said it was getting very late. And still we watched our tree.

"It's not even Christmas Eve," said Mother, suddenly practical. "Let's finish our supper now."

Father lighted the lamp and we all blew out the candles. Elizabeth and I cleared the table; Grandmother washed the dishes, and I, with mittens over the bandages which once again covered my hands, dried all the big things while Elizabeth dried the little ones. Edward was very busy amusing Big Hank. John, Carl, Mother and Father buckled their boots, put on their barn coats and went out to milk and feed the cows, to feed the horses and to bed them down, to drop down the hay from the loft for the morning's feeding. Everything had to be done before the long winter night turned cold.

The next day was a day of such scurrying that we would have known it was Christmas Eve had we not had a gleaming tree before us. Mother had to fix the lutefisk in milk sauce for the evening's supper and the black currant jelly for the Christmas dinner; Grandmother had to pluck and clean the ducks so they would be ready for the roasting pan in the morning.

And now we had to prepare the sauna: Big Hank had to fire the stove and John and Carl had to haul the water in five-gallon milk cans; Father had to tramp through the snowy woods in search of cedar boughs. Elizabeth and I had to bring out clean bath towels, spread them on the beds and place clean clothes in them for each member of the family; then we had to roll up the towels in neat bundles so that the clothes would stay inside and not fall out into the snow and disappear until spring. We had to find fresh pine soap straight from Finland, for on Christmas Eve the sauna was as important as the leaf house on Midsummer Eve and like the leaf house, was ready just as we were beginning to think that it might not be.

"It's time for supper," Mother said. Father lighted the tree again. We sat down at the table and were as quiet as could be, for on Christmas Eve Mother said grace. We waited and then she said it softly as if God were standing by. "Dear Father, bless us for we are Your children. Give us good health if that is Your pleasure. Give us life and then the gentle grace to live it wisely." She kept her eyes closed; perhaps she added her own prayer, since God was listening. Then she opened her eyes and said, "Eat, children." We did, as God hovered somewhere above the roof of our house; the candles flickered, and Grandmother's bell sang its own song of Christmas.

By now we were in a great hurry because Mother said Santa

Claus was fast approaching, and we had to be in the sauna when he passed by in his bell-ringing sled. Hank mumbled something about businessmen and churches getting rich on Christmas, but no one paid any attention. I was so spellbound by the candlelight, the sound of Grandmother's bell, and Mother's wish that God give us grace, that I believed in everything—churches getting rich, businessmen getting rich, our getting rich, in Jesus, in Santa Claus, in reindeer and camels, stars and angels, believed the whole muddled package and wished that every day were as full of contradiction as Christmas.

We children hurried to the sauna with Mother, washed ourselves with pine soap, poured buckets of water on ourselves and each other and then rushed into the dressing room to dry and dress ourselves in the dim light of the kerosene lantern. Father came to fetch Edward because he was little and might get lost in the snow. We hurried after them. Above our heads the bells of Christmas rang, over Bethlehem the angels raised their voices, and as the camels swayed over the desert sands, we scrambled up the snowy path to the house. Father opened the door.

There glowing in the light of its candles stood the tree, and beneath it and beside it, all the wealth of Hadley and Woodland. A bushel of giant apples, another of oranges, a wooden keg of nuts, another of peppermint wheels, jars of hard candies, boxes of chocolates and dates; toy cars, skis, dolls, and a kiddie car for Edward; ironing board, pots, kettles and dishes bought before they could grow to adult size; Tinkertoys, Erector sets and a glass-eyed bear for Edward; playing cards and checkerboards; books and games; everything heaped on the floor because Santa Claus was in such a hurry to be gone. And because Elizabeth and I were girls, Mother gave each of us a beauty kit. Elizabeth's box was pink; mine was blue. Inside each box was a mirror, a jar of cold cream, a bottle of hand lotion, a nail file and a comb.

That's how it was on Christmas Eve when I was seven and for many years after, though Santa Claus like elves of all times disappeared; he rode away in his sled and never returned. That's what Edward said the next year.

"Let's have tea," Mother said. And we did. We ate cardamom biscuits, candies, nuts and apples. Then Father said, "If the road is open we'll go to church in the morning."

The storm had not come; the road was open. All of us except Big

Hank, who stayed home to roast the ducks, bundled up and then squeezed ourselves into the car and rode through the white winter world into snow-roofed Woodland. There was our red brick church, its bells ringing and chimney blowing smoke into the air. We went in as quietly as we knew how, sat down, saw red hats, blue hats, black ones and green, an angel standing on the tip of the tree, heard the organ, ate the candies which Father had stuffed into our pockets, and then dozed until "Silent Night" raised us from sleep.

We went back to the car, and as we drove home we peered out upon the Woodland streets, the stores full of Christmas, the houses alive with lighted trees, doors bright with red-ribboned wreaths, and lawns busy with manger scenes. One lawn had a camel standing in the snow. "Is it real?" asked Elizabeth.

"It is!" I said. "I saw its tail move."

"You didn't!" said Carl.

"It's real plaster," said Father.

"See! I told you, Carl."

"Real plaster isn't real camel," said John.

"Yes, it is."

"Don't quarrel, children," said Mother. "It's Christmas."

"We're not quarreling, Mother," I said. "We're just talking about camels."

Down through Hadley, where the taverns too blinked Christmas. Only the countryside was without decoration, except for snow hanging from tree branches, farmhouse roofs and fence posts.

Despite the clutter underfoot, the cars that whirred from one end of the house to the other, the towers and the games, despite the miniature pots and pans on tables and chairs, Mother made the Christmas dinner, which we ate at noon and into the afternoon and evening. Between the duck and the pie, we fed the cows, horses and chickens their feasts of grain, the rabbits their greens and carrots, and the dogs their bones, which they growled at all afternoon and then buried before nightfall. The cats, not concerned about Christmas now or ever, sniffed at the cream we set out for them and walked away; eventually they licked the pan clean.

In the evening, we children brought out our presents for the adults. John always saved his money to buy a book for each; Carl always made something out of wood. Now he gave a miniature logging sled to Mother and Father, a sled so beautiful all it lacked was a team of small live horses. He gave a wooden box to Grandmother and a cribbage board to Big Hank. Elizabeth had drawn a picture for each; Edward, who had saved all the feathers he had found in summer, gave away three, but a moment later wanted them back again. I had bought plain white handkerchiefs at Kresge's and embroidered initials on each, and small flowers on Mother's and Grandmother's.

We gave each other time to play with one another's toys. One hour with a book equaled one hour with a checkerboard; a half hour with a car equaled a half hour with a doll. "What am I to do with your doll for a whole thirty minutes?" Carl asked. John said we could keep his half hour. We insisted he had to take it.

Elizabeth placed her doll in his lap. "There! Hold it."

"I don't want your doll!" He put the doll on the floor and brushed off his new trousers.

Carl turned my doll upside down on her head and made her legs dance in the air. "Be good now, Carl," said Mother, her eyes on the boiling teakettle.

"Well, I'm supposed to play with it while she breaks my car."

"I'm not breaking it," I said.

"Fight nicely, children," said Father. "Shout softly." He was playing checkers with Big Hank and had only one ear open to our bickering. And then because he had spoken and might just begin to listen to us enough to separate us, we stopped arguing.

During the next week, one after another, all the neighbor children came to see our tree, our presents, to eat candies and cookies and to play with us. We didn't ask what riches Christmas had brought them; we knew ours had been richer. It wasn't just the gifts. It was the sense that normal life had stopped for us and that we now lived in an enchanted world where anything, even the ancient camels, could appear before our eyes. We had only to stop and listen to the bells of Christmas.

Even Tony Koivunen came to look at our tree and the clutter of toys and stayed all afternoon. Though he was five years older than John and almost as tall as Father, he crawled along the floor after the cars, played with our dolls and helped us cook in our toy pots. He was trying to be kind to us and we wanted to like him, but there was something disturbing in Tony. I didn't know what it was. When the sun began to set, Mother said it was time for us to get our chores done and for Tony to help his parents.

"You sure had a good Christmas," he told us as he was stooping to buckle his boots. "I ain't seen nothin' like it."

A whole week had passed and now we had to watch the new year come in, creep around the corner and sneak in the door and hide things under the tree. But first we had to find out what would happen to us in the coming year. We melted babbitt metal to find out. At the stroke of midnight, in the light of the tree and one small lamp on the table, John and Carl poured the silver metal into cold water. Once for each of us. Maybe twice if the first pouring didn't turn out right. We saw cars, horses, boxes, trains and castles. Elizabeth and I believed in their magic power; we told Edward he should believe us. And we put the silvery trinkets under our pillows, there to do the work of changing our fortunes.

On New Year's morning, we rose early to find the tree lighted once more, and beneath it the clothes which Santa Claus in his haste to be gone had forgotten to give us. Blouses, shirts, nightgowns, pajamas, sweaters, jackets, mufflers and mittens, boots and rubbers. Everything practical—almost. Elizabeth and I got identical blouses, creamy white with an edging of lace on the collars and cuffs. Mother said that years ago when she was young, she had a blouse with lace on it, and she wanted us to have one too.

"No toys?" asked Edward. And Father found one small package for him—a wind-up car. Edward was too young to know that we needed clothes for the winter ahead.

"The sun is rising," Mother said. Father hurried out. Then we saw a yellow light against the windowpane. "Now I wonder what that could be," she said, and we all ran to see. There fast in the snow a circle of lighted sparklers spit out their harmless sparks, cast a glow upon the leafless basswood, the snow-covered cooler box and Father standing hatless in the cold. Mother rapped on the window. "Come in! You'll freeze." Father came in and we had breakfast. Carl had hot chocolate; John had Postum; Father, Mother and Grandmother had coffee; Elizabeth, Edward and I had milk, and all of us had cardamom biscuits with raspberry jam. Big Hank was still asleep.

Mother wanted to keep the tree another week because she liked the candles; Father liked the chocolates. Father went to town the next day and bought two boxes—one of candles and one of chocolate-covered cherries, but before we could eat the chocolates or burn the candles, school began again. One day when we came home, our tree stood tall in a snowdrift. As the snow came down and the cold winds blew, the lower branches disappeared one after the other until we could touch the tip, where the angel had spread his golden wings all the days of our holy Christmas.

5

SOON AFTER THE HOLIDAYS, Father hitched his horses to the big logging sled and, runners squealing on the snow, drove away to the lumber camp. The days were short and the snow was deep. The wood for our stoves had to be carried in, the water for the cattle pumped and carried to the troughs, and the hay dropped down from the loft and brought to the stalls. Twice a day and sometimes oftener, the barn had to be cleaned, for the cows were calving and needed special care.

Not a week had gone by before Big Hank began to grumble. "If I get the wages of a lumberjack, then I ought to be a lumberjack and not a barn hand." Once Hank got to mulling an idea, he couldn't get around it. In Finland, barn hands were the lowest of the low, and it wasn't any different in America. Within a few hours, Father had become a capitalist because he owned a pair of dray horses and hauled timber to the mines. One capitalist serving another—that's what it was. He filled our whole house with his grousing.

Mother tried to soothe him; Elizabeth and I tried to amuse him with our games. Nothing helped. He stayed unhappy. But one day when he was reading his anarchist newspaper, he saw an announcement of a new lumber camp in Michigan. That's where he'd go! Right in the middle of a cold winter when he was at his stiffest and clumsiest.

"Big Hank, you'll ruin yourself with your stubbornness," said Grandmother.

94

"I can stand the cold," he said, and began gathering his belongings.

The next morning, Big Hank came down dressed in his heavy moleskin pants, wool shirt and big boots. He had his knapsack packed and in his hand. After eating a big breakfast, he put on his mackinaw and fur-lined cap and struggled to get his knapsack on his back. Without a word, he left the house.

Grandmother wanted to hire Toivo Salmi at once because he liked being with us, but Mother didn't want to hire anybody. We would manage by ourselves as all the pioneer families had in years past. We'd be saving money and could help pay the taxes.

For a week, Mother's confidence intrigued us. Before going to school and again in the evenings, John and Carl helped in the barn. Mother, John and Grandmother did the milking. Carl fed the calves, chickens and ducks. Elizabeth and I washed all the dishes and did as much of the cleaning as we could. We felt as useful and daring as Mother. We were frugal pioneers, struggling through a hard time.

But as the days wore on, we grew tired of it. When we came home from school, Mother and Grandmother were in the barn and didn't come back to the house until it was almost dark. We'd have to hurry through dinner because the cows had to be milked and all the other chores done. And through the whole long evening, Mother didn't stop working.

On Sunday night, John and Carl would fill the boilers, and in the morning Mother would wash the clothes. As we walked back in the cold light of afternoon, we saw the frozen clothes hanging stiff on the lines outside. Wherever we looked, we saw the snow swirling about and threatening to smother us all. Never had we had so long and lonely a winter.

But Mother kept her cheeriness. "Life is like that in America," she'd say to Grandmother, and went on talking about the early pioneers and how the women had endured. "Men made the decisions in those days too."

"And we've made a few ourselves, Louise," Grandmother said. "You can hire Toivo or write to John so he'll know that Hank has left." She didn't care how many hardships others had had. Saving money wasn't worth sacrificing one's health.

As we walked to school, I'd begin to worry about us. I thought the snow would fall and drift forever. Long ago, Father had told

95

me that once upon a time, all of Revier was covered by a mountain of ice. What if another was moving down on us and we wouldn't see it coming? Not in time. What would happen to us then?

Nothing. The glaciers were gone and would never return, the boys said, but soon they began to argue about work and who had to do the most. They bickered all the way to school and I knew they didn't know if the ice was coming or wasn't.

It was Elizabeth who was my comfort. Every night before she fell asleep, she'd turn to me. "Mary, do you know what I wish?"

"I think so."

"I wish that when we wake up, Father will be eating breakfast," she'd whisper into the dark.

"I do too, Elizabeth."

Then she'd settle down. As the wind wailed in the night and the frost cracked in the siding, I listened to Mother and Grandmother talking in the kitchen.

One night I heard Grandmother say that she regretted selling the Woodland house and buying Alex's land. Had she known how hard our lives would be, she would never have done it.

"I wouldn't want to be anywhere but here," Mother said.

Grandmother's sad voice was like an echo of the wind outside. What could she do now? She had depended on Otto to pay back the money to Father. So useless it had been to try to keep Otto out of prison. And now he'd never pay his debt. How could a man be like that? But it was she who had been foolish and now Mother and Father would be burdened for a lifetime and her own grandchildren would suffer.

Mother consoled her. We had all we needed and Otto would have to live with his conscience. Soon our days would be easier. Big Hank would return in spring to help with the planting. By then he'd be tired of the lumber camp.

"I don't know if I'd let him in again," said Grandmother.

"But where can he go?" Mother asked. No one would have him, though when he worked he was as good as any man could be. His childhood had been so hard that it was no wonder he lacked sense, but he too needed a home. Grandmother Anderson had always let him come back and we could do no less.

As I listened to them, I began to feel that we'd get along until Father arrived and that nothing could happen to us. Everything had already happened years ago. Somehow we'd have to make Grandmother feel better, but how we could do that I didn't know. If I were older, I could do more. I'd have to wait. That was all.

On Saturday morning, I woke up to the sound of Father's voice and then Mother's. She was talking about Hank's leaving. I shook Elizabeth. "Wake up! Father's home!" We scrambled out of bed as fast as we could and ran into the kitchen. He was sitting at the table. He hugged us and gave us each a piece of his toast.

Whenever Father was upset, he didn't say much. He'd listen so intently that we became aware of his feelings by his silence. It was Mother who was talking and explaining how helpful we had been. She had saved a whole month's wages.

"A month's wages!" he said. "And suppose we had had a blizzard. Then what would you have done?" He got up without finishing his coffee. He put on his coat and went into the barn to take care of the cattle. Mother followed him. Elizabeth and I cleared the table and sat down to wait for them.

When they came back with the milk, Father was still quiet. He paid no attention to Mother until he was done with separating the milk and had brought the cans into the porch to cool. Then he sat down at the table. "Next time anything like this happens, you let me know, Louise. And if Hank comes back while I'm gone, you tell him I don't want him here."

"The poor man has no other home," Mother said, and began to talk about Grandmother Anderson again, how she had been a friend of Big Hank's mother and how, out of loyalty to her dear friend, she had always looked after Hank, cranky though he was. It was a beautiful story of duty, devotion and Christian tolerance. Once Mother began telling stories, we knew that Father couldn't win. If Hank had the wits to stay away until the weather was warm, Father's anger would melt.

Later in the day, Father and the boys went to ask Toivo to work for us. The next morning while we were having breakfast, he came in and brought a great blast of cold air. I was so glad to see him, I wanted to stay home from school. We weren't pioneers anymore! We were just ordinary people and didn't have to "endure" as pioneers did from one end of the year to the other. But I soon learned that we still had to. Though the long trip from our house to the loading site added three to four hours to his day, Father slept at home every night because we needed a grown man around to protect us if a blizzard came. Now Mother was anxious from the time he left at five in the morning until after eight when he returned. Once when Toivo took us to town to do the shopping, we saw Father perched high on his chain-bound load. The horses had their oat bags on; their long gray tails were whipping in the wind. We waved to Father and he saw us. Right behind him was another driver with his team and load. Mother said that when the men were hauling timber to the mines, they always had to drive together because they needed four horses to pull the sled up the big hills.

"That's a job I'd never take," Toivo told us. "It's worse than in the mine."

I asked Father if that was true and he said it wasn't. The mines were worse. Still, a horse could slip going down a hill or break a leg or get frightened and try to outrun the heavy load. But he always carried sand to put on the slopes, and to increase the traction, he wrapped chains around the runners. He had never lost a horse or a load. "If the driver stays calm, the horses feel it."

At last the warm winds began to blow again. The ice-packed roads turned soft, and the forest floor to slush. Father came home with his team and his sled, and Hank with a bag of pink peppermints. Now the Montfer rose, to roar in the night and to steal into lakes on our land. Then Lindbergh skimmed the whole Atlantic, skinned the froth off the waves and lived to tell his story.

"Where is the world going?" asked Grandmother.

We didn't care where the world was going. We took to the air. From that moment on, paper planes flew through our kitchen, down from the hayloft, off the sauna roof and over the shed, the house and the stable. Grandmother said we were going mad.

Carl built balsa wood planes. He stood on one side of the pond, Elizabeth, Edward and I on the other. "Here comes the *Spirit of St. Louis!*" Over the waves and down in Paris. We wound up the rubber-band motor and sent the plane back. "Here comes the *Spirit of St. Louis!*"

That was the momentous spring when all of us wanted to be engineers, all except Edward, who didn't know what an engineer was. Carl built a crystal set and wore earphones. He heard the news, scribbled it on a piece of paper, and I announced it from our radio station located between two chairs.

John, who was trying to do his arithmetic problems, kept look-ing at us. Though school had ended, he wanted to work out all the problems in the book. "Why don't you kids do something useful?" he asked.

When I said we were, he blocked both ears with his hands. But after our station went off the air, he suggested to Carl that they make telephones out of tomato cans and wire, and then string the wires between the woodshed and the porch. They were busy for a long time, and finally allowed us to test their equipment. One after another, we shouted ourselves hoarse. By then the leaf house was rustling its last.

I remember those summer days when everyone was happy that the Fourth was only a few days away and I was sad because it would soon be over. On such days, it was hard to find enough to do. Elizabeth, Edward and I would go to fetch the mail early and hope that just as we got to Revier Road, the mailman would ride up and, through the open window of his car, hand us our mail. "You folks sure have a lot of mail," he'd say.

We always did. Father's *Daily News*, Hank's anarchist paper, Grandmother's church paper, and if we were lucky, Sears' and Ward's sales catalogues and the *Saturday Evening Post*. If the mail hadn't come, we'd walk to the Salmis'. Often they had nothing but Bible tracts in their box. Since even one would lift Mrs. Salmi closer to heaven than she usually was, Reino and Rachel would come back with us. We'd divide our mail and because Edward was the smallest, he always carried the letters tight in his hand.

When we got home, Mother would read us the letters if they were personal ones which began, "Dear Louise, John, Grand-mother Harper and children." That's how Aunt Harper with the piles of hair began her letters, written in a large bold hand that covered pages and pages of ruled paper and told us all the news about relatives everywhere and at the very end would say what had led her to write in the first place. "I'm coming to visit." That's how we learned of her son, Thomas, and his wife arriving from St. Paul and of their intention to visit us, not on the Fourth but the day after.

While Elizabeth and I were drying the dishes and picking up the toys, Rachel was looking at herself in the mirror and Mother was telling us stories about her cousin Thomas. He was her favorite, only two years older than she. "He's always looked just like my father," she said. And I remembered that long ago I had blended their characters into one adventurous young man, who had skied across the frozen land in Finland, jumped on a ship, come to America and then skied down the streets of Woodland. But now I knew who had skied where, that Thomas was born in Woodland and that he had gone to St. Paul to become a successful man.

We were excited and since they weren't coming on the Fourth but after it, the celebration would last for two days. We would call Mother's cousin Uncle Thomas, his wife Aunt Ellen, and we'd be as well behaved as we knew how. They loved children, Mother said, but they hadn't had any luck in adopting one.

"Why don't they get a dog?" asked Carl. "That'd be a lot cheaper."

Mother said that wasn't nice. If people wanted children and couldn't have them, it was sad. A big house and no children in it! It was a tragedy.

I don't know how the conversation went after that because all I could remember was that asthmatic children were sometimes sent away to relatives in the city. Anna's brother, Elmer, had been sent to Detroit to live with an uncle, who had kept him a whole year, taken him to a big hospital and bought him a lot of medicines. When Elmer came back, he was fine, but as soon as the clouds began to roll over the hills and the fogs to rise from the Montfer, he started to wheeze worse than ever, just as I did. Dr. Burton had said that if there were a big hospital nearby, he'd send me there.

Maybe it was my remembering all that and then remembering the bad winter which I had tried to forget. Maybe it was the rustle of the drying leaves of the leaf house and Mother talking of the lovely days of her childhood when she and Thomas were young and Father unknown to her in another place. I only knew that I felt alone and that I too would have to go away. Carl said that it was all in my head and John that no one in his right mind would send me anywhere; I wasn't strong enough. But I was. I was a lot stronger than Elmer and he had been sent away.

The Fourth came in full color. At noon, Mother packed us a lunch and Father drove us to Lake Superior. We found driftwood, bleached to a ghostly white, stones as smooth as glass, and rocks round, flat and oval like the ones on top of the fireplace in our sauna. Father built a fire, and when I dropped the wieners into the sand, he said, "That doesn't matter," and we ate them grit and all. We walked on the blinding beach and the water licked our shoes. We threw stones into the waves and Father's skipped six times and then fell out of sight.

"Now I want to go home," said Edward. When we climbed back into the car, he said, "And I'm hungry too." So on the way, we stopped at the creamery for our gallon of ice cream, and then at the Salmis' to ask Rachel and Reino to come to our house. Toivo was at home and wanted to come too, and Paul Ojala, wandering down Revier Road and going nowhere at all, jumped on the running board and rode back with us.

We ate ice cream. The boys lighted firecrackers, and after lighting a whole package all at once, Paul said he'd had enough for one day. Away he loped across the field, leaped over rocks and bushes and was out of sight. That spring he and Toivo had helped us plant the potatoes, and as they had walked along the furrows, they had thrown the sprouting tubers at each other. "I'll come anytime," Paul had said at the end of the day. "Working is fun around here." Away he had gone, then as now, more graceful than any of us.

The next morning, Mother scrubbed the kitchen floor again and laid a new hand-woven rug at the door. Grandmother put away her spinning wheel and the wool. The whole house was as neat as if we weren't going to live in it until the Harpers came and left. We all dressed up again so we'd look our best; we sat and we waited. We hurried through our lunch of soup and sandwiches and then hurried through washing dishes. And we waited some more.

Precisely at two o'clock they came in their big black car. We all went out to greet them. They were efficient: quick handshakes for the adults, a pat on the head for the children. They appraised us briefly. They gave a glance to the ripening fields, and another to the exterior of the house. Then they went inside and we children stayed outside because the boys wanted to examine the car, which was newer and shinier than any car they had ever seen in our yard. Elizabeth and I sat on Big Hank's bench.

"I don't like them," said Elizabeth. "They didn't even talk to us." She thought awhile. "When are we going to call them Uncle Thomas and Aunt Ellen?"

"I don't know. Maybe when they leave."

I could no longer bear being outside. I wanted to hear what

101

everyone was saying, so I went in and asked Mother if I could set the table for her and she said I should. She put out her cakes and cookies, and mixed an egg into the freshly ground coffee. Grandmother and Aunt Harper always liked coffee made in that way because that was how the cooks made it in Finland when guests came to call, but Aunt said she herself was too stingy to waste an egg.

While Mother was busy at the stove, Thomas talked about his hardware business, his house and the adoption agency. He said they were having a lot of trouble with the agency people. "They keep asking us why we want to adopt a child. I even told them I could send the children to college."

"And that they'd have rooms of their own and all the privacy that children need," Ellen added.

Father wasn't saying much and neither was Mother. Aunt Harper and Grandmother were comparing their flower gardens and weren't paying any attention to Thomas and Ellen.

Mother poured the coffee, so clear it sparkled in the sun. I thought the table looked lovely with the white damask cloth from the Woodland days and our best Sears, Roebuck dishes. But Ellen was on a diet and couldn't eat anything and Thomas wasn't hungry. "When you're in business you try to keep down your waistline," he said. All he'd have was one cup of black coffee.

Aunt Harper made up for their lack of appetite. She had two pieces of cake and three cookies and a big spoonful of whipped cream in her coffee. "You're the best cook, Louise. You could take a few lessons from her, Ellen." And she winked at Mother.

Ellen didn't answer her but started to talk about the new bathroom they were putting into their house and Thomas about expanding his business. The more I listened to them, the more convinced I was that they weren't interested in adopting anybody. They were telling us how big their house was and how much money they had. They seemed to have so much, they didn't know what to do with it. I asked Ellen if they had any pets. Pets? Pets make a mess in a clean house and she didn't like that. And I asked her if the neighborhood children ever came to play at their house.

"You sure ask a lot of questions, don't you?" she said to me.

"Just keep asking, Mary," encouraged Aunt Harper. "That's the only way you ever learn anything."

I looked at Mother and she shook her head. I went outside and Elizabeth, Edward and I walked to the woodlot to pick wild flowers. "I thought if they tried to take you, Mary, I'd get into the car," Elizabeth said.

"Would you really have come with me?"

She assured me she would have and Edward too. I told them about the big house and the private room, and we decided that if the Harpers had taken us, we'd have stayed in the room and not come out. After a few days, they would have had to bring us back home.

Because I had been so worried before the visit, I thought of it for a long time. The way they had looked at us and at our house made me think they didn't like any of us. Not even Mother. Otherwise they'd have eaten what she had made for them. When I asked her if Thomas was really like her father, she said, "Good heavens, no! My father would never have had to worry about adopting children. They were around him all the time."

Some people who left to go to the big city and came back to see us were a lot like Thomas and Ellen. Once they got a house in Detroit, Chicago or Minneapolis, they couldn't talk about anything else. Some of our visitors from Woodland and Hadley were strange too; they were always getting new bedroom or dining room sets. "I just gave the old one away," they'd say, as if they were giving away a gallon of milk to the neighbors.

Our sauna visitors weren't like that. They didn't seem to care about houses or furniture. They were interested in taking a bath in our sauna, which was built like the ones in Finland, and in newspapers, jobs, politics, religion and the prices of things in the stores and shops, and they didn't talk about clothes unless they got them on sale. Best of all, they didn't worry about diets. They ate anything we gave them.

Saturday was always sauna day—the best day of the week and a small Time of the Great Anger. In summer when the weather was sunny, we brought out all the bedspreads, blankets, quilts and pillows to air on the line. Because we were busy polishing and scrubbing, we didn't always have time to prepare lunch and Father would make a quick trip to town and bring home some hot Cornish pasties—not as good as the ones Mother made but good enough —and the biggest watermelon he could find. We'd pump water

103

into a washtub and let the melon cool off and we'd eat it outdoors.

By three o'clock in the afternoon, Mother would be saying, "I'm getting so tired I can't see straight." As soon as she said it, Elizabeth and I felt too weary to move, but no matter how tired we were we had to bring in the bedding, fix the beds, make the cakes for the sauna visitors and supper for the men working in the fields. Father always said he didn't care what he ate. Big Hank did, however, and we all had the feeling that if he didn't get his meat and potatoes, he'd go on strike and wouldn't lift another forkful of hay onto a hayload.

When we all sat down to eat, the whole place was so clean that even Big Hank noticed it. Had we not spent the day scrubbing, sauna night would have lost half its splendor, for there was something in the combination of smells—naphtha soap, fresh air and the smoke from the burning wood in the sauna grate—that raised Saturday to the top in the hierarchy of weekdays.

On some Saturdays, old friends of Mother, Father and Grandmother would drive in to surprise us. On others, no one came and Mother would say, "I wonder where our sauna visitors are."

"I suppose we can get along by ourselves for one Saturday night," Father would answer, hidden behind his newspaper.

"I suppose we can," Mother would say regretfully, as if one more sauna night had slipped into eternity and only we were the cleaner. "We'll have to eat my cinnamon rolls tomorrow."

But on busy Saturday evenings, after everyone had gone and we had dried the last coffee cup, she'd say happily, "Now look at that —only a small pan of biscuits left and not a crumb of cake. I'll have to bake again. Tomorrow Aunt Taimi, Uncle Eric and the girls will come to visit."

And they usually did, though they weren't visiting as much as they were encouraging Mother and Father to leave St. Paul's Church and join theirs. Mother wouldn't, but she thought Father should if he wanted to, because before their marriage he had belonged to Taimi's church, which was the same as Pastor Grandfather's.

"I didn't belong to it," said Father. "I was pushed in when I was a boy." He preferred the organ, the bells and the choir at St. Paul's. Taimi's church didn't have anything; people there sang off key.

Uncle Eric was tall and thin, with tracings of iron dust on his pale skin. Aunt Taimi looked like our dark-haired father. She always dressed her three girls alike, probably because they were only a year apart in age and once she began cutting out a dress, cutting two more wasn't much extra work. This time, they had on peach-colored voile dresses embroidered at the neck, white stockings and patent leather shoes. Dressed like that, they couldn't do anything, but they couldn't have anyway, because in their church Sunday was God's day and all they could do was wait until it was over.

Helga, the eldest, was a year younger than I; Helmi was Elizabeth's age, and Hilja a year younger. The two smaller girls always waited for Helga to speak and when she did, they repeated exactly what she had said. If Helga laughed, then Helmi and Hilja laughed. We had a whole afternoon of hearing everything three times.

Still, when they all got into their car and drove away, raising a cloud of dust into the evening air, I asked Mother, "When will they come again?"

"Next Sunday perhaps."

"If not sooner," said Father, sighing deeply.

The following day, Mother said she wanted to buy dress material and shoes for Elizabeth and me, so as soon as the wash was pinned to the line, Mother, Father, Elizabeth, Edward and I rode off along our winding road. All the fields were bare now, stubble-bearded except for a telltale haystack here and there. Beyond, the blue hills draped themselves in the haze of late summer and below them, the trees were beginning to change color. A splash of pale yellow, pale pink and deep scarlet squandered over miles of forest.

"It'll be an early fall," said Father.

"Another summer gone."

"Yes, and soon another year."

"I can't believe I'm thirty," said Mother.

"And I'm thirty-six. We're getting on in years."

They were so much at peace with each other then, I wanted to keep that moment forever. And they did too, because Father suggested that when the leaves were at their brightest, the two of them drive to Marengo and see Grandmother Anderson's old place and Mother's aunt's house. "The places won't look the same but the roads will."

"It was always so pretty there, almost as pretty as Revier."

"Yes," said Father.

At once I wished that the frost would come to paint all the leaves. And when I saw the steeple of St. Paul's, I prayed that Father would never again have to haul timber to the mines and that no one would come to talk about his house no matter how lovely it was. But I knew the frost would come when it was ready and the mines would always need timber. Some houses were lovelier than others and people would talk about them. I could wish and pray all I wanted and I couldn't change anything.

Father and Edward went to the hardware store and Mother, Elizabeth and I to look for shoes. We found them—sturdy brown oxfords with thick laces, and because the clerk said he had a sale on patent leather slippers, Mother bought us each a pair. All four in the same size. "I can't wait to show them to the white-stocking cousins," I said.

"From now on, their names are Helga, Helmi and Hilja," said Mother. She went off to find the dress material, saw a print she liked and decided it would suit me.

"I like it too," said Elizabeth.

Since there wasn't enough cloth for two dresses, Mother chose a light brown with yellow roses and held the fabric in front of Elizabeth. "Would you like that?"

"I want the blue," said Elizabeth.

Mother tried to persuade her, but I didn't. Once Elizabeth made up her mind, she'd never give up. Had we stood there a month, she'd still have wanted the blue.

"I'll take the brown," I said. "If I want to look at blue, I'll look at Elizabeth."

We rode home with our four boxes of shoes and our rose-covered material. As Mother was sewing the dresses, Elizabeth and I stayed near so she could put them on us anytime she had the need. And as we waited, we would take out the shoe boxes from under the bed, and we'd look inside and marvel at the scent. "They're the best-smelling shoes we've ever had," I said to Mother.

When she had finished making our dresses, she too could not say which of them was the prettier and which color was more becoming on me and which on Elizabeth. The brown one was more formal, I thought. Just right for the oldest daughter in a family. We would wear them on the first day of school.

Then it was time once again to walk across the empty field, to climb the steep stairs and to meet the teacher, a new one. Lovely Miss Aho had chosen one man in preference to the roomful of us. "I'm Miss Gurney," said the new one, neither as lovely nor as soft-spoken as Miss Aho. "I shall now read your names." She mispronounced every one save Morgan. "Four Morgans? Are you Finnish too?"

"Yes, ma'am," said Carl.

"Same family?"

"Yes, ma'am."

A titter. Then laughter.

"What's so funny?" asked Miss Gurney.

"I said 'ma'am,' ma'am," said Carl.

Louder laughter.

"Silence!" Miss Gurney set the windows rattling.

Thus began Elizabeth's first year, my third, Carl's fifth and John's seventh.

There was much that could be said for that year. I didn't wheeze as much as I had in the earlier years. I accepted my ability to read when sitting at my desk though I still preferred reading in the cloakroom. Moreover, I learned that the clock was the most important piece of equipment at the Revier School. Without that round, bald-faced machine which Mr. Wiita wound up each Monday morning, Miss Gurney would have lost direction; with it she marched like a soldier through the maze of assignments from grade one to grade eight and never once got off the track. Precision, structure and predictability were the goals Miss Gurney set for herself, and in themselves they were honorable ones. No one could say she did not teach; no one could say we did not learn. She taught and we learned, and we learned more than was good for us.

On that first day we began our work as if we had practiced all summer for it. We read, wrote, spelled, added, subtracted, multiplied and divided; we remembered and forgot. Then after we had pounded every eraser on the porch railing, washed every blackboard, and drawn every shade to half mast, we sat for one minute in total silence. "Dismissed!" said Miss Gurney. One after the other we filed out the door.

As the boys ran ahead, Elizabeth and I walked home at an even pace. "Did I do everything right?" she asked me.

I said she had. I saw Father plowing the field and a lone crow flying through the air between us. Farther still, I saw the boys climb the stairs to the house. They were already home; we had a long way to go. I saw Mother standing on the stair and waving to us. "Let's hurry," I said.

"I can't."

"All right." I remembered that I didn't run when I was in first grade. I wheezed all the way home. Now I could have run, leaped or flown the whole mile. At least once. Maybe then I would wheeze again.

"I like Miss Gurney," said Elizabeth.

"I'm sure she's better than Miss Malone was."

All the same, I had the nagging sense of everything being strange and hostile at Revier School, as it might have been if Miss Malone had a roomful of bandaged wheezing girls whom she dared not touch except with a ruler. Yet I liked the building—the walls and windows, the maps, the blackboards and bookshelves. I liked the smell of floor wax and Lysol. But that wasn't enough.

As we walked across that empty field, I was as frightened as I would have been if I were alone on the shore at Lake Superior when the north wind was blowing hard and driving the waves over the sand. I would turn away and run, but the waves would chase me, and though I would know that Mother and Father would come to find me, the waiting would seem endless. And now I had a whole long year before me and no one could save me from it.

6

 WHEN WE WERE YOUNG, we were secure in our unbordered world. It stretched from Revier to Helsinki to Bethlehem, to the Czar's Russia and to Lindbergh's Paris and to any other place we thought or dreamed of. But as we grew, our world narrowed and the borders closed. Revier became our only home. Suddenly we realized what the people of Hadley and Woodland thought of us. Moreover, we sensed that we were not to evaluate them, but that they were to evaluate us. They could question our competence, our intelligence and our worth, but we could not judge theirs. We were too backward and too alien. And we were children.

That we had remained ignorant of our place in the world was largely a result of communal nonrecognition of prejudice. Most of the people in Revier had suffered traumas far worse than the snobbery of Hadley or Woodland, and since snobbery always stopped short of business deals, the Revierites didn't care. Or if they cared, by appearing unhurt they shielded their children. The shielding stopped at the schoolhouse door, however. Within, the child was vulnerable. If a teacher was humane and unprejudiced, the child could remain sure of himself for years. Otherwise he could learn on the first day what it meant to be a citizen of Revier.

Miss Malone had not been prejudiced. She had been silly and incompetent, but our brains were no softer than those of children elsewhere. Basically she liked children even if she didn't like me.

Miss Aho liked us all, even me. She had parents who had been born in Finland; she spoke Finnish at her home, which was in a village no larger than Revier. We learned nothing about prejudice from her.

Had Miss Gertrude Gurney not come to Revier School, we might have escaped learning for years on end how others regarded us. But she came, and henceforth we were peasants. Whatever we knew had no value anywhere beyond our village and no value to her as a teacher. She was there to teach us basic skills and that she did. For that we respected her. Had we not, she would have been far less successful in shattering our inner selves, and our childish acts of rebellion would have been a greater source of solace than they were.

"Were you born in a barn?" We heard the question daily.

"Yes, Teacher," we'd answer.

"Do you want to be a dumb farmer all your life?" We heard that too every day.

"Yes, Teacher. I want to be dumb."

All the same, we were fascinated. Don't think about the teacher, we'd tell ourselves. Don't think about anything except the sound of words strung together. Look at the globe and its patches of red, yellow, green, pink and brown, all floating on blue seas. We're here, Teacher. We're here in your world!

What if I made a boat and sailed down the Montfer River, down, down, past the Beaver Dam and beyond, down to the lake and across? What if I never came back? What would you say then, Teacher?

What if I made wings and leaped from the door of the hayloft? What if I flew to the North Pole and then back to the South Pole? What would you say then?

I answered the question for her. She wouldn't even notice. Not Miss Gurney from the great city of Hadley. Not until she called the roll. Then she'd say to Carl, "Will you please tell your sister that I expect her in class. At once."

"She's at the South Pole."

"I don't care where she is."

But I wouldn't come back. What do you think of that, Miss Gurney? I'd sooner freeze than become a peasant in your school. A small error. It's not your school. It's ours. I'll come back to it then. But one day, Miss Gurney, I'll show you.

How can you show me anything?

Silence.

Mary, I asked you a question.

I would never answer. Miss Gurney would stand behind her desk forever waiting and waiting. I'd walk past her desk, but I wouldn't see her. Then she would know what it means to lose as we had lost.

That year when I was eight, I became the sole owner and keeper of a shining blue history book. On its pages, one explorer after another sought a route to India, where the riches lay, the silks and spices, the gold and precious jewels. Magellan circumnavigated the globe; Americus Vespucius, Pizarro and Balboa sailed their ships on the high seas. What are low seas? And Ferdinand and Isabella gave Christopher Columbus three beautiful ships, *Nina, Pinta* and *Santa Maria,* all with sails flapping in the wind. The sailors wept when they saw land, came ashore and kissed the ground. Maps, lines and dates. Time goes forward and the earth becomes round, spinning like a ball with oceans clinging to its sides. Why doesn't the water fall off? Where would it fall if it fell?

Ponce de León, not wanting to grow old or to die, looked for the Fountain of Youth and grew old. Sir Walter Raleigh, not caring about age, threw his best coat into the mud to save the royal shoes.

"Learning will never lead you astray," said Grandmother, over and over.

I still read the old dusty books in the cloakroom, where I again went to pay for my transgressions, the new books which the librarian brought from Hadley, the textbooks which belonged to my brothers, the dictionary and the encyclopedia. When I didn't read, I made up words—words which rhymed and sang, words which could be Finnish or English or Italian—words so strange that my skin turned cold. Somewhere in the world someone was saying these words and giving them meaning. But where? Someday I would know.

"Why do you memorize whole poems when I ask you to memorize one stanza?" asked Miss Gurney.

I remained silent.

"And two pages of problems when I assign one?"

I did not answer. I would do any amount to be better than Anna, who did what Miss Gurney asked her to do, and thus more than

Arthur, who lagged behind us. Even if I were no better, I would do the impossible to baffle Miss Gurney.

Like Anna, Elizabeth was a model student. She read when she was asked to read; wrote when she was asked to write. She was already perfect and was confident. Furthermore, she was too young to come under Miss Gurney's disdainful glance.

Bewildered by the loss of his mother, Eino Ojala did not escape, however. He never combed his hair, he never washed his face, and he came to school in the same clothes day after day.

"Doesn't your mother ever look at you?" asked Miss Gurney.

"His mother is dead," said John.

"Your father, then?"

Eino didn't hear her.

"Eino, I asked you a question."

"Yes."

"Do you sleep in the barn?"

"No."

But he may have. Who could tell where Eino slept his nights? His father would surely forget to tell him where to sleep. And when Mother told Paul to look after Eino and to find out from Miss Gurney what he could do to help him, Paul said, "Me? I'm not going to fight with her." He was more interested in harvesting our potatoes than in solving Eino's problems. Besides, he had problems of his own; he didn't want to be home any more than he had to. He'd fish or hunt or run up and down the road rather than stay at home with his silent father. And because Eino had no one to care for him, Miss Gurney sent him home day after day. He was to wash, comb his hair and change his clothes. Dutifully he left when she told him to go, stayed away for hours and then came back as bedraggled as before.

"It's not his fault," I said once.

"Mind your own business, Mary," replied Miss Gurney.

Instead of talking about our own feelings, we talked about Eino, who was more helpless than we were. We thought of ways to help him, but we never succeeded in our attempts. Miss Gurney kept too close a watch on us and the clock.

The older students wondered what Miss Gurney did on her weekends in Hadley. Our speculation ended quickly. What could she do? Correct papers. Write exam questions in purple and then reproduce them on the hectograph. Add up grades. Fill in report cards. Had she done anything else, some small indication of it would still be visible on Monday mornings. A smile perhaps. A faraway look. But there was nothing.

She stood tall behind her desk just as we had left her on Friday evening. Black hair, parted in the middle and held at the sides with metal clasps; clear brown eyes and flawless skin. Gray or brown skirt matched with a gray or brown cardigan sweater over a white blouse. She wore oxfords as sturdy as ours.

That year we waited more fervently for Christmas than ever before. Perhaps the snow, the sleigh bells and the store windows in Hadley would inspire Miss Gurney to abandon reason for a week of carols, poems, secrets and Santa Clauses on windows. But nothing except a hectograph pan inspired Miss Gurney. We had an impoverished tree trimmed with last year's paper chains, an hour of carols and a bag of popcorn each.

At home we celebrated the holidays as we always did, only now Big Hank had decided he too must buy gifts. He had been on strike for two weeks and disabled with a wrenched ankle for another week. Since Father always paid him whether he worked or didn't, Hank felt remorseful just before Christmas. He bought Elizabeth and me brown coats with fur collars and cuffs, and the boys navy wool jackets. He was proud and so were we. They were splendid clothes fit for any occasion, Mother said.

And they were. A few days after Christmas, Father said that we could wear our new coats and jackets, and he would drive us in the big logging sled to the lumber camp. Covered with blankets, we sat in the sled as the runners squeaked over the snow, past the Wiitas', over the hill and down, past Revier School, the Ojalas', past a few shacks belonging to bachelors too old for marriage, and then down the logging road to the camp.

Father showed us the flatcars piled high with lumber, and the office where Mr. Payne sat and handed out paychecks. After Father got his check, he took us to the bunkhouse with the double-deck beds lining the walls and the big potbellied stove which heated the whole bunkhouse and sometimes overheated it so much that all the bedbugs began to scurry from one bed to the other. And the lice too. That's why he always slept in the small bunkhouse, which was too cold but had fewer bugs. "You can see it from the back window," he said. We looked out and there it was, an unpainted building not much bigger than our own house.

Just then I saw a bug climbing up the bedpost near the window. "There's a louse!" I moved away because I didn't want it to leap into the fur of my new coat.

"That's not a louse," said John, very grown up now. "That's an ordinary bedbug." He examined it carefully. So did Carl, and said it wasn't moving very fast.

We walked through the mess hall, which was right next to the sleeping quarters. To the side was the kitchen. As we walked in, I saw at once the enormous tree-stump chopping block. It was so large we could all sit on it at once. And the stove! It was three times as big as ours at home. But the wood crackled inside and the teakettle steamed on top, just as at our house.

From a room behind the kitchen, a woman came out, and after her a little girl. They were both very dark, with straight black hair and black eyes. Then I remembered that Father had said the cook was an Indian. Father introduced us, and Mrs. Deer introduced her little daughter, Angelina, and gave us oatmeal cookies as large as saucers. While we ate them, we stared at the solemn little girl who didn't belong in the kitchen of a lumber camp.

After we had eaten our cookies, Mrs. Deer showed us the oven, the cupboards full of gallon cans containing vegetables and fruits, gallon jugs of catsup and mustard, and hundred-pound cans of flour and sugar. She was like any other housewife showing her guests the special qualities of her house. "Every day I cook something different," she said with pride. But whatever she said, I felt that she ought to have a kitchen of her own with Angelina there beside her.

When Mrs. Deer began to take out the big kettles and pans and to put on her apron, Father said we had to get home to do the milking. As we said good-bye and thanked Mrs. Deer for the cookies, Angelina stood like a small statue beside her mother. As soon as we were outside again in the snow-packed yard, I asked Father if he too thought it sad that the Deers didn't have a home.

"They have a home, Mary. They have an apartment right next to the kitchen."

"But where is Mr. Deer?"

"He's there too. He does the maintenance work, fires the stoves and helps Mrs. Deer with the cooking."

Still, that wasn't enough. "Wouldn't they like to live in a tent? Mr. Deer could hunt and fish."

"They would freeze, Mary," said Father. "Mrs. Deer went to school to learn how to be a cook, and Mr. Deer learned to do maintenance work. Why should they live in a tent?"

"No Indians ever lived in tents around here," said John.

While Father went to the storehouse, we argued about Indians. I said I knew there had been Indians living in our woods because as Elizabeth and I walked along the paths I could feel that someone had walked there long ago. "Don't you feel it too, Elizabeth?"

"Sometimes when you mention it, Mary."

Father came out with a wooden box of dried peaches and one of dried figs, and went back in for two more lugs, one of apricots and one of pears. Just as he had finished covering the boxes with a horse blanket, the freight train came hooting out of the trees and stopped at the landing where the loaded flatcars stood waiting. The engine kept pulling the train apart, first one way and then another. At last, there was enough space for the loaded flatcars. The engine pulled them to the main track and pushed all the cars back together again. As the train slowly moved away, we counted the cars and read the names. Canadian Pacific, Santa Fe, California, Rio Grande, Great Northern, Louisiana, Erie Lackawanna, Ohio. Flatcars with rails, flatcars with rods, Florida, Pennsylvania, Land of Sunshine, Santa Fe once more and then the caboose.

"I guess that's it," said Father as the train hooted its last. Father seemed as sorry as he was when the last float rode by on the Fourth of July. We climbed back into the sled and covered ourselves with blankets. By now the sun was hanging low and falling into a bank of dark clouds. The wind was rising too and driving streams of snow before it over fences, bushes and hillocks onto the road, and filling every track and trail that man and horse had made. Every empty field had its own swirling cloud of snow, even the school-yard. The porch had a drift halfway up the door, though the windows blazed in the setting sun as if to remind us that the fire burned there still under the front register.

By the time we reached home, the snow was beginning to fall out of the clouds that now lay low above us. The lamps were lighted and the tree as well. "I'm so glad you're home!" said Mother. "I thought you'd never get back."

The house smelled of pea soup, hot bread and raspberries, of

115

candles and Christmas. The table was set; the milk pitcher was full. Suddenly I thought of Angelina Deer at the lumber camp and wished that she could share our homecoming. We sat down to eat in the festive light of the candles. The wind howled outside and whipped the snow against the panes. "It'll be a real blizzard this time," said Father. "I'll have to string the ropes between the house and the barn."

"Let's string one to the sauna too," said Carl.

"We won't be going to the sauna in a gale like this," said Grandmother.

"We'll string the ropes anyhow," Carl said. "At least we'll see where the path used to be."

"First the ropes to the barn," said Father. I felt the tension of the storm outside and the warmth inside. I had to admit that no one could survive in a tent; one would need a house of some kind. Or go deep into the woods. Perhaps there under the trees one could have a tent.

I could hear the wind rattle the porch door and whistle around the chimney. "Will the storm be very bad, Mother?" I asked, and she said it wouldn't, but all the same the wind howled for three days. Every crack and crevice had snow in it, in the porch, the stable, the shed and the barn. Every building was an igloo, plastered over with snow. The west wall of the house was banked with snow to the eaves; when we looked out the window, we saw nothing but a white wall. And while the storm was wailing, a cow calved. Father spent the whole night in the barn to care for the cow and her baby calf. In the morning, Grandmother brought the cow her pailful of medicine, and came back with a half bucket of eggs. "It's colder than it's ever been outside!" she said.

Carl got out his crystal set and earphones. At least we'd know how cold it was in Woodland, and then we could subtract ten degrees from that figure. Revier was always colder than any other place around us. We waited. "Minus forty-six," he said at last. "So it's minus fifty-six!"

"It can't be," said John. He went outside to scrape the snow off the thermometer on the north wall of the house. He came back. "It's only minus fifty-two."

"Well, it gets heat from the house," said Carl. "I'd say it's minus fifty-six."

We all wanted to go to the barn now to see how cold it was and to see the calf at the same time. Mother said it was too dangerous. It was safer for us to stand in the porch for a few minutes, but we wouldn't because it wasn't cold enough there. And we never found out how dangerous it was, for after a few days the weather turned warm again, though it was still below zero. We dressed in our heavy clothes and went out to see the new calf, all snug and warm in her little stall next to her mother. Edward thought that Reddie was a good name although she had only a few red spots on her. We agreed. We could call her anything but she would grow up into a Finnish cow because Grandmother renamed the animals as she took care of them.

Because the snow kept blowing around, we had an extra week of Christmas that year. No one could get anywhere except on skis or snowshoes. Tony Koivunen skied to our house and said that a cow had calved at their place too. His mother had a cold and his father had "busted his foot with an ax," but he didn't seem to be worried and neither were we. Things and people were always "busting" at the Koivunens'. Someone was always falling off or into something, in good weather and bad. We couldn't tell whether they were more clumsy than the rest of us or just didn't care if they mangled themselves.

Father and Mother began to talk about the snowstorm again and asked Tony if the road was open. He said it wasn't. "I don't care if it never opens. I get around on my skis."

"Well, it should've been plowed by now," answered Father. "You'd think we never paid taxes around here."

Mother too worried about the road being closed for weeks after each storm. "We could die out here and nobody would care."

Three weeks went by before anyone from the township board came out to look at snowbound Revier. The wild wind had filled the hollows between the hills, covered the fences and bushes, and buried the road under twenty-foot drifts. As soon as the skies cleared, however, people had to begin moving about. Mr. Lahti brought Miss Gurney bundled up in his horse-drawn sled; she told us that she had fared well in Hadley. The mailman came riding on a saddle horse. Within a few days, the snow had packed into a solid mass. When the plow finally chewed its way to the Big Hill in Revier, the motor stalled. Two trucks drove up to work on the plow and got stuck in the drift. A tractor, out to rescue the three, slid into the ditch. Another week passed before the road crew arrived to dig out all the equipment.

Father always complained about Revier Road. Not only was it closed most of the winter, but from one end of the summer to the other, no one filled the potholes or cut the brush along the road-sides. People were too patient, he said. It was time for someone from Revier to run for township board. "I think I'm going to run."

Mother didn't approve of local politics. If someone was in need, she'd go, but electioneering was something else. "You'll just make a lot of enemies."

Father didn't seem to care. He had cards printed, hundreds of them. They all read: "Elect JOHN P. MORGAN for Supervisor." Mother would look at the cards and shake her head. "I never thought we'd get into politics."

When spring arrived, Father would stuff a stack of his cards into his pocket, ride up and down the muddy roads of the township, stop at every house and leave his card. Usually he'd go in the evenings or on Saturday or Sunday afternoons. If we had finished our chores, we'd go along to tell him he'd win the election. On the last Sunday before the election, we made sandwiches and took along a sack of apples and a box of cookies, and off we drove, as noisy a carful of politicians as there ever was in the history of the township.

The election finally came. Mother, Father and Grandmother went to the Range Hall to cast their vote. Big Hank didn't go because he was a citizen of the world, he said, not just of the United States. John told him that he was still a citizen of Finland, where he was born, but Hank said that by living and working in America, he had earned American citizenship even if he hadn't applied for it.

"You could vote for Father now if you had papers," I said. We always called whatever it was that one received when one became a citizen "papers," though none of us knew exactly what they were. I thought they were like baptismal certificates without the angels scrambling up the sides, and in Roman print on thin paper like that of the *Daily News*. Whenever I thought of "papers" the pages grew in number; now I had forty-eight, one for each state. They were all neatly folded together and stuffed into a big brown envelope.

Grandmother couldn't show us hers because she had lost them after she came to Revier, but since she was already a registered voter, she was safe. Someday, Father always said, we'd get her new ones, but Grandmother said she certainly didn't need papers to prove she was a citizen. She was one!

In the evening, Father and Mother wanted to go to the Range Hall to watch the final counting. They told us not to wait up for them because they would stay until the last vote was tallied. Mother was nervous. "It'll be a shame if he loses," she said to Grandmother. "He's worked so hard all spring."

Grandmother said that no one had ever won an election by staying at home. In fact, no one had tried to win by driving around with a carload of children.

"His pride will be so hurt if he loses," said Mother.

"Don't worry about his pride," said Grandmother. "He's had the best time in years."

When we woke up in the morning, we had a supervisor in the house. Father had won by a large margin. To celebrate the occasion, Mother made pancakes and blueberry sauce and because we were late finishing breakfast, Father brought us to school in the car.

Everyone in school knew that our father had won the election because Toivo Salmi, who was now driving the milk truck, had gone up and down the road even before he could pick up the milk tanks and had told everybody that we had a supervisor in Revier. The other children were more excited than we were, because now if they had problems they could come to our house and Father would solve them. But Miss Gurney didn't join us in our exuberance. "Settle down! There's an election somewhere every day of the week."

Maybe there was, but this election was special. Father's name would be in the *Daily News* and the *County News*. If Carl was lucky enough to tune in just at the right time, he might even hear it announced from Woodland. Perhaps Grandmother's newspaper would print the news and Big Hank's anarchist paper. Then everyone would know about Father!

"They already do," said Liina Wiita, who at sixteen was about to finish her long stay at Revier School. "Mr. Morgan could run for President."

For that comment alone Miss Gurney said she ought to keep Liina for still another year, but she couldn't. Liina would be ready for the world by the end of May. We decided that Miss Gurney was jealous of Liina's good fortune and ours too. Why else would she tell us that she didn't want to hear another word about readiness for the world and the township board of supervisors?

Miss Gurney may not have wanted to hear, but I wanted to talk about Father's success. Thus when Aunt Taimi wrote telling us that they'd be coming over to show us their new pair of twin girls and that they'd bring Grandfather Anderson along too, I could hardly wait for Sunday. We hadn't seen Grandfather since he went to preach in Minnesota two years ago. He surely wouldn't know about Father's winning. "I'm going to tell him that you won," I said to Father.

"I don't know if you'll have a chance, Mary. Grandpa's not interested in politics."

"Not interested? Wouldn't you be glad if John or Carl won an election?"

"Sure, but Grandpa's been worrying about doomsday so long, he's forgotten all about voting."

Father was right. I didn't have a chance. Right off, Grandfather asked us whose children we were. Elizabeth and I said we didn't know and Edward named every member of the family. When Grandfather told him that he was God's child, Edward frowned. "No, I'm not, Grandpa," he said, and went into the bedroom. John and Carl were clever. They gave the right answer.

Grandfather had his Bible in his pocket and we knew that he wanted to give a sermon because he had probably missed holding his accustomed Sunday service. We had already had a whole morning at Mrs. Salmi's Sunday school and weren't prepared for more religion just then. Besides, Grandfather's sermons were always long. Even Father was looking out the window and was as far from our kitchen as he could possibly be, while Big Hank sat in his chair and stared at Grandfather as if by staring he could silence a preacher who was bent on ruining our afternoon.

Mother said that we children should go into the bedroom to watch the babies. That meant that if we didn't want to, we didn't need to keep both ears open and that she would be satisfied if we remained reasonably quiet. Elizabeth and I whispered twice and I prayed with all I had that the babies would wake up, but they slept as Grandfather read the Bible passage, explained it by repeating it in his own words and then explained the explanation by reading parts of the Bible passage.

After Grandfather's sermon, everyone sat down at the table to have coffee and cake, but Grandfather decided to say grace, which turned into another speech because he hadn't said all he wished to say the first time. And still the babies slept. After we were done eating, Aunt Taimi finally uncovered one of them and began to feed her. She was so small that her head was only half the size of her mother's milk-filled breast and yet she suckled as efficiently as the kittens who tugged at their mother's belly.

I asked Aunt Taimi if she knew which baby she was feeding, but she said she didn't. Eventually she would have to find a way of identifying the girls, though just now it didn't matter much which was Vieno and which was Vera. Then Helga, Helmi and Hilja said that they liked the babies, but they wished that there had been three of them. Then each of them could have a baby.

"That's too many to feed," I said. "Even kittens do better if there are only a few at one time."

"I would have to give them bottle milk if I had three," said Aunt Taimi. "I wouldn't have enough breast milk for that many."

After she had fed both babies, she changed their diapers, bundled them into their pink receiving blankets and placed them back on the bed. Within minutes they were sound asleep and didn't wake up for the rest of the afternoon.

When we were by ourselves once more, I asked Mother if the babies had been baptized and she said they had been. Grandfather had come all the way from Minnesota to christen the little girls.

"And you and Father weren't the godparents?"

"They always have someone from their own church," said Mother.

I didn't think that was fair. Now that we had two new babies in the family, Mother and Father should have been allowed to be their godparents. Mr. and Mrs. Kaari had been mine though they had never gone to church. They had always gone to Communist Party meetings, however, and that must have made them responsible godparents in my parents' eyes. Why was St. Paul's Lutheran worse? It wasn't, said Father. Everybody goes to the same heaven.

The next day in school, I told Miss Gurney about the twins, but she didn't seem to be any more interested in babies than in the one-eyed chick, the knock-kneed Reddie and the bedbugs at the lumber camp. No matter what we told her about our lives, it bored her. I knew it did and for that reason I told her about Big Hank not having shoes when he was a child and Grandmother's brother being a palace guard; about Grandmother's spinning wheel and mother's butter churn. Then for weeks and weeks I didn't talk to her at all. If she asked anyone, "Were you born in a barn?" I would tell her more about animals, barns, the Finns and Revier than she ever wanted to hear.

For once, I didn't want to annoy her. I wanted to talk to her seriously. I thought she'd like to hear about Grandfather, who spent all his time preaching, and the Kaaris, who were my godparents though they didn't go to church. I wanted her to believe me and to think that it was nice to have godparents like them.

She didn't say anything. Nothing at all. She sighed and looked at the ceiling.

When Miss Gurney had first come to Revier School, we talked to her about the Kaari place, how lovely it had been and how the Kaaris had had a post office where they sold candy, gum, cigarettes, pipe tobacco, stamps and money orders. "They sold candy and tobacco in a post office?" she had asked, not at all concerned about the burning down of a house, barn and mill and almost everything else worth owning, but about candy and tobacco, which were important only because they made one half of the Kaari kitchen look a bit like a real store and we had no other in Revier.

"Her veins are full of ice water," Carl had said. Maybe they were. None of us could pass through the Kaari yard and forget the sadness.

At home when we talked of the Kaaris, I had the feeling that some of the vacant air which hung over their burned-out home had followed them to town and made their life so empty that nothing would ever fill it again. It would only get emptier. Even the children had gone away to work, and the Kaaris had had to move from the narrow house into an apartment. "We could go to see them sometime," I said to Mother.

She agreed and one Saturday after the haying was finished, we did. She said we couldn't stay long because Mr. Kaari was ill and tired easily, but he'd enjoy having some fresh berries and new potatoes.

Their apartment was right above a tavern on Iron Street. They had three small airless rooms; the living room had a single large window and in front of it a table with a yellowing fern in a coffee can. On one side of the window was a door to the kitchen and on the other a door to the bedroom, where Mr. Kaari was lying down. Thin and wasted himself, he wanted to know if I had been able to go to school most of the year. I told him that I had and that I only wheezed sometimes. He said he knew just how I had felt because now he wheezed day and night.

Mrs. Kaari made us coffee and gave us cinnamon rolls which she had bought at the A & P. She just didn't have time to bake anymore. "Do you remember, Mary, how you and I would sit at the table and drink our coffee together?"

"Yes," I said, and the whole place came back to me in a rush of pleasant memory as fresh and sweet as a spring breeze from the cherry-blossomed hills. "I remember."

After we had had our coffee, Father went to sit with Mr. Kaari in the bedroom, so narrow it scarcely held the bed and one dresser. Elizabeth and I sat on the couch, and Mother and Mrs. Kaari stayed in the kitchen. They were talking and weeping by turn, for they had a good reason. Mr. Kaari wouldn't live long.

The next day, Elizabeth, Edward and I walked to the Kaari place to see if the raspberry vines had come back to life. They had. While Edward scrambled around finding pieces of glass, nails and Mason jar tops in the debris where the house used to be, Elizabeth and I picked a lard pail full of berries. "If they were here we could stop there after school, Elizabeth."

"They'd be nice to us, Mary."

"If we had a storm, they'd let us stay the night."

We came back across the dusty, stubbled field and frightened the grasshoppers into whirring flight. It was so hot, Hadley had to be burning. How could Mr. Kaari breathe in such weather? It was worse than the cold of winter.

Mother and Father brought the Kaaris their raspberries and a bouquet of Grandmother's roses. Mr. Kaari no longer knew where he was. He had asked Mother why she didn't sing as she had when Father and Mother moved to Revier. For days and days, he had waited to hear her voice coming from the trees.

He died on the third of August, on the hottest day in our memory. The girls, Laima and Olga, came back from California and the boys from Detroit. The boy who had gone to Russia and never returned could not be notified; no one knew where he was.

We went to the funeral—all of us, even Big Hank, who rarely went anywhere. We gathered together at the Workers' Hall in Woodland, where the Communist Party held its meetings. There were posters on the walls and pamphlets and printed notices on a big table near the gray coffin. The paint was peeling off the doors; the windows were covered with dust. No one had remembered to sweep the floor. There were no flowers to remind the living that when Mr. Kaari was with us in Revier he had walked over the flowering meadows every day of summer.

The speaker wore a black suit, a white shirt and a black tie, just as all preachers wear when they give a sermon at a funeral. His was a sermon too, not about heavenly reward but about capitalist greed. It was this greed which had killed our comrade. Like a preacher, he said the same thing in many ways, and like a preacher he gave little comfort. Then he asked all workers to unite in the memory of Comrade Kaari.

Mrs. Kaari asked Mother to sing and she did: a Finnish hymn so lovely and peaceful that no one could quarrel with its meaning. Her voice filled the air and brought love and caring back to remembrance in that grim and shabby place.

When Mother was done singing, she said, "No one should leave us without our tears." Then she wept and others did too. I would have, but the tears wouldn't come. Elizabeth and I held hands. I wished that we had picked some wild flowers from the Kaaris' field and brought them to place on the coffin, but we had been in a hurry to get ready and I hadn't had the time.

We said good-bye to Mrs. Kaari, who was leaving with her daughter. She would write to us from California, she promised. She did write, but I never saw her again, only snapshots taken in sunny places where flowers grew all around her.

That's how it was in Revier. People always left, never to return.

When we went back to school, Miss Gurney was at her desk. Perhaps she had been there all summer and was annoyed now because we hadn't even once climbed the stairs to bang on the door of Revier School. Perhaps she was annoyed that we had come back. Now that we were there, however, she read the roll and noted that she saw one new name, Angelina Deer.

Angelina was as quiet as she had been in the kitchen of the lumber camp and as somber a child as ever had walked into the school. Though she studied her reader, none of us could tell if she could read or if she just looked at the pictures. Elizabeth and I showed her the schoolroom and the toilet downstairs, where she would certainly need to go sometimes. We held her hand and asked her if she remembered us. She nodded her head.

We helped her write the words which Miss Gurney wrote on the blackboard; we asked her to find the words in her book and she did. We asked her if she could talk. She nodded her head but said nothing. During the noon hour and during recess, she sought us and stood beside us as if she were about to say something, but she didn't. Finally we assumed she couldn't talk. We stopped trying to encourage her and played wordless games with her.

Just as we were leaving school for the Thanksgiving holiday and walked out into the gently falling snow, Angelina looked at us and smiled. "It's snowing," she said. We never saw her again, for the Deers moved away. Later, when Elizabeth and I walked in the woods, we often talked of Angelina Deer, the pretty Indian child who had come and gone. I thought we would someday meet her there in the shadow of the trees, where she would be neither tongue-tied nor solemn, but free to voice whatever she felt.

"Do you think she liked us?" Elizabeth asked the next summer when picking violets on the banks of the Montfer.

"Yes," I said, "because she did talk to us once."

But how could one really tell with an elfin creature like Angelina Deer? Perhaps she would always come and go her silent way, and everywhere people would wonder, "Did she like us?" No one would ever know for sure. She was like beautiful Ann, who had made people think and dream.

When we returned from our holiday, Elizabeth asked Miss Gurney if she didn't feel lonesome for Angelina.

"Why? How can one miss a child who never talks?"

"Well, I wish she were here," Elizabeth said. On the way home she told me that she still liked Miss Gurney but not as much as she had before.

After that I didn't tell Miss Gurney anything about our lives. I read. I read every book in the bookshelf at school and all of Carl's dog stories—*Call of the Wild*, *White Fang* and *Bob, Son of Battle*. Then

Mrs. Wiggs of the Cabbage Patch, Little Women and *Huckleberry Finn.* Anything and everything jumbled together. *David Copperfield* went on forever; a half would have been enough, but I read on. *Gulliver's Travels* and Richard Halliburton's *The Glorious Adventure.*

Sometimes for days I drew pictures, and did page after page of arithmetic problems. I wrote poems and stories; I used big words which I had to look up in the dictionary and the encyclopedia.

We didn't complain about Miss Gurney anymore. John had gone to Hadley High School in fall and told us we were lucky: we had only one teacher looking down on us. He had Mr. O'Reilly, the superintendent, and Miss Hanson, his English teacher. On some days he came home, slammed down his books, changed his clothes and went to do his chores in the barn. He wouldn't say what had happened at school. "I'll show them," he'd say, and studied until midnight six days of the week. He'd get on the honor roll every month; he'd stay on it for the whole four years.

And he did. There were more teachers who were not prejudiced than there were teachers who were, but Mr. O'Reilly's bias against the Finns and their ways and his disdain of the farmers living north of Hadley set the tone for the high school. Revier was a wilderness. Who but the witless would build a home there? Who but the Finns, who hadn't had the sense to make a go of it in their own godforsaken homeland? Other immigrants had settled around Revier, but the Finns had tainted the whole area because they had been the first to head north.

We were so accustomed to conflicting notions that we didn't think anyone would care what we were, but Mr. O'Reilly did. He was an Irish Catholic and a Republican. Most of the Finns were Lutherans or evangelicals or atheists; their political leanings tended toward the left, though we had enough Republicans among us to make a reasonable balance. To Mr. O'Reilly, however, we were all in the same heap of sauna-bathing anarchists.

What could our parents say? They couldn't protect us from scorn without denying us an opportunity to learn, but they supported us in their own ways.

Mother was proud of being a Finn, a St. Paul's Lutheran and a Revierite. We were the salt of the earth. Stubborn, hard-working, clean-living and honest. That's how pioneers had always been. Where would the country be without people like us?

Father's pride wasn't in being Finnish or being in Revier. A Finn was no better than anyone else; Revier hadn't been the home of his choice. To him, learning was something one did because it led further. Who could know where? The sky was the limit. He was pleased with our successes and when we lost he consoled us. By never trying, one could be certain of never failing, but there was no adventure to that.

Grandmother accepted our Finnish heritage as a fact. We had to speak the language; the rest would follow. We were in Revier because we hadn't gone elsewhere. She wanted us to learn but not to use our skills for moving out of our station in life. To her mind, there were two kinds of people: the wellborn and the other. Each kind had its place; each had equal dignity. We belonged with the other and remembering that was more important than attempting to do something which could land us among the wellborn.

That's one way of looking at the world, Father would say, but he hoped we'd learn not to care what others thought of us. If one waited for approval, one never did anything that made life worthwhile. In a hundred years, no one would know or care who said what or why or when. Mother wanted us to be courteous. Grandmother urged patience. Big Hank, anarchist soul that he was, had one answer to everything. Strike. Had we followed his lead, we'd have learned nothing.

Because our parents rarely spoke of intolerance, neither did we. Perhaps they knew we were rebels and wanted us to be good, kind, accepting ones. What we had, however, was the freedom to act as we saw fit. That was more important to us than a discussion about something they were too powerless to change.

7

MISS GURNEY LEFT US and Mr. Dominic came instead. He was our teacher for four years, and my last at Revier School. Every day he walked the two and a half miles from the highway where the town school bus left him off, and every evening he walked back. He never missed a day, nor did I after he came, unless I was too ill to stand. Sometimes on the coldest days of winter when no one else dared to face the weather, I'd go to bring him the milk and cream he needed for his ulcer. We'd be alone, just the two of us with all the books, the maps and the globe to ourselves. He never said, "Why don't you stay home? Give me one day—one day of nothing but bare walls and windows, clean blackboards, untramped floors, silence, and dry heat rising out of the floor register." He might have, but he didn't, and I was certain he needed me there to assure him that his effort wasn't wasted.

Thin, tense, angry when we were stupid, delighted when we were not, Mr. Dominic coaxed, punished, lectured and cajoled. Think. Think. No more inkwells flooding over; pencils would do. No more Palmer Method workbooks; just learn something. For God's sake, learn. He told us about the university where he had gone, and worked his way through. He told us about living our lives well in order to reward our mothers and fathers who had had no chance. That made us no-chance children too, but we could change it. We had time.

He brought olive oil for my hands and face. "Don't use water, stubborn girl. Look at this."

I saw the sores on my hands and my arms, and I didn't see them. "It doesn't hurt at all."

"Of course it hurts." He'd rub the oil on my skin. "You're just stubborn. Just stubborn, that's all. You wheeze and you don't admit that either. You don't admit anything. Foolish girl." He paused. "Well, maybe that's what it takes. All the same, keep your hands out of water!"

He brought his wife to school. She too had eczema, he said, and she used oil. But I couldn't see the rash. She was just an ordinary girl, neither pretty nor ugly. A year later she came in with their baby, a baby like any other, soft and rosy.

Sometimes in spring when the days grew long, he played baseball with us, forgot that we had lessons to do, and forgot that he had papers to correct. "My God, we've wasted an hour. Back to work!" We went in, breathed the close, chalk-laden air. He'd open the windows and the door. We sat, half inside, half outside, with the sun flooding over us and the wind blowing in, fluttering the map against the wall, and lifting our papers off our desks.

He was ambitious for us and wanted us to know that he was. He saw more in us than we saw in ourselves, but just as he wanted to add to what he saw, he also wished to subtract. We had to leave behind one set of superstitions for another, and one way of feeling and being for another which was more suitable.

We knew, however, that no matter what went on at school or in our heads, the cows had to be fed and milked, the horses harnessed, the fields planted and harvested, the food cooked and the house cleaned. The endless work from dawn to dusk and long after wasn't outside our realm; it was ours as much as anyone's. As children, we enjoyed no privilege; an hour's study was an hour's burden upon another.

Our parents assumed that we would do well; Grandmother insisted. "Read your lessons," she'd say crossly whenever we were resistant to learning. "Don't waste your time." We didn't. To waste was to add to our sense of guilt.

Thus Revier School became our place of work and expiation. Our success there was a proof that we had not been wasteful of our parents' time and trust. When the school day was over, we could work to compensate them for their effort in our behalf.

Yet success in school left its mark upon us. We no longer belonged totally to the rock-fenced fields and silent places of our island world; we no longer felt as deeply the kinship between ourselves and the wild creatures with whom we shared the land. We sensed the loss, but to whom could we explain this losing and severing? To the town-bred teacher? How could he understand? What did he know about our feeling of helplessness at hearing in the night the wild geese lost and flying so close that we could pluck them out of the sky? How could we explain our identification with these bereft birds? After all, geese will be geese.

And if lost geese were just geese, what were we? Was there no value in us just as we were? Whom could we ask? Our loving no-chance parents? Ask them, and tell them that we did not wish to be like them? Of course not.

"Always remember where you came from," Grandmother said, sensing our estrangement.

We remembered well enough, but remembering was no help. What good did it do to remember and then reject it? We didn't ask her, because we knew she thought that we ought to be more humble and modest, and that remembering would make us so. It didn't. We stayed uneasy. That's all.

Only in our close and cluttered kitchen with the wood crackling in the stove, the pots nodding on their uneven bottoms, the bread browning in the oven, and all of us there together did we feel a momentary ease. We'd have a cup of tea, and then begin our chores, the boys in the barn, and my sister and I in the house: the feeding and milking, the putting in order, the making of dinner, the washing of dishes, and the tending to the smaller children— all to be done before we could sit down around the table for our evening of study, which once more removed us from our time and place.

That spring, his first at Hadley High School, John reached man's estate. Never again would he be a child, for in our village once we reached the age of fourteen or fifteen, we were eligible to attend the confirmation school at a Lutheran church or go to a summer camp run by the local Communist Party cell. After two weeks of either church school or Communist camp, we were certified adults. Some of the young people had double certification, first by the camp and then by the church, for the camp in spite of its secular concern had one serious drawback—it was not fun at all. It was incredibly dull. The church wasn't. There was no difference in the mode of instruction; one memorized pages of material that no one understood, answered questions, sang songs and listened to lectures. Yet after two weeks at the church, one had a steady boy or girl friend, and after two weeks at the camp, one had nothing but a campful of comrades. There was no comparison. The Lutheran Church could provide earthly love with its certificate of adulthood, and the Communists couldn't.

John was prepared for confirmation school. He had had years of Mrs. Salmi's Sunday school class, read and spoke Finnish well, and knew the good-natured pastor at her church. Every day instead of attending high school he went to Woodland, and there at the church repeated all that he had learned over the years. In the evenings, he memorized whole pages of new material, and rattled it off to us to show that if there was joy in locking the girls' toilet, in climbing out of basement windows, and in hiding behind the altar during the noon hour—though of course he didn't—there was an element of seriousness in the business of becoming grown up.

Our parents bought him a dark wool suit to wear, a white shirt and a dark tie. So attired, more handsome than he'd ever been, John prepared to leave for the final rite at church. My parents were dressed in their best, and Carl, who was going along because he would be confirmed the next year, looked almost ready for confirming but not quite. One could tell, people said, though I thought that if he had on a black suit he'd be ready enough.

On that wet and soggy Easter morning, we waited for them to leave. They'd stay the whole day, have dinner in the church parlors, and then hear the choir late in the afternoon, after all the communicants had "passed" their oral questioning and had "partaken of the holy feast"—thin wafers and a thimbleful of grape juice. Everyone was ready now. John, never caring much what was underfoot, ran ahead at full speed to the car. In a moment he was back again, all arms and legs, his hair tousled and his new suit dripping snow and mud.

I could have wept for the change in him, from a handsome young man to an unhappy child, ashamed and angered by his clumsiness. At that moment, if he had told me ten times that I was the ugliest girl in Revier, I'd have loved him still. Mother and I wiped him off. There was nothing new in falling down on Easter Day, we said. People fell all the time, broke their legs and arms, fell face down on the church stairs, broke their teeth and glasses, and never got into church. In fact, Easter was probably the most dangerous day of the whole year! That's what we said, but we might as well have said nothing. John was miserable and so were we.

All that day we waited at home, as we did long before at Grandmother Anderson's funeral in Marengo, when we were left behind to eat orange slices and to wait forever until everyone came back to the house. The same cold gray air was around us. Finally, late in the afternoon, we heard the car coming down the road. As Father drove into the yard, he blew the horn, and we ran outside. There was John, truly adult now, and my parents as proud as only parents can be when their child answers questions loudly, clearly, and correctly too. The day had been splendid. "Even the dinner wasn't too bad," said Carl.

After several weeks, we received a big envelope in the mail, and inside, wrapped in tissue paper, a big photograph of the confirmation class. The dark-suited boys were in the back and the white-frocked girls in front. In the center of the first row, flanked by two girls, sat the pastor, with the Bible in his hands and a beatific smile on his face. John recited the names of all the students and identified the girls he liked and the ones he didn't. And for nights on end, he told us stories about the escapades, jokes and foolishness they'd shared on their way to becoming adults in two weeks.

Eventually we would all be certified adults. Carl would become one next year; I, two years after him; Elizabeth, two years after me; Edward, two years after Elizabeth. One after the other, we were marching toward that remarkable goal. We could only wonder how exciting it would be for each of us as we approached the final stage when we declared ourselves Christians forever.

Mother told us about her experiences, how her class had hidden the hymnals and locked the church door so that the poor long-suffering minister had to bang on it until someone heard him. One boy rang the church bells; another skipped school for an hour and returned with gum and candy for everyone.

Big Hank's confirmation school had been all business. He said the minister rapped the students' knuckles to remind the fledgling Christians that God is loving. But Hank had learned the Bible and for that he was grateful. Otherwise he would have had nothing to talk about with Pastor Grandfather.

Grandmother didn't say what had happened to her in confirmation school and neither did Father. They had probably had a very dull time, since neither of them remembered anything about their experience.

Now as we looked at John in the photograph of newly declared adults, he stared back at us with an unfaltering gaze. He really had changed! One thin wafer and a swallow of grape juice had elevated John from boy to man.

Once we were done with this two-week exercise, we were expected to put away our childish concerns. When we regressed, Grandmother or Hank, and sometimes even Mother, reminded us that we were behaving improperly. "You've been through confirmation school. You ought to know better!"

Father never said that. Perhaps the magic hadn't worked on him as it had on John that spring. Maybe he didn't think the rite important. He never talked about it, but sometimes when just the two of us were together, when I brought him his coffee to the field, for instance, and he stopped the horse and sat down with me, I thought he was sad and wanted to be elsewhere, away from the rock-fenced fields of our place.

We'd say nothing much at all, just look across the field cut off here and there by fences, and up at the sky so wide that it reached the end of the earth. Sometimes he saw a cloud he liked; sometimes a tree so rare in color that we would never again see it in our lifetime; sometimes a deer leaping over the fence and disappearing into the woodlot. We'd share the silence. Then reluctantly he'd get up, thank me politely for bringing the coffee, and pick up the reins again.

I'd watch him for a while. What did he think as he followed the shifting hindquarters of old Maud? There was nothing to see but the furrowing earth and the tired legs of that poor beast. What did Father really think as he plodded over that uneven ground? Whatever he thought, I felt sorry for him.

One day during the noon-hour break, Maud laid herself down

on the grass near the house. There was something ominous about her repose, for she usually roamed about, munching the tender grass in the shade. We went out to see her, that great mound of flesh and bone. Her heaving side was gleaming with sweat.

Father fetched her a blanket; we placed cold cloths on her forehead and rubbed her neck. Then she opened her mouth as if to tell us something, but her voice was gone and nothing came of her effort. Her tired old hide shivered; her back legs twitched nervously.

We brought her sugar lumps with liniment, we rubbed her heaving sides, and we talked to her. She opened her mouth again and a white froth flowed out and dribbled onto the green grass.

"Now she's better," one of us said.

Then the ribbed sides and knotted limbs stopped moving. "She's dead!" Father said. We stood there looking down at her.

Hank said that someone should go to the fox farm to tell one of the men to come out with his truck.

When we heard what would happen to Maud at the fox farm, Mother began weeping into her apron, which she always held cupped to her face at a time of crisis.

Elizabeth and I said that Maud ought to be buried.

"You can get five dollars from the fox farmer, and we can keep the skin," said Carl, hiding his feelings behind practicality now that he would be an adult in less than a year.

"That's cruel," I said.

"She's dead, you dummy!" said Carl, and because I punched him, he whacked me.

"She was just a horse," Carl said.

"She wasn't just a horse!" I shouted.

"Well, she wasn't a cow and she wasn't human."

We yelled at each other until Father told us to stop. Elizabeth stood beside Mother. Edward pulled grass, and placed it in neat little bundles next to Maud's nose.

"I guess we'll bury her then," said Father.

He and Carl worked all afternoon to dig a hole big enough to hold Maud's enormous carcass. Neighing in protest, the other two horses dragged the body to a shadowed glade beside the river, and there we buried her.

Elizabeth and I planted wild violets on the raw earth. We wondered if we ought to mark the grave with a cross, but then we decided that if Maud were alive, she would stumble over it. Instead we made a picnic lunch for us—Elizabeth, Edward and me—and while we ate we talked about the wonderful exploits of Maud, who had died at thirty-three.

During that summer when I was almost eleven, we dwelt in a world of proper secrecy, expectation and wonder. Mother was pregnant. We wouldn't have said "pregnant," however. It was a word we didn't use. If we had spoken of it, we'd have said "heavy with child," a Biblical term describing a condition of Gothic-lettered importance. A blessing. A gift from God's storehouse. But we didn't talk about it. To do so would have invaded the privacy of Mother and Father, whose cooperation had been necessary to bring about this remarkably exalted state.

It was our summer secret which we kept from each other through all of haying, harvesting grain and threshing. Even Elizabeth and I, though once when we were left to wait at Kresge's, the two of us looked at baby sweaters, booties and pretty ribboned bonnets in blue and pink. Elizabeth liked the pink; I thought the blue ones were prettier. We saw a christening dress, all lace and embroidery, suitable for a girl perhaps, but certainly not for a boy.

"Here's one, Elizabeth," I said. I had found a white pique suit, double breasted. "Isn't that neat? It's dignified."

"I don't think that's for christening."

"It doesn't need to be fancy, does it?"

Just then we saw Mother coming through the door and we hurried to meet her because we didn't want her to know that we had been looking at baby clothes. "It's almost like Christmas!" Elizabeth whispered.

"I know," I whispered back.

"What's the matter with you two?" asked Mother.

"Nothing. We were just looking at Christmas things," I said.

"At this time of year?" asked Mother. "I wouldn't begin planning yet. Heaven only knows what we'll be buying at Christmas."

All summer long, Father tried to be especially kind, but in his attempt to anticipate Mother's wants he was often clumsy and ineffectual. Once he got up from the table to fetch her a cup of coffee and as he was pouring it, he spilled some on the stove. The sudden sputtering and steaming made Mother turn her head and

135

ask, "Now what happened?" as if every time he did something, there would be an awful hissing and steaming in our kitchen.

Once when he saw that she needed help, he got up too quickly and pushed the table. Ever unsteady on its three small legs, the cream pitcher overturned. "My goodness! That thing is always on its side," Mother said. Then she added at once, "But it's the prettiest one we have."

Fortunately she remembered in time. Father had bought her the blue glass bowl and creamer on their last wedding anniversary. "I'm so fond of them I'm always putting them to use," she said, patting Father's hand. Then she held up one side of the tablecloth and Father the other. Elizabeth and I ran for towels, and Edward for the stool which Mother was to have under her feet when she sat down. We were always in motion that summer when Mother was with child.

If we had an idle moment, Grandmother asked us to help Mother. "Your legs are young and nimble," she'd say, "and your mother needs her rest." We worked harder than ever in the house, and when we were finished we helped Grandmother in her garden. Even Edward worked now, brought kindling, fed the chickens, brought the ducks to the Montfer to feed on polliwogs and fish, and in the evening brought the waddling birds back to the barn. Meanwhile the books, which Mr. Dominic had given to us at the end of the school year, waited on the shelf under Grandmother's flowering begonias and verbenas. We didn't have time to read.

When we went back to school, we didn't tell Mr. Dominic why we hadn't read anything. We just said we had been busy, and he said he had been too, because they had a new baby who cried a lot. We didn't say anything about Mother to Paul Ojala, but we should have. Father had asked him to help with the potato harvest, and had told him to come right after milking. He didn't. During the noon hour, we saw him racing down Revier Road, past the school, up the hill and down. Then Mother was certain that the harvest wouldn't get in. Still, nothing impressed Paul; he had his own schedule and was as cheerful as if he had a hundred years to do whatever work there was to be done at home or anywhere else. "Don't you be upset, Mrs. Morgan. We'll get things done," he said.

And Mother was worried because he ran around with Tony Koivunen, who had a bad temper, especially when he drank. She said Tony needed all the sense he had. Paul agreed. Tony had

136

gotten angry and pushed Mr. Koivunen out of the hayloft. "But don't you think about it, Mrs. Morgan. I can take care of myself."

"I hope so," said Mother, drying her eyes. She too must have thought of Mrs. Ojala, whose death had left her sons lone and unguided.

Whenever Paul began working at our house, he'd return day after day even if there was nothing to do. Now he was riding the horses bareback and trying to lasso hats, old boots and milk cans. All he did was raise the dust if the ground was dry; he never picked up a thing. John and Carl were experts and tried to teach him, but he gave up. "I'm not going to be a cowboy anyway," he said, and went in to talk to Mother.

We thought he was growing more handsome every year. He had long-lashed blue-green eyes that reminded me of Lake Superior close to shore, where the water caught the color from the trees. His hair curled around his ears, and now that he carried a comb in his shirt pocket, the top of his head had waves over it instead of the wild tangle which his little brother Eino still had. "I got to keep looking nice for the girls," he told Mother, as he stood before the mirror in the kitchen.

"You look very nice, Paul," said Mother.

"If I ever find a girl, Mrs. Morgan, I'll come straight over here to let you see her."

"I wouldn't be in a hurry."

"Well, I don't want to be an old man before I find somebody."

When Paul was with us, so was Eino unless school was in session. "Don't you ever stay home?" Paul would ask him. "Mrs. Morgan has enough work without having a bunch of kids around."

By late October, all the potatoes were gathered into the shed, all the pumpkins heaped into the empty spaces in the garage and all the rutabagas, carrots and beets safe in the cellar. The huge purple and pale green cabbages were still in the porch. In the mornings before the sun had warmed the air, the frost was thick on the ground. Sometimes a flake of snow danced in the wind.

One Saturday, we woke up to find Mother sitting at the table and watching the pendulum swing on the wall clock. "It's time, John," she said to Father. He put on his coat and ran hatless to the car; we heard him leave.

Hollow-eyed, tired, Mother sat at the table and held on to the edge. She was quiet and totally unaware of us as she rocked herself back and forth, in another realm out of our reach, waiting for that momentous hour when a new being would be ready to come to our house.

Grandmother asked John and Carl to bring in some more wood and to fill the kettles and the copper boiler. They began to run at once, in and out in a frenzy of activity as if their speed and agility would hasten the process of birth.

"Don't run! For heaven's sake," said Grandmother, "there's time."

Elizabeth, Edward and I had been standing still, just watching the boys run about. Then we too began to hurry. We cleared the table, swept the floor, washed the dishes and made the beds.

"Stop running, Mary, and make some sandwiches for yourselves and the boys," said Grandmother.

"Where's Big Hank?" I asked.

"He's at the Salmis'."

I was almost done making the sandwiches when Father drove back into the yard. Mrs. Maki had the black bag I always remembered as the one in which I had come; she placed it on the kitchen table and took off her gloves. She shook hands with us all and hung up her heavy coat on the nail. "I'll just have to have a cup of coffee first," she said, "and while I'm sitting here doing nothing, you boys get me a clean bucket full of clean straw."

Everything was normal now. She sat at the table opposite Mother and drank her coffee. Soon the boys came in with the bucket overflowing with straw. "Thank you, boys. I should hire you as helpers. I usually have to get my own straw, to make sure it's clean." She was calm and unhurried. And then as she looked at Mother, she got up. "If you young people can find something to do for a little while, I'll get going here."

John and Carl still had chores in the barn; Elizabeth and I had to sweep the floor and change the beds upstairs. Edward would come with us. I gave the boys their bag of sandwiches and a bottle of milk; I gave Elizabeth ours and poured us a bottle of milk too. Then we went upstairs and the boys into the barn.

We worked. And we waited for hours. Below us we heard a great hustling and bustling which we might have heard on Christmas Eve had we not been in the sauna at the moment that Santa Claus

138

came to bring the toys, years ago when we were so young we thought of nothing but Christmas and the Fourth, and believed everything, however improbable. I thought of our baby lying on the clean straw in the clean bucket. Then I heard the first faint infant cry.

I told Edward that Mrs. Maki had brought us a baby though we all knew how babies came, but after the months of secrecy and not talking about being with child, it was pleasant to think that the smiling, good-natured, button-nosed Mrs. Maki came with a baby, all snug and warm inside a blanket smelling of Johnson's baby powder.

Then Father called to us, "The baby's here!"

We scuttled down the dark and narrow stairs. There sat plump and smiling Mrs. Maki with a bundle in her arms. If we sat down we could each hold him for a few minutes, she said. We did. He was the most beautiful baby I had ever seen.

For two weeks, every morning before we went to school, Mrs. Maki came to bathe the baby and to tend to Mother, who stayed in bed. I'm not sure why, for many other women were up within a few hours. Perhaps Mother suffered still from the effects of the fever she had had after Carl was born; possibly staying in bed for two weeks was considered a new method of maternal care.

In any case, Mrs. Maki came and we waited for her coming, because we could watch her bathe the baby in a new washtub placed on two chairs. First, she poured in the hot water from the kettle, then she spread a blanket on the bottom of the tub, and finally, after checking the temperature of the water, she placed the baby on the blanket. As soon as he was in the water, he began to squall. We called to him. "Oliver! Ollie, look at us!" But he didn't. He turned red and shook all over. The two purple patches, one on his chest and the other on his knee, turned a deeper shade still.

Mrs. Maki said that his crying was normal, but the purple markings bothered her. She had never seen such marks before. Perhaps the doctor would know what they were. Dr. Burton saw nothing unusual. "Just blemishes. They'll fade."

Mrs. Maki was doubtful; still, he was a golden-haired, well-formed baby. He certainly appeared healthy. Then when he was six weeks old, Oliver became gravely ill. Every day after school was over, I'd run home across the fields, and hope that when I

139

walked in the door, Oliver would open his eyes, look at me and smile as the twins had, but as soon as I saw him, I knew he was no better. Day after day, he just lay on our parents' bed, his eyes closed, his skin hot and dry, and his heart pounding like a small hammer inside his chest. Sometimes he cried plaintively, and I'd rock him until I was dizzy myself.

The doctor gave medications, but they didn't stay down. Every time we lifted or moved him he vomited. "The medicine helps," I would say. "I think he's much stronger." I thought that if I repeated the statement often enough it would become a fact.

And gradually he did improve. The fever left him, he held his food, and his heart beat normally. His limbs were still weak, and he slept unless we awakened him, but he was better. When I held him, he seemed too motionless, and not at all as he had been earlier when he flung his arms about.

Weeks went by, one watchful day after another. We had forgotten how he was before his illness; we accepted him as he was now, carried him about, and anticipated his every need. I had saved the money I'd received for my birthday and now bought him bonnets and boots with ribbons from Kresge's in Woodland; I worried about him whenever I left him, as if he were my responsibility alone. Soon he wept whenever I left him; he clung to me more than to Mother. "He'll be all right," she'd tell me.

As Mother often said, he was a blessing in our house. He was loved, dawdled, rocked and carried more than any child anywhere. He was growing; he was pretty. Yet, there were those sudden piercing cries of pain, even in his sleep. Even now when he was nine months old. "Some babies do," Mother said, comforting herself and us. "He doesn't cry much otherwise." And he didn't now that he was over his illness.

One evening when Mother and Father were milking the cows, Elizabeth and I took Oliver outside into the leaf house. The leaves were already dry and beginning to fall. He was fascinated by the rustling sound; he caught a leaf and examined it, then brushed it against his bare legs. He was delighted with himself. Then the wind shifted to the north, and I thought he would get chilled in the sudden cool breeze. I picked him up and began carrying him into the house. Just as I reached the top of the stairs, I stumbled, and as I went down, his head hit the edge of the doorstep. He turned pale and closed his eyes. He didn't cry; he didn't move. At that moment, I was certain that he was dead and that I had killed him. I carried him to his cradle. Then I ran to the barn to tell Mother and Father.

The whole family was in motion. Everyone was scrambling into the house to see what it was that I had done. By this time, Oliver was crying the sad, hurt cry that he sometimes gave us for no reason at all, but now he had one, and I was at fault. Mother and Father examined his head; there was only a small bruise. He'd be all right. But how could he be? I must have injured him.

Then one day a few weeks later, Grandmother and I were alone. I had waited for a peaceful time with her, a moment when the two of us sitting together could forget our usual reserve, forget that I was young and she was old. She was at her spinning wheel and I was rocking Oliver. I asked her if she was sure that I hadn't injured him. She said she was certain of it. If babies were damaged that easily, they wouldn't live through the first year. But Oliver wasn't well and had never been. Perhaps when he was older, Dr. Burton would be able to help him. "We'll have to wait," she said.

Had I been the cause of Oliver's ailment, Grandmother would have told me. She wouldn't try to protect me from the truth. She would console me and tell me I couldn't help falling. "Maybe when I'm older, I can take him to a big hospital," I said, "and then he'll get well."

"That's our hope too, Mary."

I thought then of Oliver on his first bed, a bucket of straw, and wondered why a baby needed it. "Grandmother, do you know why we needed the straw for him?"

She said that the straw hadn't been for Oliver, but for Mother. Had she had trouble delivering the baby, Mrs. Maki would have poured hot water on the straw, placed a clean towel on it and then had Mother sit on it. Maybe midwives in Finland no longer used the method since everything had changed so much, but Mrs. Maki had always had the straw ready and she had never lost a baby or a mother in all her years of practice. Only once had she had to use the straw at our house and that was during Edward's birth. He was the smallest and the weakest, but he too came out.

"And lay on the straw," I said. The image of this Christmas bed was so tender I wouldn't let go of it, especially if the straw was covered with a clean towel.

"No, we bathed him and put him in the cradle."

Then I asked her if it was hard for the baby to come out, and she said that it wasn't. Mrs. Maki had all her babies in the warm sauna all by herself. And I could see her going into the heated sauna when she was heavy with child and coming out again a moment later with a bundled baby in her arms. When the men came in from the field, there was a new child in the Maki house.

Asleep in my arms, Oliver stirred. I got up and placed him in his cradle, wound the spring and set the small bed in motion. Then I went out to hang his diapers on the line. As I walked back and saw the naked trees, I remembered again that dreadful day, and wished there had never been a leaf house.

Though Grandmother said I hadn't injured him and everyone else did too, how could I ever be really sure? I could ask the same question a thousand times and get the same answer as often, but I still wouldn't know. Whenever I heard Oliver cry, I remembered falling with him. Nothing could change that now.

8

IT WAS DURING OLIVER'S FIRST SUMMER that we children became fully aware of the events in the outside world.

There had been talk before of times getting harder elsewhere, of people losing their jobs and life becoming less certain. Yet that couldn't hurt us. What could happen in Revier? In the best of times, the farmers hadn't earned much for their labor; the foods they raised on their rock-strewn land had brought them little in the marketplace. Besides, the season of growth was too short; a late spring frost could destroy the newly planted crops and an early frost in autumn a summer's work. We were accustomed to that. To supplement their incomes, the men could always work in the lumber camp, their own woodlots or the mine. They could do carpenter work as Father did.

Our farm had fertile soil; the Northfield was free of stones and coal black. Our yields were good, our cows high producers and our chickens fast growing and early maturing. In our woodlot, we had hardwood to feed the stoves and furnaces of Hadley and Woodland, wild fruit and berries everywhere to eat and to sell, and sap in the maples for making the best syrup around. As long as the townspeople had money to pay for our produce, for the new houses Father built, for the repairs and improvements on the old, and as long as the mines needed timber, our lives were secure.

As the Great Depression began to move across the country, however, our livelihood was threatened as well. The price of farm products began to fall. Week by week. No one could shield us from the reality; no one could protect us from the consciousness that we too were victims of the disaster. There was in the air we breathed a sense of doom we had never before experienced. Father was always looking for work; Mother was always reassuring him. "It's going to be worse than anything we've seen," people would say. And it wasn't the economy alone; it was the change in the climate as well. The droughts and high winds brought dust that covered the young seedlings; the rain came down dark and thick, turning the green plants brown The universe had gone awry.

We called the years that followed the Days of Arrivals and Departures. The farmers couldn't find jobs and had to exist on their depressed farm incomes. They couldn't pay the interest on their mortgages; they couldn't pay their taxes. One by one, the families left; new ones moved in, but they had no money to buy machinery and farm animals. Soon the fields were overgrown with sumac and hazelnut. To the east and west of Revier, some farms were vacant for years; the windows in the houses were broken, the barn doors open and the fences falling down. As we looked upon the desolation, we saw the futility of the effort lavished on this beautiful but unproductive corner of the earth.

What would happen to us in Revier? Nothing, Mother said. We all had enough work to do and food and shelter. We didn't need to worry. There might be some foreclosures, but surely not many. We in Revier would always manage. In the big cities it was worse, though even around Hadley and Woodland the small mines were beginning to close down, a day at a time. Next a three-day week; then a three-week layoff, and back to work again at reduced hours for those who weren't fired.

Uncle Eric was working two days a week and couldn't find another job. The Montfer mine, always the biggest employer, was no longer hiring. Now he wished that he were there, but he wasn't. And who could know? Perhaps the Montfer would close too; there were rumors that it would. He'd be no better off and maybe even worse. He might have bought one of the mining company houses and been left holding it forever. "What am I going to do?" he asked Father. Over and over, the same question.

One day he and Aunt Taimi and the children left town. Eric's brother, who had a trucking business in St. Paul, needed a driver.

He had a place for them—a small house he owned. Until they could find something better, they could live there free. A roof over the head and food on the table. That's all you could expect these days. You couldn't plan ahead. Thinking did no good. The best anybody could do was to accept what came along, whatever it was. But who could live like that?

Mixed in with the gloom of those years was an uprootedness. Take off. Go. Leave everything behind. Or box everything, stuff it into the car. Pack a knapsack; hop a freight; ride the rails. It was that spirit which stoked the minds of young and old. Our world expanded once more. We looked outward for comfort. "Hallelujah, I'm a Bum" became our favorite song, and "going west" more immediate than going to heaven.

Mandy's niece and her husband gave us their radio, the Harvard Classics and the five-foot shelf to hold them. "We're off," they said, and drove to California. They never returned.

Some of the young men we knew hopped the trains, rode west and came back again. "There's nothing in the West," they said. I saw an empty desert from our place to California and the blue sea. The green land had turned barren, the dry dust rode the wind, the train whistles hooted in the night, and the cold young men huddled in boxcars.

The lumber camp where Hank used to go when he became angry with us closed. He couldn't go there and he couldn't "go west" because he was too old, he said. Where could he go? Where could any of us go, with one mine after another closing tight and not a dollar bill loose in the whole town? "We'll think of something." Everyone said it. Soon after Mandy's niece arrived in Los Angeles, she wrote to Mandy. Everything was fine in California; they had a nice place and the weather was beautiful. They even had two orange trees in the backyard!

Lured by good weather and two orange trees, Otto and Mandy decided to leave at once. They sold their house and all their furniture. At age forty and forty-five, they would begin a life all over and open a business in Los Angeles. Maybe a laundry. Maybe a restaurant.

It was Saturday afternoon when they came to see us. They brought books and magazines, another radio, a cabinet, a big dictionary and an old encyclopedia—the last of their possessions. In the morning, they would pack their suitcases and start off early.

They had their sauna bath. Mother made them coffee, and while they sat with us for the last time, they kept up a steady chatter as if a moment's pause would destroy them. Suddenly they got up. They were in a hurry, they said, because they still had to see Mandy's relatives.

With a few old books he no longer wanted, an old radio and an old cabinet, Otto had paid off a debt which had mortgaged our house and our land. I thought of him limping across our fields and Mandy calling me an old soul, of the gray dress which was first mine and then Elizabeth's, of birthday trinkets and prison tales all bundled together from the past of our lives and bound for California, flowering along the shores of the Pacific, as near or far as Grandmother's northern seas.

"I'll never see them again," Grandmother said softly.

Mother put her arms around her. "Maybe they'll come back."

Father brought them each a cup of coffee and sat beside them. They didn't say anything for a long time. "It's so hard," Grandmother said. "He was like a son to me. Not the best, but a son all the same."

Elizabeth and I went outside. Edward joined us. "Maybe it'll rain real hard tomorrow," he said. "Then they can't go."

"They'll have to," said Elizabeth. "They don't have a home."

And as they talked the first star came out and then another. I wished that we too could go somewhere. But we wouldn't. We'd stay and wait for people to come to our house, and they always did.

The Watkins' man, one eye blue and the other brown, drove in to recite his wares: lemon pudding, vanilla pudding, butterscotch pudding and chocolate; black pepper, white pepper, cinnamon and nutmeg; raspberry, strawberry, grape and cherry nectar; carbolic salve and camphor salve, white liniment and red. Mother always bought one item.

The fisherman peddling fish, ice cold in slivers of ice. "Fresh. Caught this morning. Whitefish, lake trout and perch."

A man selling winter jackets. A furtive man. God knows where he got a carload of jackets. "Selling them wholesale."

People from Hadley and Woodland. "Just thought we'd drive in for a visit." They'd go away with a bushel of produce for a quarter.

And the lonely lumberjacks turned into bums shuffled down the railroad tracks, followed our dusty road and sat on the stairs. "Are you hungry?" They wolfed down eggs, fried potatoes, bread and a quart of milk. God bless you, lady. Mother gave away loaves of bread. "It's a sin for people to starve."

The old bachelors from their shacks walked over to reminisce, young men to look for work and the homeless for a night's shelter. Everybody was moving about. The gypsies rode into town and camped for a week in the Woodland park. They wandered through the streets of Hadley and Woodland, the women in long skirts, embroidered blouses, scarves, beads and dangling earrings; the handsome men, black-eyed, black-haired, with bandannas on their heads. People said the gypsies would drive down to the farms and steal everything, including blond, blue-eyed children. But they didn't steal anything. They left as they had arrived, in a long caravan of covered trucks.

On one steaming August day, the old bachelor lumberjack Aksu came to our house. His right hand was wrapped in a dirty towel. Several weeks before, he had had an accident while working on some old lumber at the loading site at the camp. He had thought he could sell the wood, but now he couldn't get anything done. He didn't know what he'd do when the nights got cold and he couldn't sleep in the shed near the tracks. Nobody had room for him. Could he have a patch of land in the pasture? He'd build a small shack on it and then he'd never have to worry again about a place to live. Mother examined his injury. How could he build anything with a hand twice the size of the other, and torn and bruised so badly it would take weeks to heal?

Father wondered if Hank would help, but since Hank stayed silent, Father thought that he would ask Toivo Salmi and Paul Ojala, and probably Tony, who was lazy but might help if he could be useful for once. If he would drive the Koivunens' truck to town, he could haul back as much lumber as Aksu needed from an old building Father was tearing down. When Hank heard that all the "neighborhood bums" would be on the job, he knew that he was needed there to keep some order.

Until his shack was finished, Aksu could sleep in the attic or in the sauna, Mother said. He wanted to stay in the sauna, because his hand was so painful he slept little and he really didn't want to

147

bother anyone. We fixed a mattress for him on the floor of the dressing room. Though we would have to take everything out again when we had a sauna bath, Aksu didn't care. It was better than sleeping in the shed at the lumber camp.

Tony borrowed his father's truck, hauled home all the lumber Father thought that Aksu wanted, and then added a few more truckloads because Aksu's estimate was too low. At last the building crew gathered in one corner of our pasture.

Aksu was there to do whatever he could with his good hand; Edward and Eino were there to carry nails and tools. Elizabeth and I were to bring food and drink to the builders and were there ready with thermos bottles of coffee. In the evenings, after he was done with his work and with milking, Father would correct the most glaring mistakes. John, who was working in town with Father, and Carl, who was doing the chores at home, were chosen to be Father's helpers when all the others had left the building site.

After one day of building, Tony quit in anger. He couldn't stand Big Hank staring at him all the time. Toivo and Paul stayed on, worked enough to keep Big Hank from quitting, and told us all that when they were done with Aksu's shack, they would build one for themselves. Aksu puttered about, tried to carry boards with his good hand and kept telling us that he had never dreamed he would have a place of his own. Eino and Edward grew tired of carrying nails, quit, and came to play at our house.

The shack went up. The windows were parallel to nothing, not even each other, the door was at an angle and the roof was one foot higher on one end than on the other. Father squared off the doorway and rehung the door, but he let the windows stay because Aksu said he didn't care that they weren't straight, as long as he had some light.

"The house won't look bad," Elizabeth said, "once Aksu hangs curtains."

"Maybe not," I said, although I knew that it would take more than curtains to make the shack as sturdy as our log sauna.

Finally the shack was finished inside and out, though Father still had to build a bunk out of the lumber that was left over, to rebolt the legs on the table and repair the cupboards he had found in the basement of the now almost totally dismantled house in Woodland. Aksu and Tony had gone to the secondhand store in Hadley, and there, just like a miracle, was a stove exactly the kind Aksu wanted and a mattress almost like new.

Now Aksu's place was ready. No one was more proud of it than Big Hank unless it was Aksu himself, and no one happier for having dealt the capitalists a blow. Who was the richer for Aksu having his shack? No one. Big Hank had seen to it that the shack was properly built and without cost too.

As the late summer days went by, we became interested in politics again. Even when Father wasn't running for office, elections were exciting at our house, especially presidential elections because they lasted longer. Father was a Socialist and Mother a Democrat, which was as close as she could come to being a Socialist. "I don't say it's wrong to be one," she'd say, "but you don't have to tell everyone how your father votes."

We didn't need to. He said it himself. "Norman Thomas is the best man on the ballot. If he were a Democrat, you'd vote for him, Louise."

Grandmother would never tell us what she was, but since she was a monarchist she probably voted Republican. She thought the secret ballot meant that she could never tell anyone where she placed her X. She said it was against the law to reveal a political secret.

And during every election, Mother urged Big Hank to become a citizen so he could finally vote. "It's not even right, Hank, to live in a country for most of your life and never go to the polls. Goodness!"

This time the stakes were high. If Hoover won, there'd be a revolution. If Roosevelt won, something else would happen but no one knew what, and if Norman Thomas won, everybody would have a job even if he didn't want one. We talked and talked. And the more we talked, the clearer it became that we liked the game of politics, the charge and countercharge, and the noise that accompanied the sport. It was a pity that Norman Thomas couldn't make as much noise as the other two.

We now had two radios, one in the barn and one in the house. There, on a cabinet right next to the oleander tree in the bedroom, was Otto's enormous black oblong box. It had a formidable number of knobs and buttons which could be turned, pulled, pushed or just let be. I never dared to touch the gadget for fear of blasting off the roof, but Father, Carl and John—the radio experts—enjoyed the ear-piercing noises, which I assumed to be the music of the spheres.

Thus, the election of '32 became an extraordinary experience. The morning newspapers brought the contestants into our midst and Otto's crazy box removed them at once to Mars if not farther. I felt sorry for Mr. Hoover, because whatever he hadn't done hardly justified removing him from earth. But with every whistle, hoot and crackle on the radio, Mr. Roosevelt, his smiling opponent, appeared more like an angel prepared to set things right by the wrong means: by magic, by sleight of hand or by prayer.

We never heard Norman Thomas speak on the radio; he remained on earth, the keeper of sense and reason. Father said everyone ought to have rallied to the Socialist cause, moderate and decent as it was, but people weren't in a rallying mood. They were in an affirming one: affirming the basic soundness of the system; affirming that whatever had gone wrong was an inadvertence which had unfortunately led to serious rumblings and grumblings; affirming that minor repair jobs here and there would cure the national ills. "Norman Thomas will lose," he said.

"And Roosevelt will win," said Mother. "You should vote for him."

After the fateful day when people went to the polls to affirm their faith, we anxiously turned the knobs on the black box, not to find out if Roosevelt had won, but by how much Hoover and Thomas had lost. And thus, mixed with the ear-piercing whistles, we found they had lost by a lot and that Roosevelt had come back to earth on a landslide. The nation was saved. Or what was left of it. God save the republic!

When all the reporting was over, Grandmother said, "Thank God! Now turn off that hideous racket."

"Those are the election returns, Grandmother," said Carl.

"I don't care what returns they are," she said. "You can read it in the paper tomorrow."

Hoover left and Roosevelt came, but the emptiness stayed. In a few years, even in Hadley one could get a bushel of grapefruit from the relief office. The next month one could fetch a bag of beans, the month after, raisins and rice, and after that the biggest, toughest oranges known to man. One could get shoes too, flannel, cotton, and sometimes dresses like tents.

Father wouldn't accept the dole. He'd find work, he said, and he did, but no one had money to pay him. He loaded the car with wood, potatoes and eggs, brought them to town, "sold" them, and came home empty-handed. People had to eat; they had to stay warm. What could they do if they didn't have money?

"My fellow countrymen," said Roosevelt, dapper and smiling. We felt a stirring of hope; the hope all but died ten times over.

Hank wanted a general strike. "Everything's got to stop," he said.

"Everything already has," I answered. "What we really need is a revolution." I saw myself building barricades. "Workers of the world unite!" I shouted from the top of a barricade. The people united and the depression was over.

Hank thought that it would never work. There'd be ten different kinds of revolutionaries killing each other, and the rich would win in the end.

"There aren't that many left," I said. "They've all jumped off bridges."

If we had been in New York, we would have seen the wealthy lining up for the great leap to eternity. For them, dying was easier than being without money. For us, being without money was a challenge. John said he'd become an engineer and be famous. Carl said he would too. The rest of us changed our minds too often; no one listened anymore.

Then Christmas came. We prepared for it as we always had, scrubbed the house, and fetched the tree. The week before, Grandmother had made her dark sweet bread from the flour which Father had milled. Now the heavy brown loaves were waiting for the holy day. We had meat, vegetables, cranberries from the bog, wild honey, maple syrup, canned wild fruit, and apples from our trees. There was no lack, not even of coffee and tea. We had almost everything, certainly more than anyone else in Revier. What we didn't have was a sack of white flour.

Mother counted the egg money in the sugar bowl. Thirteen cents. That's all. None of us had any money. At once our one need, a sack of white flour, was exaggerated a hundredfold. Now we were really poor! We had never experienced being poor before. It was as if we had no wood, no water in the well, and no roof over our heads. We could not have our Christmas biscuits, our cakes, nor the pies for the Christmas dinner, just as the old widows and the lonely bachelors in their shacks wouldn't have and had never had.

Mother said that we were no better than the rich people who jumped off bridges. "We have so much food, we could feed everyone in Revier. We don't need cakes."

"How do you explain to children that Christmas isn't Christmas?" Father asked.

"By saying that Christmas is Christmas even if the milk check comes after Christmas. We can buy flour then," Mother said. "It's good for children to know that we can manage with less."

"I could sell the wood."

"Wait till after Christmas," Mother answered. "No one will give up his last dollar now."

The next morning, on the eve of Christmas, Father loaded the sled with wood, hitched the horses and drove off. Mother waved to him. After he was gone, she stood there at the window and watched the snowflakes, like miniature wind-driven balls of fur, float down between the barn and the house.

Darkness had come before Father returned. Life was even worse in town, he said. Even the rich were hanging on to their money.

"Did you bring back the wood?" Mother asked.

"What for? We can't eat it!" he said. "What could I do? The Rowlands didn't have any wood, and they didn't have money either. I left half the load there and took the rest to the grocer."

He carried in a hundred-pound bag of flour, a twenty-five-pound sack of sugar, and a box of cocoa. Then out of a Kresge bag he took a big green toy lizard and a foot-long pencil. He didn't wrap them, hide them or place them under the tree; he just handed the lizard to Oliver and the pencil to Edward. Without looking at the rest of us, he left to unhitch and stable the horses.

Had I owned anything, I'd have given it to Father, given all the Christmases past, the bell-ringing sleds, the books, toys, clothes and surprises, to show him that he had brought us Christmas as he always had. We had a sack of flour, sugar to spare, and cocoa besides. The rest didn't matter, for we could always pare down our wants, and then whatever we got made us richer.

But how we felt made little impression on Father, for to him Christmas was the day for giving and he had little to give. He had not been able to give Mother fifty or a hundred dollars to spend on our presents; he had not been able to buy surprises—the nuts, dates, chocolates and peppermints, the giant oranges and apples, the special cheeses and the bucket of pickled herring. Nor could he provide the surprises any other day either. The new coats and jackets, the dresses and shirts, the fur-lined boots and tasseled caps, were there in the stores, but he couldn't buy them for us no matter how hard he worked.

As time went on, he found paying jobs when others could not; he was a carpenter for the county, the assessor for the township, and then a foreman on a PWA project. He hammered new roofs on old barns and built new houses out of old ones. His days never ended, for the farm work had to be done no matter how he labored elsewhere. The money came in and went out again: to the dentist and doctor, whom we young ones had to see when we needed them, though our parents did not go themselves; to the bank for the mortgage, and to the township for the taxes. Hank and Paul and Toivo, who helped with the planting and harvest, had their daily wages, and we had our books and magazines.

We sold milk to the dairy, and eggs, ducks, rabbits and produce to the grocer in Hadley, and used the money to buy the food we couldn't raise for ourselves and the animals. The snorting piglets grew into pigs and in the autumn Father turned them to ham and bacon, smoked in the sauna. The fat calves became veal, the mean old roosters, stuffed chicken, and the old white ducks, our holiday fare.

"We don't lack a thing," Mother always said when Father was silent and worried.

She made old things do. She ripped old coats apart, washed the pieces and made new jackets; she made skirts out of trousers. She pieced, patched and mended, and when the garment was beyond piecing, she cut it into ribbons which she rolled into balls and gave to the carpetmaker, who made them into colorful yard-long rugs that slid on the floor.

153

When we shopped for flour, we shopped for the print on the cotton bag. Two bags made cottage curtains for the windows, another bag added a valance; three bags made a dress or a blouse and a scarf. Feed sacks became pillowcases, sheets, covers for quilts, and when sewed together into one huge bag and stuffed with straw, a mattress as prickly as a thistle. We spread quilts on them, sneezed for nights on end, sniffed Watkins' liniment and then pronounced ourselves cured.

"We're not poor," Mother told us. "If we were, we wouldn't have a thing to share."

Thus we became "not-poor." We were not-poor and proud, we said. If only half the roof fell in, we'd want the rest of it to tumble down so that we could prove our ability to scramble out from the debris. We had to climb our own Mount Everest every week, sometimes every day. Once we became not-poor, we became rich. We just didn't have money.

But who needed money when the river iced over for our pleasure on every clear purple-shadowed night? When the Big Hill turned hard and slick for our wood-runnered sleds? When we flew our toboggans down the other side of the hill, missed the trunks of the trees by a hair, hugged each other as we never dared at any other time, only then because we endangered our heads, arms, legs, backs and our lives on that swift ride down. It would be sad if we hit the big elm! There'd be such a wailing—worse than if the Montfer swallowed our village.

"You can't die! You've got to help me with my algebra," someone shrieked into the night. But nobody died; nobody broke anything. Perhaps the elm tree wasn't there; perhaps there was no danger at all, though the elm was somewhere, and we could always move it for our enjoyment.

During the noon hour on school days, we danced in the basement at Revier School. We had no music other than the cracking of the burning wood in the furnace, but we danced the waltz, the polka and the schottische, and didn't feel the lack of a tune.

"What a waste!" Mr. Dominic would say. "You could be outside getting fresh air."

Fresh air? Who needed fresh air? That's all we had, mornings, evenings and nights. Our lungs were bursting with fresh air. What we didn't have was an open floor all week long.

He said we were oblivious of the facts around us, but we weren't. We were being the not-poor young. We knew that Father's annual cash income had gone down to a fourth of what it had been—dropped below a thousand dollars. How far could our income drop? We wouldn't think about that. We had enough food and we had shelter. What more did we need? We were lucky to be where we were; other people were worse off.

Mandy and Otto hadn't fared well in California; their laundry business had failed and they were on pension—relief, that's what it was. Uncle Eric and Aunt Taimi hadn't improved their lot either. The trucking business had gone bankrupt and Eric and his brother were jobless; they too had gone on relief.

Father grew silent and remote. Why couldn't he be satisfied if we were? Why couldn't he take pleasure in our exuberance? It wasn't his fault that the world outside Revier was a shambles.

"Our children will get along as people always have," Mother said. Our lives were no worse than before, and in a lot of ways much better, because ever since Father got on the township board, Revier Road was open from end to end.

Father thought he wouldn't run the next time; the township had no money and soon it would make little difference who was in charge. Mother didn't agree. He ought to run for chairman. Something good would come of it.

She no longer waited for Father to make decisions. She made them, hired Paul when the need arose and told Hank to stop being childish and he did. If one of us wanted to keep an animal she thought was useless, she'd say, "We're trying to make a living here. We're not running a feedlot for idle stock."

Perhaps it was Mother's steadfastness and refusal to give in no matter how little money we had that made Father accept the condition of our lives as temporary and to hope once more. We were always unified in a special way when he was at peace, for it was he who joked and told stories about himself, not heroic tales but funny ones with a poignancy that made us all feel protective toward him.

As we gathered around the supper table—Big Hank and Grandmother at opposite ends, John and Carl opposite Father, who had Edward on one side of him and Oliver in his high chair on the other, Mother, Elizabeth and I between John and Grandmother— Father would say, "Well, how did it go today?" We each had our turn to talk. John and Carl told ever new stories about the superintendent, Mr. O'Reilly; Miss Brock and Miss Hanson, the two crabbiest English teachers in the world; and Mr. O'Connell, the principal, the kindest man who walked the earth. Father listened to every word they had to say, for he was again living with them as he had before.

He listened to the rest of us too: to Edward, who had long since begun his steady progression from west to east at Revier School, and to Elizabeth and me. Yet our tales were less fascinating than John's and Carl's. To keep up with theirs, we'd have had to tell lies, for once we got through the excitement of Christmas, we studied from one end of the day to the other. Besides, it was Father's story we wanted to hear and not our own.

With the mantle lamp shedding its light on us, he began telling us the story about the train wreck long ago when he was no bigger than Edward and looked a lot like him too. Edward smiled. It was a hot day. Father was picking strawberries along the railroad tracks, and whenever he looked up from the ground he saw the sun glowing on the rails. That made him feel hotter than ever, for now there were a million suns shining around him. Then he heard the whistle. Down roared the train, faster than any train ought to go. Suddenly he heard an incredible noise. He ran for his life.

From a distance, he watched the train scream to a halt in a cloud of steam and dust. When everything was quiet again, he went back to see what had happened. There, lying on their sides, were three freight cars broken open and thousands and thousands of watermelons scattered around. He had never seen one before, though he had seen pictures of them and knew they could be eaten. He asked the train crew, now looking at the wreckage, if he could have one melon. "One? Take them all before they rot!"

He couldn't take any home because his stepfather, our Pastor Grandfather, wouldn't have let him keep them, but he took four, one after the other, heavy ones, so heavy he could hardly carry them, and hid them in a cold spring near the tracks. Every day he went there to eat watermelon.

Some of them spoiled before he could eat them. Still, he remembered that summer as the best one in his boyhood. The trouble was that every summer thereafter, whenever he heard a train hooting down the track, he waited for a crash. But there never was another and he had to wait until he was a grown man before he got to taste watermelon again.

"Poor dear," Mother always said after one of Father's stories, because she would have protected him then had she been there. Since Father usually waited until Friday to amuse us, we didn't need to hurry to our chores. There was a special quality to those winter evenings—a quality which could hold throughout the weekend.

On Saturday mornings, Mother, Elizabeth and I would examine our collection of sugar and flour sacks to see which prints we needed. Then Mother put on her hat and coat—a red hat with a feather in its band and the fur-collared, fur-cuffed coat in as royal a red as there ever was—no worse for having belonged to Mandy's niece before she left for California. Father wore his favorite coat, a sheepskin, and a matching cap. As Mother and Father stepped out arm in arm, we watched them walk to the car, and saw the red against the white snow, the gray barn and shed, the green firs and Father's tan coat. He always turned to see if we were at the window. We were, for there was something which lifted that Saturday morning journey out of our everyday world and into another.

"I wish they'd come back soon," Edward said, as if that bright world had departed with our red-coated mother and our sheepskin-clad father and wouldn't return until they walked in, their arms loaded with bags of A & P staples.

"Did you buy anything else?" Edward would ask.

"I think we did," Mother would answer.

Father smiled. "We went to the bakery too, to buy day-olds."

The day-olds were probably more like week-olds—doughnuts, cupcakes, longjohns, Bismarcks, raisin buns, sweet rolls and molasses cookies—all jumbled together in a big box. "All yours for a dollar!" the baker always said. We called them "all-yours," the weekend surprise box. Any child who came to visit was free to hunt through the scrambled collection and find what he wanted. Rachel liked the jelly-filled Bismarcks; Reino, the apricot sweet rolls; Eino ate anything but looked at everything. Even Paul would take his turn. By Monday morning they were all gone.

Even Oliver would toddle to the box the moment he saw Father bring it in. He had taken his first steps on Elizabeth's eleventh birthday in February. All day we had encouraged him to hold on to his green lizard's tail instead of us. Within days he was walking everywhere, always with the lizard in one hand and the other hand held out to ward off danger. Still, he bumped into chairs and tables. He stayed away from the stoves, however, and knew where they were without looking at them.

His babble was constant now, though there was no sense to it yet. It was a mixture of distorted Finnish and English, of trills and guttural sounds which we could not imitate no matter how we tried. In this early walking and talking stage, he showed us how fast he could learn, though what he was learning and how he was learning it remained unanswered questions. Grandmother thought that the outstretched hand and the strange speech were symptoms of some disorder far more serious than that of skin blemishes.

Dr. Burton did not agree. Oliver had a chronic ear infection and enlarged tonsils; he screamed because swallowing was painful.

Yet he didn't scream when he swallowed food—only randomly in his sleep or at play. And why was a change of weather so irritating to him? He knew long before we did that a storm was coming.

Dr. Burton didn't know. Children differ. All he could say was that Oliver was a normal, well-developed and bright little boy. Some of his problem was in us. We were too concerned and too doting. "We'll wait and see," he said, and gave Mother medications for the ear infection and the sore throat.

A doctor ought to know. That's what we said and wanted to believe. "Oliver has to be well," I said to Mother, and remembered the leaf house again and the summer which now seemed so long ago I could recall nothing of it except falling on the stairs.

"He'll learn to talk, Mary."

We tried not to be too protective, but we were attentive to every cry and responded to any demand. If one of us overlooked him, the others didn't.

I hadn't talked to Elizabeth about my guilt. It hung in the air and bewildered her. "You don't let Oliver do anything, Mary."

Although I knew I fussed over him too much, I couldn't stop.

It was at such times that I'd burst out in anger and, by reminding her that I was older and had to be more responsible, alienated her for days at a stretch. There was no way I could reach her then. Eventually she'd tell me that she wished she had a best friend somewhere.

But we had no other girl friends with whom we could share our interests. We were the Morgan Girls, a single entity, too bookish, quiet and near to our mother to be good company. Still, I'd have liked Elizabeth to have a friend of her own, though I never felt I needed one. Perhaps she decided she didn't want one either, because one day she told me, "If it weren't for you, Mary, I'd probably mumble to myself for the rest of my life."

Elizabeth always wanted new and pretty things to wear. Yet there was no way we could get them without sewing them out of flour sacks. "I'm tired of wearing bags," she'd say good-humoredly but all the same rejecting what we had plenty of—sacks. And there wasn't one thing I could do to earn even a few dollars. Not in Revier, where no one had a dime to spare. I'd have gone to high school a year early if Mr. Dominic had let me. There I could have found some kind of work, but he thought I ought to spend my time reading and gave me a dozen books for the summer ahead. When I told him I needed money to buy us clothes, he said they weren't important. "Time is the only thing of real value if you want to learn something. You'll be earning money soon enough."

It was our discussion about flour and sugar sacks that prompted Father to squander a whole week's milk money by sending us off to find dresses at Penney's. We found them—pin-striped broadcloth, blue for Elizabeth and red for me—prim and proper dresses with white collars, white cuffs and white belts. Mother thought we could easily have gotten material to make four outfits for the price of those two, but Father insisted he was tired of listening to the machine rattling away one weekend after another.

Since Carl was going to confirmation school in spring, I asked him if he'd mind if I went with him. We could probably get by on the same five-dollar fee and I'd save half the price of my new dress.

"You look no more than twelve, Mary. Anyway, there are no sales in the confirmation racket."

He may have been right, but he just didn't want me to go with him. He wanted to become an adult first. He had already been delayed a whole year because we hadn't had the money to buy him a new suit, but after working at the dairy during the past summer he had bought all his school clothes in fall and a suit besides.

Unfortunately, the benign minister at Mrs. Salmi's church had died and the hellfire preachers had taken over. Since Carl thought that two weeks of ranting was intolerable, he chose Grandmother's church as the lesser of two evils. Though the minister there was scarcely sympathetic toward sinners, he was too well-educated to bellow at them. He presented his Christian belief as a detailed road map to heaven.

Carl and his fellow confirmants were not preparing themselves for heaven, however, but for earthly pleasures. Once they were confirmed, they could join the choir and the Luther League and be assured of two dates a week. Who could ask for more? Besides, said Carl, he might even learn something.

Carl enjoyed himself, didn't worry about his lessons because he was sure that no one had ever failed in confirmation school, and assured us that the rest of the class was a lot dumber than he. Who could deny heaven to those who were stupid? Surely not God! Then if God chose to stand so firmly on the side of the dull, He'd have to stand as staunchly beside the bright. Carl said he was glad that he'd had geometry first, because there he'd learned that with just a few facts and assumptions he could prove anything. We knew at once that he was turning into a man.

After battling another year of Mr. O'Reilly's scorn, John and Carl were both on the honor roll. "It's like getting out of jail," said Carl, and to celebrate we made a big dinner, and placed candles on the cake because it was John's seventeenth birthday. Everyone came over: Toivo, Paul, Reino and Rachel. We fooled around the whole evening in the cool spring air, heavy with the odor of lilacs growing wild all over Revier.

The joy we felt was as heady as any we had experienced long before on holidays. It was as if all the Miss Gurneys and Mr. O'Reillys had been shipped off to hell, never to return. It wasn't that alone. Both John and Carl had summer jobs: John at a big dairy farm in Michigan and Carl at the dairy in Hadley. They'd be earning a dollar and a half a day, and John would get room and board besides.

"You guys will be loaded before the summer is over," said Paul.

He had to stay home to help his father and couldn't take on more than the part-time work he did for us.

John came home on weekends to eat our cookies and to ignore us, and every morning when Toivo picked up the milk cans, Carl went with him. As they drove down Revier Road, we could hear the cans banging away to the skies. "Lucky stiffs," muttered Edward, and got a stern look from Mother. Our job was to tend to the garden, poison the potato bugs, take care of the house and pick berries.

"If I never see another berry, I won't care," said Elizabeth. "Next winter, I'll choke on them."

Yet when we saw the rows and rows of green Mason jars glistening in the sun, we felt proud of ourselves. Not in all of Revier was there a mother who could can two hundred quarts of wild berry concentrate and another hundred of tomatoes and pickles. No mother was more pleased. And every evening, Father counted the jars. "Look at that! Our cellar will be full to the ceiling. We'll eat like kings."

Had we been able to sell our potato bugs, which multiplied by the thousands, we'd have been as wealthy as any lord who ever walked upon the earth.

9

ALL OF THAT SUMMER, we were more giddy than we had been before. Surely the worst would soon be over. But what if it weren't? What would we do then? We didn't want to think of it.

Our activities were often planned by Eileen Larson, whose family had moved to Revier three years before. Her knowledge of recreation, she said, derived from years of Girl Scout meetings. Tangled with her knowledge was a sense of mission to bring culture to the lesser breeds—to us—who had missed all the wonder and lore of scouting, in addition to having missed living in Hadley, where she was born.

Since our farm was the most scenic in our village, we had Eileen's picnics there, always near the river. We had gallons of Kool-Aid, baskets of sandwiches made of store-bought bread and a mayonnaise spread, and sticky white cake covered with a half inch of chocolate frosting. These picnics never lasted long; the boys were soon in the river and in the trees; they galloped through the hazelnut bushes and kicked up the dust along the road. Eileen would gather the girls together, set us into a ring, and lead us in the songs she'd learned at the Girl Scout meetings. She hadn't much of a voice, nor did we know the songs, but our noise brought back the stampeding boys. They built a bonfire; Eileen brought out the marshmallows, which we impaled on sharpened sticks and then watched, entranced, as their white flesh turned brown.

After that the picnic was over for us. Eileen stayed on with the boys. She was "practicing" her kissing. She was only two years older than I but she already had a list of twenty boys, including my brothers, whom she had kissed and evaluated. Because it was a "study," she kept a notebook. According to her records, my brothers were "all right." Why they weren't the best, I didn't ask. I thought she might have been more generous with her praise because they were my brothers, but Eileen's great source of pride was her honesty. "I'm a Girl Scout! I can't tell a lie," she said always. All one had to do was ask her how her practicing was coming along. She'd tell you. Even when and where she had done it.

When I first met Eileen, I thought she wanted to be an actress, for she had great dramatic skills and used them often, especially during her last year at Revier School. Her best act was the faint. She'd raise her hand and say, "I have a headache!" Then she'd slide out of her seat onto the floor and just lie there.

The teacher ordered the boys to fetch cold water, and while he tried to get her pulse, the boys dipped paper towels into the basin of cold water and placed them on her forehead. Others opened the windows and doors for fresh air. The rest of us waited until Eileen sat up and asked, "What happened?"

Several times the teacher sent her home. Then other girls began to faint, but their faints were poor compared to Eileen's. They went down with great thumps which shook the floor.

Soon after Eileen decided that she would become a nurse, and never fainted again. No scratch escaped her attention; if anyone became ill, she was there to take a pulse, read the thermometer and bathe a forehead. Mother said that Eileen was "good-hearted" as a nurse ought to be, but my brothers thought she was doing too much kissing which had nothing at all to do with nursing. Her list continued to grow, and so did her interest in helping the sick. Her scouting didn't suffer either, for while we were studying and cleaning the house, she often went on week-end camp-outs and hikes with the city girls, ate a lot of wieners and canned beans, and finally, after a lot of splashing in the various water holes, earned her badge in lifesaving.

Her badge wasn't nearly as impressive as her black wool tank suit, however, for none of us owned swimsuits. We swam in our cotton underwear, and in all our lives hadn't thought of water as anything but wet. We didn't dress to go in, we undressed, and after the first plunge were just girls in wet underwear. Eileen dressed and was a figure of glamour. We could see at once that even if we'd been stark naked, we would have been as safe as we were at St. Paul's Lutheran Church on Sunday morning; but the moment she leaped into the water, the boys were after her, and when by some accident she became isolated, she'd begin shrieking "Help! Help!" as if she were drowning.

One Sunday afternoon, we all gathered at Lake Hadley, where Eileen had won her lifesaving badge. She said the water there was usually "nice." That was another of her passions. Water had to be nice, though we'd jump into anything wet if the air was sixty degrees. We usually swam in cold spring-fed pools, muddy pools, in the river, which carried the sewage from Hadley, and in Lake Superior, which was rarely above fifty degrees. Nice, but icy. The others were nice but dirty, nice but shallow, or nice but muddy. If there was more water than there was dirt or mud, we would jump in.

Since Lake Hadley had no beach, the water wasn't as nice as at some other lakes, which did, but there was a long pier jutting out into deep water and that was nice. She'd done her lifesaving there, Eileen said, because there was no sense in trying to save people in shallow water. They just wouldn't be serious about being saved.

Eileen had dressed at home, and had her father's long-sleeved shirt over her tank suit. All she had to do was pull on her cap, shed the shirt and race down the pier. She leaped in and after a few minutes she surfaced. "Come on! It's beautiful!" By this time the boys had their shirts, shoes and stockings off and were racing after Eileen.

The rest of us took our time. We had the whole afternoon of watching the glittering surface of the lake, the canoes sliding over it, and the constant splashing which marked the location of Eileen and her Kissing Boys. I was standing near the end of the pier when Eileen's younger brother came flying headlong down the boarded walk. "Watch out!" he yelled, and ran straight into me. I went down to the muddy bottom. I was choking down there, floundering and churning about with the chubs and minnows.

When I regained my senses, I was on my face in the grass and

164

Eileen was whacking my back. She was pushing and counting breathlessly, and probably using every bit of the knowledge she'd gained in her lifesaving class.

"She's dead," someone said.

"No, she isn't," said Eileen between counts.

"Would you get off?" I said. "I want to sit up."

"Just lie down," she said, whacking me a few more times.

I finally pushed her off and sat up. Then there was a big argument about who had thrown me in and why; another argument about Eileen's lifesaving technique, which hadn't worked at all since my brothers had had to drag us both to the surface. Then Eileen told me how to respond if anyone tried to save me again. "Just relax," she said. "You almost choked me."

It was all crazy, as our lives usually were when Eileen was around. What sense we had individually or together was lost in her enthusiasms, but all the same, she added several new dimensions to our lives—Girl Scouts, swimsuits, kissing lists, wiener and marshmallow roasts, and the possibility of being silly and harming no one by it.

Mrs. Salmi heard about our escapades and probably about our dancing, which she considered sinful. Even if she had not heard, she could see that we weren't preparing ourselves for heaven, but were wasting our valuable time in fooling around. She knew how it was when one was young. She too had gone to a dance hall once, though upon hearing of it, the Lord sent her a message ordering her never to go again.

Since the Lord wasn't sending us any messages, she decided to act in His behalf. In addition to the Sunday school for the young children, she would have a Bible class for the older ones. We were to meet every other Friday evening to do what we did in Sunday school, only we would do more singing, hear a sermon and listen to Bible lessons read by older people.

After a few meetings, we realized that the important part of the evening was not the sermon nor the readings nor even the hymn singing. What was important was the dating after the coffee and cakes were all gone, and for that the young people came from the nearby villages in Michigan to the east of us and from our own villages in Wisconsin to the west. Usually the boys from Revier dated girls from Michigan. That is, they brought the girls to their homes, and the boys from Michigan brought our village girls to their homes.

Elizabeth and I were still considered too young to be brought home, for we remained at age twelve the whole summer and long after. Other girls grew older, attained "reputations" for themselves and were sought, though a reputation was something no girl would admit to having. It wasn't good. It was bad. It was the kind of thing Mrs. Salmi prayed over. We didn't have a reputation, so we walked home alone through the dark and eerie pasture, hushed except for the gurgling of the river and the faint sounds of cowbells in the distance.

We attended every session, however, simply to watch everyone else. Sometimes old people came too, but they did because they were hungry for the Word of God, and didn't seem to care at all that they weren't asked to read or preach, which was a special honor. They sang with us and drove our organist, one of the high school boys, to playing faster and faster until some of the women were a half stanza behind. The old men bawled off key as they sat together on a bench against the wall. No one minded them. It was the old women, with their cracked soprano voices, who turned our songs into medleys of nonsense.

Out of the confusion of our weekday lives, Mrs. Salmi gleaned order. She arranged Sunday afternoon church meetings now that the haying was done and the pasture still green. No matter that the ground was strewn with cow droppings, and the trees noisy with crows. No matter, for everything had a place in God's world. The farmers put up planks on sawhorses to provide tables and benches. The women cooked stews, baked cakes and pies, brought out their preserves, boiled huge enamelware pots of coffee, and then, last of all, brought out the fresh buttermilk. Always buttermilk. No itinerant preacher drank anything but buttermilk. Perhaps coffee too was sinful, and on its way down stained the soul. Anyhow, the preachers never drank a drop.

After the preaching and singing, the minister drank a glass of sacred milk, packed his hymnbook and Bible, and went off to the next village, and another meeting. Heaven departed with him. We ate and roamed about. The girls looked for boys, and the boys for girls. While the flies buzzed over the table, the young women breast-fed their babies, and the older women, in flour sack scarves, sat and gossiped on the benches. Lost in the dangers of the past, the old men in their ancient suit jackets and faded overalls sat apart, talked about Finland, the storms at sea, the mines and the lumber camps.

The younger men, like Father, sat on benches across from one another. Their talk was about planting and harvest, prices and Roosevelt. Sometimes I sat there beside them and listened to their quiet, even tones; I sensed an anxiety and grew fearful myself. There would be a harvest, at least something, wouldn't there?

Now and then on a Sunday evening when the chores were done, John would drive us and Reino and Rachel to Woodland to hear one of the borrowed preachers at Mrs. Salmi's church. As we bounced along the red snake of our country road, the boys in their suits and we girls in our pin-striped cotton dresses, as bright as on the day we bought them at Penney's, the misty veils from the swampland drifted under the fences, under every bush and tree, hovered under the noses of the cows feeding before nightfall, and then ran along the road ahead of us. The heat of the day still lingered in the cloistered areas where the road threatened to lose itself in the trees, but night was coming and we reveled in our wheeling freedom.

We were always early. We climbed to the empty balcony, took the first rows, and waited for the preacher to damn us all. Down below, the people straggled in, town people and country people, old women in scarves and young ones in hats, bent old men and straight, sunburned young men with shining faces, and snickering adolescents like ourselves, seeking the balcony, halfway to heaven.

The bells tolled above our heads. The usher closed the doors purposefully, shutting out the sinful world. There in the dim light of evening, as the solemn bells rang, we felt one short moment of reverence. The organ silenced the bells, grew louder, and shook the beams. We were in the presence of the Lord.

At that instant, down below us, a voice broke out in song. The organ caught up and we were off. We sang to outdo each other, one stanza after another, five, seven, ten, the longer the better, always in Finnish, which made no sense to any of us because we had never thought that those words strung together in the hymnal might by chance have some meaning. We just sang.

As the organ pealed its last notes and the straggling worshipers sang the final phrase, the preacher came out. He passed the altar scene of Jesus on the Cross and then rose miraculously into the pulpit. "May God have mercy on your souls," he began softly.

All reverence gone, we nudged each other in anticipation. For five minutes, God was merciful to us; we had come to this House of God to worship and to cleanse our evil souls of sin. We had done the right and godly thing. We had come out from the darkness of night into the light of day. But that wasn't enough. We were still too complacent. We were too comfortable. And that would be our doom. We would never get to heaven. Never! We were conceived in sin and were stained by it. His voice rose and fell like the waves on the shores of Lake Superior. Our sinful souls responded with a delightful drowsiness.

"But you can be saved!" he shouted, just as we were confident that all was lost. "You can be saved!" he repeated in a whisper. Now the miracle cleanser of stained young souls, the blood of Christ, flowed over us and like the Montfer River at flood tide swept everything in its path. We were left stark naked.

"How about a tank suit?" someone whispered.

"His face is getting redder," said another.

"He's perspiring."

"The other minister used to have a glass of water on the pulpit."

"But you will not be saved!" he ranted at the congregation.

"Now we're not saved. He should make up his mind!"

"You will be damned! You will go to the cauldron of hell and the *bubbles shall rise to the top."*

We were now a good distance toward hell. We danced, played cards, went to movies and listened to the radio. We painted our faces like whores.

"Let's all go to Hadley," someone behind us whispered.

We scorned our parents and we spit upon our teachers. Our sins were like cordwood, piled one on top of the other.

"You deserve no mercy." On he went, the logger of sins. At last, perspiring, red-faced and hoarse, he left the pulpit.

Before the organ had stopped shaking the rafters, we were tumbling down the narrow staircase from the balcony and out into the cool night. We stuffed ourselves back into the car and drove to the ice cream stand, where we could buy a triple-dip cone for a nickel.

Snuggling on the back seat of our Ford, we lurched along the country roads. The lights blinked in the farmhouses, and the darkness swallowed everything between. Now and then, wild eyes peered from the bushes. Sometimes, frightened by our rattling, a mass of fur crossed the road in front of us. Was it a fox, a coyote, a raccoon or a skunk? Or was it a dog?

Then we were home. Grandmother was still dozing at her spinning wheel, Father was reading his newspaper and Mother was combing out her long hair. Oliver and Edward, too young for damning, slept in their beds. Sitting around the kitchen table, we described the events of our evening. Father thought the preacher reminded him of Pastor Grandpa Anderson. Grandmother wondered if we couldn't have learned something if we'd listened. Mother said that if we didn't like the preachers, we shouldn't go to hear them.

But we did like them! Where else could we get a whole evening's entertainment costing a nickel for each of us? Nowhere. And we could certainly not have listened more. We listened to every word and probably could repeat the sermon from start to finish. Besides, we liked being damned, for it placed us in the human race.

We derived no such assurance at St. Paul's, where the minister, properly trained, gave sermons so dignified and lacking in drama that there was no joy in hearing them. He was a stern and astute judge of human frailties, but he didn't judge from the pulpit. When he said, "The Lord be with you," he implied that it was our duty to keep the Lord within hailing distance.

The self-anointed and unschooled rabble preachers were unwelcome at St. Paul's. They were left to free-lance in the countryside and in the other Finnish churches. Some preached only in the revivalist churches, which were separated into sects, each claiming sole knowledge of the road to heaven. Some were Holy Rollers, and some were not. My brothers, who had been to the Holy Rollers' church, said it was a lot like the Range Hall on Saturday nights, only no one had booze and no one was ever seriously injured. They said the meetings were "too rough" for Elizabeth and me. Maybe they were, but getting rid of us for an evening was advantageous.

Mother insisted, however, that they take us to several of the weekly open-air concerts in Woodland. Her cousin's husband,

Jack, played the violin and we were to listen to him not only because he played well, but because the violin was a good one, made by the cousin's brother. That's all the brother did. He made one fiddle after another and people came to buy them. Of course, he couldn't do anything else because he was a hunchback, and had one leg shorter than the other. He did well to toddle from work-bench to workbench.

We told this story to Rachel and Reino and to anyone else who would listen. We said we liked to hear this particular violin played by Jack. I suppose that sometimes we actually did hear him, but certainly not often. Once my brothers had decided where we ought to meet again, my sister and I milled about just as everyone else did along the walkways circling the platform and were deaf to the sounds coming from it. We found other young people, asked them if they'd seen anyone, and since they always had, we continued our meandering search. The only instruments we heard well were the drums, which drowned our own chatter. Sometimes the concert was good and sometimes bad, depending altogether on the number of people we had met in the hours of walking around the platform on which Jack fiddled away the summer evening.

Since my brothers were adults now, they had access to the family car whenever they needed it. Besides, Uncle Roy, Father's half-brother, who had just moved to Hadley, had a new car which he was willing to loan to them so that they could go off separately, and they had no greater problem than deciding who would take the Ford and who would take Roy's new Chevrolet.

At that moment, Uncle Roy was the wealthiest member of the whole family. His wealth was accidental. Years before, he'd worked in the mine for one week, but a week was long enough for him. He ran his head into a beam and promptly claimed that he had suffered a permanent injury to his nerves. Maybe he had, though we had trouble deciding just how much hitting the beam had altered him. He was Uncle Roy before and after, no worse and no better. Still, he knew the law, just enough of it to know that if one sues for all, one gets some. He got several thousand dollars. Within a day Uncle Roy had a new Chevrolet, a new topcoat, a new suit, new shoes, a silk shirt and a silk tie. He looked like a Rockefeller loose in our bedraggled town.

At the end of summer, the dealer repossessed the car, but not before Hank and my brothers had a lot of mileage on it. Roy said it wasn't anyone's fault. He'd just forgotten about the payments and now he couldn't pay because he was as broke as everyone else. "I thought you'd paid for the car," said Father.

"I did. I gave the man a hundred dollars and told him I'd pay the rest."

Not long after, Roy left town to find work and did. This time he'd work hard, save his money and buy a car for cash. "No more payments," he said. "No, sir!"

But his plans never got anywhere, for his head had always been in the way of machines, overhangs, beams, rods and rails, and was once again. We had the feeling that if Roy didn't have a head at all, he'd be better off. He made the best of having one, however. He sued the construction company. Again he was doing what he did best—proving beyond a reasonable doubt that he had suffered permanent nerve damage. The poor man could talk about nothing else.

Long ago on one of those rare occasions when Pastor Grandfather spoke about earthly affairs, he had said, "Roy is as he is." He certainly was! For once we had to agree with Grandfather.

The whole summer had gone by more swiftly than any summer before it. We had done our housework, taken care of Oliver, tended the vegetable garden, watered Grandmother's flower beds and picked the berries on the raspberry hills. The men had gathered in the hay and harvested the grain; the season of growth was drawing to its close.

It was evening. I had prepared Oliver for bed; his cradle made a steady clicking sound as it rocked to and fro. Father was reading his newspaper; Mother answering the letters which had come from her cousins in Finland. Grandmother and Hank were reading their separate news of the world—hers in Gothic print and his in Roman.

The rain was beginning to fall on the hushed earth. Gently, in a whisper of sound, I had seen the mist move over the late summer hills and screen them finally until I could see only the shadow of the trees in the pasture.

Edward was building a model plane. He was intent; the tip of his tongue between his lips moved as he tried to fit piece to piece. "Mary," he said. "I can't get this right."

If he couldn't, I probably couldn't. He was adept; his small fingers rarely failed him.

"All right. I'll hold the wing and you apply the glue."

But I wasn't thinking of the plane. My hands moved.

"Mary!" he said. "Elizabeth, you hold it."

At that moment, had I been able, I'd have taken back the whole summer, begun all over again and preserved the silences of evening for reading.

"Mother."

"Yes, Mary?"

"Did you ever feel that you wasted a whole summer?"

"No, I don't think so," she said. "We always had a good time."

"We can't just sit at home, Mary," said Elizabeth.

It would have been better, I thought. I felt the loss of time more keenly than ever.

"What's the matter, Mary?" Father asked. "Are you feeling old at thirteen?"

"A whole summer—just gone." I was closer to tears than I had been for a long time. There would be other summers, of course, but never this one. In all her years of living, Grandmother must have felt such losses. "Grandmother, did you ever feel you just wasted whole months of your life?"

She put down her paper, and looked at me. "Yes, dear, whole years sometimes," she said.

If I had read as Mr. Dominic had wanted me to, I'd have finished the books he had given me to take home. But as mindlessly as the rest, I had followed Eileen and her "gang," listened to her recite her kissing lists and been damned ten times at least. And I had known I would regret the loss of time, though I had thought I could retrieve it later. Make it up and not really lose it.

"Is it still raining?" asked Mother.

"Yes," said Edward. "Maybe I can fly my plane tomorrow."

But he couldn't. The steady rain fell for three days and turned our yard into rivulets of mud. Then the clouds lifted; the weekend came with clear skies. The gleaned grainfields had the soft green of springtime and the vegetable gardens the bright color of full summer.

Mr. Wiita walked over to bathe in our sauna. His own was so

poor, he told us, he was afraid it would burn down if he heated it. But we knew his sauna was sturdy enough, only he was too frail to carry the wood and the water there. Each time we saw him, he was bent closer to the ground.

"How is Liina?" I asked him.

"She said she was going to get married," he said. "She even bought herself a white dress, but I guess the young man thought going to California was easier."

We had never had a wedding in Revier. Only funerals. Mrs. Wiita's. Mrs. Ojala's. Arthur's father too had died. Mr. Kaari. Always endings, never beginnings. Liina's might not have been a marriage of great promise, but at least it would have had some.

It was peaceful and clear that evening. We sat outside after sauna. The sun was falling into its bed of clouds; filled again, the river ladled along. We heard Paul yodeling down Revier Road and the echoes chorusing back and forth from one wall of trees to the next. He must have been on his way to the Koivunens', for he didn't appear out of the trees in our pasture.

"Maybe he'll come by tomorrow, Liz."

"You say that every Saturday, Mary. You always wait for him."

We heard the news early the next day. Father had turned on the radio to hear the morning report on the Woodland station. After the initial whistles and crackles the voice came out of the box. I was setting the table and not paying attention. Someone was in the Hadley jail; someone was in the hospital—the usual harvest of Saturday night.

"My God!" said Father.

I listened then. Tony was in jail and Paul was dying. The police were investigating; Tony was in for questioning. Apparently the shooting had occurred after an early evening hunting trip.

Soon after, Eino ran in. He was pale and breathless. "There's no one at home now!"

Breakfast was ready. "Come and eat, Eino," Mother said. "Your father must be at the hospital. You can stay here."

We all sat down. Eino took off his cap and sat on it. He looked like a small child still, though he was Elizabeth's age. He was thin and with his large eyes wide and staring he seemed even thinner.

"The sheriff came last night to tell us," he said. "I wasn't sleeping yet. Father left and I was all alone."

"Eat your breakfast, Eino," said Mother. "Your father will probably come back soon."

"Tony shot Paul," he said, "and I don't know why. Paul wouldn't hurt anybody." He began to eat, but the tears were running down his cheeks.

People told all kinds of stories. That the two had fought over dating a girl. That Paul had threatened Tony; that Tony had fired in self-defense. Rumors. Perhaps it wasn't Tony at all.

Paul lived for a few days. There was nothing left of his insides, the doctor had said. Death was a certainty. We wanted to see him; I wanted to bring him a bouquet of wild roses which grew along the rock fence. But no one other than his father and an older married sister, who had returned to take care of the household, was allowed in the room. And so he died, that carefree boy who had spent days after days with us.

The service was at home in the living room of the lonely Ojala house. We had gone there the evening before, soon after the undertaker had brought Paul in his coffin for one last visit. Now we were going again, Father, Mother, Grandmother, Big Hank, Edward and Oliver in the car, and John, Carl, Elizabeth and I on foot across the greening fields. We had nothing to say to one another; we just walked in the summer sun, over the field, the haunting Kaari place, past the Wiitas', up the hill, past Revier School standing blind on its acre of weeds and then to the Ojalas'. The yard was full of cars; the shining hearse stood by. We went inside. There was the gray open coffin. There were the bouquets of red, white and pink gladioli. There were the neighbors, all but the Koivunens. Near the coffin sat Mr. Ojala in his black Sunday suit; always silent, he seemed now like stone, as dead as his son placed to rest. Eino in his brand-new grown-up suit appeared even younger than he had a few days before. He held his sister's hand; she was as impassive as her father.

We went to the coffin; Paul was in his suit, his white shirt and his tie. We had never seen him dressed in a suit, only in bright-colored shirts, cowboy hats and denims, but he was properly attired, poor lad, for the last formal occasion of his earthly visit.

The minister from our church came in; the women preparing the lunch in the kitchen went silently about their business. Come what may, our bodies must be nourished. Mother had asked the closest neighbors to bring cakes and sandwiches.

We sang two Finnish hymns. The minister gave a sermon, but I did not hear it. I heard the prayers. Our Father; the Lord giveth and the Lord taketh away; The Lord is my shepherd, I shall not want; God turn His face upon thee.

John, Carl and four other young men carried Paul in his satin-lined bed to the hearse. Father, the boys, Elizabeth and I followed the procession to the cemetery. The sky, which had been clear in the morning, was leaden now; the wind had shifted to the lake and brought the chill of early fall. We gathered around the broken earth and the bearers moved Paul to his resting place.

One rose on the coffin; one prayer; dust to dust.

The gravediggers were standing by. The rain was coming and they were in a hurry. Mr. Ojala stood there. "Come, Father," said the daughter, tugging at her father's arm. "Come. It's time to go."

He just stood there. The diggers began filling the grave. The stones made a hollow sound as they struck the lid of the coffin. At last Mr. Ojala turned away into the wet wind.

We went back to the house to eat sandwiches and cakes with our coffee. Eino and Edward sat together on the stairs leading to the attic and talked quietly. The sister, Lempi, went around thanking everyone.

The rain poured down all that night. I couldn't sleep; I thought of Paul in the stony earth of the cemetery. We should have tried to save him, but we hadn't and now it was too late.

"Whatever will they do?" asked Mother, wiping her tears on her apron. It was morning; we were making breakfast. She was talking about Eino and Mr. Ojala.

They would adjust. That's how life was always. And surely not a week had passed before we heard again the echoes flying from the wall of forest. We were startled, but when we looked out across the field, there was Eino yodeling his brother's song and leaping over the stones.

Tony insisted on his innocence, but when the matter came to court and he saw the jury, he broke down. Yes, he had shot Paul. Yes, they had argued, only Paul hadn't been serious. He had laughed. And when he, Tony, picked up his shotgun to prove that he was angry, Paul had laughed again. "Come on, Tony," he had said. "You wouldn't dare shoot." All Tony could think of then was that he did dare, and that Paul couldn't make a coward of him. So he shot.

Tony went to prison and his parents moved away from Revier. People said they wanted to be nearer to the prison so that they could visit Tony. And Toivo moved to the Ojalas' to take care of them. Sometimes Eino and Mr. Ojala rode along with Toivo as he picked up the milk cans. "It's not much of an outing for them, but it's something to do," he said.

Paul's death marked the end of our first brave battle of the Depression years. We were never as exuberant again and our lives never the same, for the bad times went on and on.

10

 A PERVASIVE SADNESS HUNG OVER THOSE YEARS. The abandoned mines caved in and the lumber camps weathered to decay. Such money as there was in the bedraggled towns flowed from Washington. Like the climate and the seasons, the federal agencies became a part of our lives because, in one way or another, they touched us all. On the first floor of the courthouse in Hadley, the relief office dispensed aid to those who were down and out. Mother went there with the widows and the old bachelors who couldn't speak English and got vouchers which paid their doctor, their dentist, their druggist and the department store.

The National Youth Administration hired the students and the Civilian Conservation Corps the graduates, who became the soldiers of a new cause—conservation. They rumbled about in their trucks, planted trees, cut fire lanes and fought fires. The public works projects kept some of the unemployed busy repairing roads, schools and hospitals. But how much money would you need to hire all who had been in the mines and the lumber camps? Too much. The towns couldn't prosper.

Everyone depended on the same lifeline—banker, builder, farmer and ditchdigger—and they all had the same goal: to hang on and survive. This common interest gave people whose hopes and lives had always been expendable a sense of equality, and a frail promise that if enough desolate lands were reforested, roads

177

widened and buildings refurbished, then possibly a more secure and equitable world would come into being.

Father believed it; that was *his* lifeline. A nation concerned about her people and her natural riches had to improve, and though it would all take a while, surely in the end life would be better for everyone.

Long ago, he had adopted Grandmother's feel for the earth which provided our means of existence. He could have cleared the woodlot and tilled the land, but he hadn't. He had pruned the trees selectively. He had kept the partially wooded pastureland in its original state as a haven for the wild creatures who dwelt there, because too many trees had already been cut and too much land left to waste. Now there was nothing to hold back the runoff from the heavy snows of winter and the drenching rains of early spring. The water rushed down from the hills, filled the Montfer beyond its capacity, sometimes overnight. Every year, the river cut deep gullies into our road and left a trail of debris along the fenceline. "The Montfer is no longer safe," Father would say, and he'd stay up to hear its roar. He ordered books and pamphlets on conservation and land use, erosion, waterways and reforestation.

But there was more to his interest than the restoration of land, important though that was to him. He was making a valiant effort to give his life meaning and, despite all the losses, to lead us outward to look at our world with fresh eyes. Don't give in. Don't give up. There's work to be done if we just look hard enough. He became a fire warden, an insurance agent, and now he would be the new road commissioner and would learn surveying.

After supper when we gathered around the table to study, Father joined us. Once he learned a skill, he could always use it. "Perhaps being a surveyor is even better than being a farmer," he said as he sharpened an extra pencil and placed it behind his ear. He had bought himself a ream of paper and brought out the box every evening. "If you kids need any paper, I have some here."

In the center of the table, we had our dictionary, an atlas, a slide rule, a protractor, a compass, several rulers and a pencil sharpener. I kept all the erasers—red ones, white ones, green ones and clear gum—and could erase anything. Mother said I had improved a lot. Years earlier, I had always made holes in my papers, had wept and had worried that I'd never learn to erase properly. It wasn't the mistakes that had bothered me, only the erasing.

Whenever I began to erase, John would say, "Mary, you're going to hand in a paper full of holes again." We'd all stop working and Carl would begin complaining about horrible Miss Brock in English. He and John lived lives of extraordinary excitement, as if something were about to erupt any moment, and it usually did, and then Mr. O'Reilly came to shout order out of chaos.

"We've got nothing like that at Revier School," said Elizabeth, proud of the peaceful, decorous and scholarly life we led there.

"What do you do to break the monotony?" asked Carl once.

"Nothing," said Edward. "We just wait till he lets us out."

For a long time, we were as silent as we could be. Grandmother's spinning wheel whirred its music; the wood crackled in the stove; the steam hissed in the teakettle; Oliver chattered in his own complex language and described the coming and going of people and cars. Sometimes it seemed to me that the whole outside world had disappeared and we were alone. Even when Toivo came, more to get away from the stillness of the Ojala house than to visit, we went on with our studying, and he waited, reading the newspaper until we were ready to have tea.

It was always then that we'd remember Paul and how he used to ride the horses home from the pasture and how he had asked to borrow the car. "May I have the key?" Have it back by midnight, Father would always say—a rule no one except Paul ever broke, though never by enough to make Father deny him the privilege he or anyone working at our house had. We'd remember Tony in his prison cell and wonder what would become of him.

Grown tired of our talk, Oliver would go to Mother and she'd prepare him for bed. Elizabeth and I took turns reading him fairy tales from the book Mother had bought us when we were young. He'd lie still with his glassy-eyed bear in his arms. We'd show him the pictures of giants, castles, kings and queens, and he'd bring the book so close to his face that his nose touched the page. At last he'd give the book back to us and we'd have to read on until he fell asleep.

It was on one of those evenings when we were all gathered together that John said he was planning to go to the university. So pleased he could only say, "Well!" Father put aside his work. Mother was worried. How would John do it? Where would he get the money? If we sold some of the cows, perhaps then it might be possible.

But no one ever sold the one source of food and steady income. One held on to the land, the cattle and the horses—the last hedge against dependence on relief. We all knew that. John said he'd work in summer and save enough to get to Madison and to school. That's all he needed.

Grandmother had been asleep at her spinning wheel, but now she was wide awake. To the university? Only the wealthy sent their children there. Ordinary people like us had no real place in their lives. For a bright man, there was still work to be had in Woodland if not in Hadley. He could study all he wanted to on the side, just as Father did and had always done.

John didn't argue with her. What could he say? He didn't care if he was ordinary. Besides, where were those good jobs? He could drive a truck in summer when the road building was going on, but what would he do the rest of the year? Not much and we all knew it—all except Grandmother. We didn't talk about John's leaving, not when Grandmother was around. Why worry her? But the thought stayed with us. Father was as joyful as if he'd been twice paid for his effort. His son planning to go to the university! And if John went, so would Carl.

Those quiet evenings merged into each other. With the snow falling outside and the wind so calm, we couldn't hear a sound other than the hiss of the kettle, Mother slapping the bread starter, and Big Hank puffing as he made his stumpy ax handles. "So thick you can't get your hand around them," said Father. "But the old guy tries, so we can't complain."

Now that the long winter had begun, it was time to slaughter the heifer and the pigs. Mr. Swenson, who had learned his slaughtering skill in Sweden, was Grandmother's preference. Mother complained that every year he needed more hot water. "Well, he's probably a little crazy," said Grandmother, "but he's clean and knows how to bleed the animal properly." No one denied that; his butchering was humane and flawless.

By the time we were done with breakfast on that Saturday morning, every kettle and bucket was full and boiling. When Mr.

Swenson arrived, he strode into the steaming inferno of our kitchen and said, "Good, good." He examined the bubbling containers on the stove and said, "Good, good." He was everywhere at once. He took off his jacket and his cap and there he was, the Viking pirate of old in white coveralls and a red bandanna around his reddish blond head. He rolled up his sleeves—on his upper right arm was a large eagle tattoo and on his left a coiled snake with a fiery tongue. With a great flourish, he opened the long wooden box he had placed on the table, took out his knives, and arranged them side by side. As he finished sharpening a knife, he put it into his mouth, held the blade sideways with his large white teeth until he was done working on another. Then he placed the first sharpened knife in the box and the second in his mouth.

All the while, he talked a steady stream of something—Swedish, Finnish, English, and maybe all three mixed together—I couldn't tell what it was. It was merely the background noise behind the sound of steel against stone. When the knives were sharp enough, he asked for two dishpans—one for the heart and tongue and one for the liver—a bucket in which to catch the blood, and a cup. "I always drink a cupful," he said. "Good for the health."

Then he rushed out hatless into the cold. Elizabeth, Mother and I were busy in the house with our Saturday cleaning, and Edward was playing with Oliver on Mother's and Father's bed. We didn't want them in the kitchen because blood-spattered Mr. Swenson was a frightening sight even to us; he ran in with the bucket of blood and later for a cup of coffee. He bloodied the cup, bloodied the doorknobs and bloodied the oilcloth on the table.

"Why does he need all the water?" I asked. "It's like a sauna in here."

"He has to get the bristles off," said Grandmother. She was beating flour into the blood and Mother was greasing the loaf pans one after the other. We'd have the traditional blood bread for lunch.

All the while, Carl was telling me how Mr. Swenson wrapped the pig carcass in cloth and poured boiling water over it. When the bristles were loose, he scraped them off until the whole hide was pink and smooth to the touch. "The hotter the water, the faster he gets it done," Carl said.

"Do you have to talk about it?" I asked him. I thought of the little pigs and the wobbly-kneed calf. Never before had I seen any of the murderous process; I had always been shielded. When I was very young, the animals had gone to the cabin in the forest. When I grew older, the facts were too glaring to avoid. I had to think that the animals wanted us to be well; hence it was only right that we ate them, their milk and their eggs. For a long time I had faced other facts as well: that the animals did not want to be eaten; that they had no interest whatever in our eating their eggs or in our drinking their milk. We ate them because we had to have a balanced diet. And now I had to accept the killer and the killing.

Mr. Swenson stayed for lunch. He talked about his wife, his children, and how he had been a sailor when he was young and to this day missed the feel of the open sea. That's why he liked to fish on Lake Superior, but one couldn't make a living at it. Besides, the lake could be rough and too dangerous for a family man.

He was probably no crazier than the rest of us, I thought. He too had to support his family. And if we had to eat meat, someone had to kill the animal. If Mr. Swenson didn't, then Father would have had to do the slaughtering, and if he couldn't, we'd have had to hire someone who had Mr. Swenson's skills. Still, when I went out to get some wood from the shed, I avoided looking up. I knew that the once lively heifer and the playful pigs, their back legs tied with a rope, hung from the rafters.

And now that we had a supply of meat, we had to share some of it. It wasn't Christian to hold on to what we had when others had nothing. What could the lone old bachelors afford but salt fish and sausage? They weren't starving; they weren't eating well, either. When we listened to Mother, we had a feeling that it was a plain sin and a shame to own more than one shirt as long as so many in the land had nothing. If we had anything, we had to give part of it away.

Mother sent Big Hank off with a roast to Aksu. When Hank came back, he said the "Raisin Grandma" was there again. She was the "Welfare Lady," a social worker, very young and earnest, who brought Aksu and the other old bachelors their monthly allotment of surplus food. She'd tell them how to cook whatever she brought them—huge bags of raisins, beans and rice. Hank, who had met her several times at Aksu's place, disliked her. "How does she think they've lived this long if they couldn't cook?" She was the symbol of the capitalist system running amok in Revier. The poor crops, the summer's grasshoppers, the crazy preachers, all the churches and the whole New Deal, represented by Raisin Grandma, ended up in the same muddled heap.

She didn't have an easy time of it. The old bachelors didn't speak English and she didn't speak Finnish. In desperation, she'd sometimes fetch Mother to translate for her. And now because Christmas was coming, Raisin Grandma was worried that the bachelors would have no holiday at all, and she couldn't explain to any of them that they'd have a better time if they had their Christmas dinner together. Mother assured her that we'd invite them to our house. Three extra mouths to feed at Christmas? To Hank's mind that was another sign that the lady had no sense at all, though it wasn't her fault that Mother invited them.

We couldn't have had a wilder Christmas. Aksu was a good-natured man, but the other two were as cranky as Big Hank. They argued about politics all day long and couldn't agree on anything except Raisin Grandma. She had some idea of their needs, however, for when the bachelors left us at the end of that noisy day, they said they hadn't had as good a time in many years.

Our Christmas at school matched the one at home. Mr. Dominic liked Christmas the way Father did—heart and soul. We began right after Thanksgiving to plan the program. We would have carols, poems and skits, but that wasn't all. We had to have a play as well. We would wear makeup and design our own costumes; we would have a curtain which opened and closed, for the first time in the history of Revier School. How? He would string a wire from one side of the schoolroom to the other and fasten sheets on it. He would attach ropes to the sheets so that they could be drawn.

Since every child had to have some part in the production of the play, he gave the older students the stage work and the younger ones the speaking parts. The play was long, with a dozen characters who had very little to say. The main character, Christmas Witch, who was determined to destroy the holiday forever, had pages of monologue which were to be delivered in a cracked voice; she was to cackle and whack the floor with her broom. She was to be hateful, dressed in rags and hideous to behold.

At the last moment, Christmas was to be saved by the Christmas

Angel, a lovely creature in white, who was to dance lightly out of the girls' cloakroom at the back, dance down the aisle, approach the evil witch, and with one touch of her wand and a polite "Farewell, Witch of Christmas," reduce the ugly crone to a heap of rags next to the front register.

The play was absurd but it was loud and lively, and so full of characters that all the young children had parts in it. Elizabeth, cast as one of the lesser angels, sang a lot of songs. Her part was bigger than that of the Christmas Angel, who seemed more important because she saved the day. Edward, as the Christmas Elf, didn't have to learn a line; all he had to do was dart about and he did.

Since I was to do the decoration, I asked Mr. Dominic if he'd let me draw three camels, three wise men and a manger on the blackboard. He thought it was an appropriate idea, but I used a whole wall of board and needed more. "What am *I* going to do? You're leaving me nothing," Mr. Dominic complained. "Oh, well, it's Christmas," he added, and gave me one of the front boards for the manger scene.

We had never had a play before and everyone came to see it— even the old bachelors. It was remarkably successful and had Mr. Dominic let us, we'd have had another. No one said anything about my pop-eyed camels. What they contributed to the festivity was a strange un-Christmaslike hue. Though I had used boxes and boxes of colored chalk to hide the black slate, I had only changed it to a lighter tone.

Before we left for the holidays, I wanted to wash off the boards. "Why, Mary?" asked Mr. Dominic. "It's a nice picture even if the camels' legs are on the short side."

"Maybe their legs were short in those days."

"And maybe they were of normal length." He looked at the camels again. "But there's something to be said for a four-legged animal that doesn't resemble a stork."

When we went back to school and walked past the blackboards day after day, we carried off the chalk on our sweaters until the camels had scarcely any legs at all. Before long we were so tired of those near-legless creatures that everyone clapped when I finished scrubbing them off. The sun coming in and shining on the clean slate made it into something totally new. "It looked as if we'd gotten a fresh paint job," Elizabeth said later.

Years had gone by since the last one. No one complained. There just wasn't enough money to take care of a country school—not when there was a high school that needed a football team, cheerleaders, a band and a lot of uniforms. We were lucky to have a teacher who was a university graduate and liked his work. "Seventy-five dollars a month is better than nothing," he'd say. "Better than going on relief." He worked at the dairy or on the road construction crew during the summer months.

John was graduating from Hadley High School. His name was in the *Daily News* and the *County News* because he was leaving with honors. That was the good part. The bad was that he had to go to the graduation, wear the flapping gray gown and listen to speeches he had heard several times during the rehearsals. Mr. O'Reilly would give the same sermon he had given at the dinner for the seniors, so there was no surprise in that. All the same, Mother and Father were excited about going. They had never seen the inside of Hadley High School and were looking forward to having John show them around.

They saw everything from the locker room in the basement to the second-floor assembly hall, and they heard Mr. O'Reilly's heavenly tones rising and falling for a half hour straight. "It was a good ceremony," said Mother. "John looked so nice and lots of teachers told us we could be proud."

Well, we were. But our enjoyment was private. A school ritual was something we had to go through so we could get on with thinking about what we'd do next.

John took out the university catalogue and began looking at the list of courses. Now Grandmother had another suggestion. Couldn't he go to the seminary and become a minister? When he was little, that's what he had wanted to be.

"I'm not even religious, Grandmother."

That didn't matter. One didn't need to be. All one had to have was an understanding of the Bible, and he had had a fine beginning. Since his Finnish was good, he could come back and preach in Woodland. He could spend his whole life studying.

When Grandmother heard that Mr. O'Reilly had refused to give John a letter of recommendation to send with his application to the university, she was even more certain that he was making the mistake of his young life. That he could get a half-dozen other letters from Hadley High School if he needed them didn't matter. Mr. O'Reilly's was the one he ought to have gotten.

And since John had refused, surely Carl would consider the ministry. If Finnish boys didn't go into the church, soon there'd be no one to preach to the old people who had come to America too late to learn English properly. Besides, a poor man's son could become a minister and even the rich couldn't hinder his progress.

Mother and Father looked at each other. Carl a minister? He'd be the biggest hindrance to his own advancement.

Grandmother wasn't alone in her convictions, for most of the old people agreed with her. When Mr. Wiita came to our sauna and asked what John would be doing now that his schooling was over, she announced the news right off.

Well, that's a big step for a poor man's son. Who would've believed it a few years back when the mines and the lumber camps were going strong? Young men could find work then. But the old rules held. Once John saw the rich man's ways, Revier would never seem the same to him. He'd look down on the people he'd known all his life, but the rich wouldn't accept him. Had he thought of becoming a minister?

"He'll do all right at the university," said Father.

No one from Revier had gone to the university before, but these days the young were scattering all over. "What's there in Hadley?" they asked. "Or in Woodland? If we've got to leave, we may as well make something of ourselves." It was a new world all right.

The old were baffled and sad. Who's going to take care of the farms? What will happen to the land? What will happen to Revier? If only the mines hadn't closed and the lumber camps shut down. The young would stay then—or would they? Perhaps all the schooling was changing the way children thought of themselves. Not as workers anymore.

"It could just be," Father said.

The boys found summer work as truckdrivers on the federal highway project, burned a deep tan to the waist, and grew back the muscle they had lost during the school year. They worked ten and twelve hours a day. How much luckier could young men be?

No one enjoyed the long days of summer the way my older brothers did. They worked at their jobs, saved their money, and waited all week for Saturday, when in the evening, fresh from the sauna, they would dress up in their white shirts, their suits and ties, and then, smelling of hair oil and shaving lotion, they'd drive off for a whole mad night of cruising through the sleeping country villages and towns. Now and then our second cousins, Julia and Violet, came to stay for the weekend. They brought their box cameras along, and took pictures of each other standing between several boys, all of them leaning toward one another as though they feared falling if they stood without support. The girls borrowed the boys' hats, and the boys grinned rakishly, for the loaning of hats to girls made them into men of the world. Sometimes they climbed into the car and waved at the black box; sometimes they sat on the hood while others stood on the running board.

"I'm so glad they have a chance to enjoy themselves," Mother said. "Our boys are so young and they've got to work so hard."

"We all do," I answered.

"Young men have a hard time, Mary."

Perhaps they did; perhaps all men did. Father turned red in the dust as he widened Revier Road now, at last, when everyone was either leaving or dying. Twenty miles away, John and Carl turned brown in the dust of another road, which would be wider too. But our lives at home were no easier and the tasks no lighter. I saw the similarity between our existence and theirs, not the difference.

On those hot summer days when the sun blazed in the sky, I tended the vegetable garden, carried water from the river, staked the tomato vines and waited for evening. Then, after the whole house was back in order, every dish in its place, the floor scrubbed clean, the stove shining, I'd go out once more to water the plants —Grandmother's flowers and my vegetables.

"We're lucky to have a home," Mother said. She thought of the homeless adrift in the land. What would happen to them all?

"We are lucky," I answered. Only nothing we had could be painted. No bucket or milk can replaced with a bright, shining new one. No shining washtubs or washboards. A bundle of remnants from Sears perhaps, enough for a dress, an apron and a quilt cover; a pair of shoes for each of us children, but none for Mother or Father or Grandmother. Everything was patched, mended, faded and old.

On some days I still was not-poor. On others, I saw nothing but the dust, the graying boards, the stains, Grandmother growing too old and my parents too tired. I could stretch the day to twice its length but I could do nothing to change our lives.

Elizabeth and I would sit on the stairs and watch Edward chase fireflies and Oliver bumble about. These were our moments of quiet talk. Since we didn't go anywhere, she was no longer interested in clothes. More than anything, she wanted new curtains for the kitchen and a tea set for Mother. "I saw a pretty one in the window at the jewelry store, Mary, but I couldn't see the price."

"I'll have some money soon. John said he thinks Mr. O'Connell will let me work in his office for a few hours a day. Then we can buy things."

"What do you think you'd like to be?" she asked me.

Oliver came to sit beside me and sought my hand. "I don't know yet, Elizabeth."

"I think I'd like to be a teacher."

Mother joined us. "My tired girls," she said. We sat together, three women of the house. "It's so peaceful you'd think there isn't a problem anywhere."

Peaceful it was—so still we could hear the cars on the highway, nearly three miles away. We were closed off in our small corner of the universe. "I guess I should get busy at John's paperwork," I said, and got up reluctantly. It was too lovely a night to spend indoors, but I had to.

Since John was always too busy to fill out his applications for admission to the university and for the National Youth Administration job, he had asked me to do it. I could print well and filled in the blanks easily enough, but the biography for the NYA job became a labor of long evenings. He had told me to finish the "stupid thing" or he'd never be allowed into the engineering school or be given a job and he'd end up driving a truck for the rest of his days. But I wanted to make the biography as true and as real as possible so that anyone reading it would know that John was more deserving than anyone else. I questioned Mother about his early years. The rest was easier because we had shared many of the experiences. I had ten pages written before John, disgusted with my slowness, asked to see the biography.

He read it once. Then a second time. "For Christ's sake, I'm only fourteen here," he said.

"I'll do the rest," I said.

"The rest? In another ten pages? Maybe thirty? God alive, Mary. I don't want them to weep. All I want is a job."

I insisted that the detail and our being where we were made a difference.

"Hell," he said, and grabbed the pencil. On one side of a page he scrawled a brief biography—so brief that it said nothing at all. "Now copy that and send the damned thing in."

I did, but I knew that anyone who read John's biography would remain ignorant of his life. No one would ever know because John wouldn't say anything. "It's none of their business. I need a job. Period. What else is there to say?"

He was accepted at the university, but he didn't get the NYA job, which he needed. "I'll go anyhow," said John. He'd saved enough money for fees. He had a suit, and he bought three white shirts and another black necktie because that's what he thought students wore. Then he left, with his suitcase and the aluminum laundry case which would go back and forth between home and university during the four years in which he studied to be an engineer.

Mother wept, as she was to weep whenever the boys went away. Sometimes I wondered if she felt more than we did, but once she began to weep I turned numb and had no way of discovering what I felt or did not feel. Perhaps she sensed that she ought to weep in our stead, for Father and Grandmother were restrained. Carl was as funny as ever, and the rest of us just watched Mother. I hoped that she would wish John well, encourage him to take care of himself, and tell him that she would think of him. But she didn't. She sent him off with the sound of her weeping in his ears. Maybe he didn't care, because he too was as numb as I. Maybe he felt braver and stronger for being able to leave despite the tears.

Before the day was gone, we all began to notice the emptiness around us even though we had our own busy lives to live. We started to wait for John's laundry box, with his dirty clothes all jumbled and mixed together—sheets, socks, pillowcases, underwear, towels and shirts. And when the box arrived, we could see him stuffing in everything he could see at first glance, and then searching everywhere, under the bed, in the bookcase, and beneath the desk, for socks and handkerchiefs. We knew he would have no sense of order, that he would manage by pure chance to eat, to fall into bed, to stumble out of it at the sound of his alarm clock, and to get into his clothes. All his energy would go into work and study.

Mother washed his clothes, dried and ironed them on the same day. We made cookies and fudge, and then somehow we packed everything, even a loaf of Mother's bread, into the silvery box. The next morning after we had gone to school, Mother brought the case to the mailbox, and then waited there until the mailman drove up.

John always wrote us a postcard thanking us for sending him the laundry and the food, and at last we had a letter too, telling us what an exciting time he was having. When he first got to Madison, he went twice a day to the student employment office, but there weren't any jobs. By the end of the week, he was down to his last dollar and had to find work or begin selling his books. He decided to sit in the office until someone found him a job. He sat all day long. At last the director appeared from her private office and was on her way out when he stopped her. She made one phone call and he had a steady weekend job clearing brush on a big estate near town. He got seventy-five cents an hour plus meals, though in most places students were paid twenty or twenty-five cents and nothing else. On weekdays, he had a meal job at a restaurant, so he wasn't hungry, but the room he had would be mighty cold in winter. There wasn't a radiator or a heat vent in sight.

"And when does the dear boy have time to study?" asked Grandmother.

"I don't know," Mother said, drying her eyes.

Father was pleased that John wasn't discouraged. "We'll send him a quilt." And we did.

When John came home between semesters, we found out that he had time to study and that he wasn't freezing. He told us about the campus, the big buildings, and running from one to the other for his classes. He talked to each of us as if he'd missed our presence, and he ate as if he had served penance since September. Mother, he said, would make a fortune if she ran a restaurant in Madison. No one knew how to cook there.

Everyone said he'd changed a lot, but to us he seemed to be as he'd always been. He slammed doors, forgot where he'd placed his gloves and where he'd left his hat, but he went out anyway, to the Michigan side of the river to tell his girl friends of his adventures. However we tried, we couldn't protect him from his obliviousness. He didn't care, he said, and he hugged us, carried Oliver on his shoulders, and promised us he'd be the biggest man in town once he became an engineer.

Before we had time to become accustomed to his being with us, he left. We brought him to the train, watched him disappear into a cloud of steam and smoke, and waved until the train went around the curve. Then we came back home to an empty house, though we were all there except John.

Even Grandmother had to admit that John was happy with his new life, hard as it was. The rich were there, but so were the working students, and no one questioned their right to attend. He had been relieved to find that out, because after Hadley High School he hadn't been sure just what he'd find at the university.

I had gone to Hadley when John went to Madison and I discovered for myself what he knew: we were intruders. We entered by the requirement of law; without the law our formal education would have ended on the last day at Revier School. But the law placed us in high school, and there we stayed together with the town children: the children of the tavernkeepers, unemployed miners and shopkeepers; and the children of the wellborn, for whom the academic program was designed—the sons and daughters of the mining company managers, the doctors, lawyers, teachers and bankers. Their children were expected to go to colleges and universities; the children of workers were expected to go nowhere; and the Finnish farm children were to become servants in Milwaukee, Chicago or Detroit. For the sake of economy, we all had the same courses in English, history, mathematics and science; Latin was an elective, and advanced mathematics could be substituted for a foreign language.

At the time of my schooling, I saw only the doors at Hadley High School. Many years later, I saw the whole building, a red brick oblong placed in the center of a well-tended lawn. Surrounded by firs and a variety of maples which turned yellow, gold, pink, red and maroon in autumn, the place had a primness about it, a propriety which set it apart from other public buildings and a neatness similar to that of a girls' school. Had I seen the whole building when I was a student, I might have been pleased by its neatness, but for me the high school had a heavy double door, classrooms, corridors and a staircase.

Still, if I missed seeing the outside of the building, I missed nothing that was offered within. None of us did. We'd learned to study at Revier School, and now we used our skill with a singleness of mind which reached far beyond satisfying our own sense of usefulness, fed by our parents' trust. We used our skill to prove that the law which placed us in Hadley High School could accomplish more than anyone in Hadley had expected of it. Absorbed in the competitive race to achieve, we became more stubborn with each year of attendance, and more like robots wound in September and spent in June.

Every morning and evening, Carl and I walked two and a half miles to and from the bus stop on the highway. In the early fall, when the frost colored the leaves and the dry reeds rustled in the ditches, we felt secure and certain of our path, but in winter when the snow was deep and the days short, we were like Arctic explorers. Bundled in snowsuits, boots, scarves and sweaters, we left the house long before sunrise, and returned long after sunset. As we trudged along the snow-choked, unplowed road, we clutched our books, notebooks and lunch buckets and froze our feet, hands, ears and noses, and then, after the blisters had healed, went back to school again.

Carried away by the thought of such stubbornness, and no doubt wanting to inject some of it into students who did not risk their lives daily, Mr. O'Reilly called everyone into the assembly hall. He was a big-bellied man, pink-jowled and nearly bald. In fact, he was much like the rabble preachers who condemned us to hell, for he loved oratory as they did, and as they, became drunk on the rise and fall of his own voice. But they at least had the Bible to chart their course. Mr. O'Reilly had nothing but his righteousness.

Now he stood before us and applauded us for our courage. He asked everyone to applaud, and everyone did, for ten minutes at least. Anything was better than listening to Mr. O'Reilly. He said that we had "an extraordinary sense of duty," and that such performance of duty demanded recognition. Therefore, mindful of his own duty as a citizen and an educator, he would "award us orchids figuratively."

Did he mean what he said? Was he impressed by our will and determination? We'd find out. We petitioned for the rerouting of the school bus.

Had we placed a bomb in Mr. O'Reilly's office he could not have been angrier. We were defiant, he said. We were probably Communists and certainly idiots.

What had happened to the law which states that no child need walk more than two miles to the nearest school? Had he forgotten, we asked, that none of us from Revier walked less and many of us walked farther just to get to the bus stop?

"There's no such law anywhere and there never was!" he said. "There's only one law, that you've got to attend until you're sixteen. As far as I'm concerned, you people aren't worth educating." He went on: We were good for nothing. We could become maids and janitors, but nothing else. "That's why I didn't give John a recommendation when he said he wanted to go to the university. He'll fail, and I, at least, will not be a party to his failure. I can't imagine what your parents are thinking!"

"They're not thinking," said Carl. "They're idiots too."

"What we really wanted was the orchids," I said.

Then Mr. O'Reilly explained what sending orchids figuratively really meant. In our words, it meant nothing.

Perhaps he had thought about the orchids, because a few days later, during our weekly assembly, he had another tale about flowers. This time he turned to lilies. We were to nurture our souls with lilies. We were to reach the heights, and then he told us how we could use lilies to get there. "There was a man," he said, "who had but one dollar between him and starvation. And what did this brave man do?" He paused again, came forward on the stage, raised his chin as if he were that dollar-rich poor man. "He bought a lily for his soul!"

We applauded him, all six hundred motley scholars that we were, applauded him as if we all had dollars to spare, and Hadley a dozen florists specializing in lilies for young souls. But Hadley, we knew, hadn't one florist to redeem her tarnished image; her business wasn't in lilies. Hadley was the red-light district of the north. On her main thoroughfare—Iron Street—eighty tavern-keepers traded alcoholic beverages, a chance to gamble, and some the services of women. Earlier the women had served the lumberjacks and miners; now they served anyone passing through the town.

On Saturday nights, the drunks lurched from door to door and above them the lights glittered: "Girls, Girls, Girls." They were women past their prime, hair bleached to lemon yellow or dyed a bright red or pitch black, women with bare arms, bright red lips and silk-stocking legs.

All but lost among the taverns were the post office, dentists' offices, four grocery stores, two hardware stores, a dry goods store, two drugstores and a bank. Even the movie house had closed its doors. The drunks and lechers didn't go to the movies and the young, who might have, didn't want to dodge the drunks outside.

Once we left Hadley, all we needed to say anywhere in the neighboring states was, "I come from Hadley," and we became at once the sophisticates of the underworld. Had we seen Dillinger? No, we hadn't. He had come there only once, but after one drink he left again to have a shoot-out at a resort miles into the pine trees. For years Dillinger's bullet slugs were on sale there; perhaps they still are.

That was Hadley. What went on there on Iron Street concerned me so little, however, that had the street not been straight, I might have lost my way. I cared about one thing only: doing well at Hadley High School. Nothing else.

Every day I worked for an hour in Mr. O'Connell's office and earned six dollars a month. I had more money than I had ever had, but had no time for spending it. Our days began at five in the morning and ended at midnight. Had I met Mr. Dominic again, I would have told him what he told me, "Time is the only thing of real value if you want to learn something."

That first year when I went to high school and all but lost sight of myself, I had to take time off to become a Lutheran adult. This was no easy matter, however, for now in addition to walking two and a half miles to the bus stop, I had to walk two miles from Hadley to the church in Woodland. Thus in order to become a Christian adult, for two weeks I had to walk nine miles a day.

Fortunately the years of training had not been wasted in Mrs.

Salmi's Sunday school, where the piles of Gothic-lettered Bible tracts grew ever higher. While the calico cat and her descendants had cleaned themselves every Sunday morning, I had learned the Ten Commandments, the prayers and hymns, and had learned about Job and his trials, Moses in the bulrushes, Jesus in the manger and Jesus on the cross. I had learned the impossibly long Finnish words and sentences in God's holy Gothic print. I had learned to read so well I could rattle off the holy writ as well as the minister himself.

The meaning of all the years of Sunday school came to me in those two weeks in Grandmother's church, that Spartan house of our Lutheran God where the bells, the pipe organ, the rose window, the altar and the minister in the pulpit turned the familiar words into sacred writ which, however, I could not accept. The birth, the trials and the crucifixion of Christ became evidence of man's cruelty to man and of God's imperial intransigence.

And that wasn't all. There was the feast at the altar. A feast! "This is the body of Jesus Christ," and then, "This is the blood of Jesus Christ," intoned over and over to thirty-five communicants, turned into a spine-chilling cannibal rite. What was Christ but bone and flesh as any other? That bony rib cage, that flattened midriff and that drooping head belonged to slaughtered man nailed to the cross to bleed out his crimson blood, and there impaled resembled a slaughtered beast rather than the Son of God.

Grandmother's pantheism was far easier to accept, unexpressed though it was and existing beside her loyalty to the Lutheran Church. Her love of living things bore fruit; her loyalty to the church was ritual. On Sunday mornings she listened to the organ music, the choir song and the murmured prayers. On weekdays she called upon God when he wasn't needed; she spoke His name in vain more often than she spoke it in reverence. Unlike Mrs. Salmi, whose real life was yet to come, Grandmother's life was here and now, enhanced but not altered by the drama of the Sunday morning service.

The myths upon which the Sunday ritual was based we learned from Mrs. Salmi. We believed in those myths only as one believes in poetry, only as words placed together to form images through sound; we related the myth to its season and the season to life as we lived it. We remembered the reward for learning in terms of frosted cakes, molasses cookies and brown paper sacks lovingly filled with Christmas candies, and associated these with God's unwavering love of children.

From this kitchen Christianity I walked ninety miles to adulthood. The route was easy—straight down Iron Street in Hadley, past the taverns blinking "Girls, Girls, Girls," up the hill to Woodland's Main Street and one short block to Grandmother's church. I could see the steeple—like a beacon—a long way off.

After the ninety miles of walking, I received a certificate bound within white satin covers and lettered in Gothic. Two weeks later I received the photograph in the mail. We had a very large class and in order to get into the picture, the newly confirmed adults at the ends of the rows had to stand sideways and lean back toward the middle. Since I was the last one in the long third row, I had to lean at a truly precarious angle.

Carl looked at my picture. "My God, Mary, what happened to you?"

"I felt sick."

I didn't say I had trouble swallowing the grape juice. I did get it down, but I wasn't certain whether it would remain there to do its work.

I now went back to high school. In English class the students had just begun reading *Romeo and Juliet*. In history, the class had finally become involved in the Civil War. Our teacher, Mr. Merriman, had done his graduate work in the military tactics in the Revolutionary War and for that reason spent months fighting the various battles. Thus by spring he was behind schedule; he had to leap straight from one war to the next—the Civil War. Of course we had all the between-wars reading to do, but I had already done that and was set to do battle again. He said we couldn't hope to get to the World War in class, but in fact we got to the rumblings of it. We had to muddle along through that conflict by ourselves.

That year the spring rains were over even before the schools closed. The air was warm, and the winds from the south brought nothing but small puffs of cloud which yielded nothing. Then the weather turned hot. The sky was an oven one day after another. Our fields, though parched at ground level, were still green, however. In the Northfield, where the river fed the morning fogs, the earth was damp and the vegetables were growing faster than usual, but the river was too low, Father said, and forests too dry.

Late in July a fire broke out in the timberland north of the river, and now and then when the wind shifted, we could smell the smoke borne high above our dry fields. The rains would come, we said every day, but they didn't.

One day the wind stopped, as if it had blown all the existing air to the north and had left nothing behind to fan the blazing sun. The cows sought the shade in the pasture; the chickens flapped in the barnyard dust. Day after day, the house held the heat from the sun and from the cookstove, which we had to use now, for the small stove outside was too dangerous in such dry weather.

Then came an evening when a light breeze from the north brought a faint smell of acrid smoke. It was the odor of dying trees. During the night the breeze turned into a gale from the northwest. By morning the fire was burning on the banks of the river opposite our farm.

The fire warden perched in his tower saw the threat and called the Civilian Conservation Corps. Dressed in khaki like soldiers out to do battle, they arrived truckload after truckload, and like soldiers they fought the enemy at the expense of those whom they protected. They tramped over our grain and potato fields and stumbled through the vegetable beds as they dragged their pumps, which then clogged in the river mud. They brought tractors and plows to gouge the earth and make it safe from burning, but the wind brought flying bundles of flaming leaves and dropped them down to set the grass on fire.

"They could lose the fight," someone said. Then another suggested emptying the house of furniture. Now the boys in khaki attacked the house, hauled everything out of it—beds, dressers, tables, chairs, cupboards—and loaded every worn stick we owned onto the trucks and hauled them off to the Salmi place. They emptied the barn as well.

In all the rush, we had forgotten the cows. Frightened by the noise and the commotion, they had gone to the far end of the pasture. They bellowed in their fear and stood flank to flank in a clump of maples as the smoke curled down through the trees. I took the lead cow by the collar; the rest followed one another along the narrow path and then down the road to the Larsons', where I left them, disconsolate in their bewilderment.

Later Mr. Salmi fetched Grandmother and Oliver to eat and sleep at their house. The rest of us stayed behind to make sandwiches and coffee in our near-empty, echoing house. Eileen Larson appeared riding in the back of a truck with the CCC boys. She was a part of the fighting force, she said. Other neighborhood girls came to help as much as to share such glory as there could be in fighting a forest fire burning out of control and threatening our worn, tired clapboard house and barn.

The young men flirted with the girls, sang songs, ate sandwiches, pumped the cold well dry, and saved our buildings. But on that first night in the empty house, with the sky red above our heads, I wondered if we were saving anything. Let the whole place burn down, every board of it, I thought, and then we could all go elsewhere like the Okies, all squashed into one car with mattresses loaded on top of the roof and the odds and ends of our worldly belongings strapped to the sides. We could wander forever.

In the morning the wind was calm. The clouds rose like mountains from the lake, covered the sky and drenched the fire, poured over the raw scarred fields and the brave khaki-clad boys. Weary but victorious, they gathered their gear, climbed into their trucks, and waved their soldiers' farewells. The next day when the rain stopped, we moved back our furniture.

Our lives settled into a routine of salvaging the fields, repairing fences, and putting into order everything that had been hastily disordered in the house and barn. For Grandmother, now eighty-five, the loss was far greater. Her flower beds were in ruins; the plants she had wanted to see in blossom could not be revived. She was just too old, she said, to do more. She slept whole long summer afternoons and then in the evening wandered about in the woodlot and gathered pieces of dead wood which she brought back wrapped in her apron.

By fall she had recovered. She began carding the new wool, and when she was finished, she started spinning. Every day she'd go out to split some wood for the stove, to feed her calves and to see the cows. She was well all winter long. In spring, she said, she'd plant a big flower garden and even a strawberry bed. Still, on some days the sadness of a long lifetime seemed to gather around her. She talked of Grandfather, of her sisters and her brother, all dead now. Sometimes she could not eat. Her limbs ached, and she complained that her back was "broken."

Yet secure in the strength of our own resilience, we saw her living forever. "She complains a little," we'd say when anyone asked us how she was. "She's fine otherwise." Her sadness was no more than the mirror image of our adolescent emotions.

When she amended her statements with "if I live," we were perplexed. One didn't die without being sick.

"Why do you always say that? Of course you'll live."

"We must all die," said Grandmother.

All but Grandmother, we thought, certain of our rightness. She did sleep often, but she could still chop her blocks of wood, hoe down the weeds in her flower garden, card and spin her wool, and read. Why would she die?

11

FROST CAME EARLY THE YEAR OF THE FIRE. We had a few brisk sunny days, and then the dense gray clouds blew in from the lake and hung over the countryside. One cold rain followed another. Morning and evening we were drenched to our skins and arrived at school as bedraggled a lot as there ever was.

Carl and I both had colds. One morning he couldn't get up. By evening he was delirious. Dr. Burton came, examined him and said that he had pneumonia. There was little to be done other than what Mother could do at home. The hospitals were full of patients in worse condition. For a week Carl thrashed about, silly even in his delirium. Then the fever left him, and he lay weak and hollow-eyed. "I'm waiting for Mrs. Salmi to pray me to heaven if she can," he said.

Meanwhile my cough grew worse, but the weather had cleared now, and the air was clean and heady. I felt free and unburdened, for the days seemed to become longer and longer. I had time—so much of it that I fell asleep in English class, and again in the assembly hall. When I began walking home from the bus I thought the road would go on forever and become steeper and steeper until it rose above the red, yellow and gold of the autumn trees. But I got home before the road lost itself in the treetops, and in the warm dinner-smelling kitchen I sat at the table, and dreamed that I was lying on the glass slab, as cold and treacherous as ice.

I woke up in a strange room with fans whirring in every corner of the ceiling. Sometimes a woman dressed in white brought me a pan of water. I saw her lips move, but the sound of the fans buried her voice. She brought a tray of food and a pitcher of water. She took them away again. Dr. Burton appeared, looked at my chest and shouted, "Who did that?"

What had happened to my chest, I didn't know. After that he was there twice a day to demand and to be angry, to tell me that it was morning or evening. He placed borders on time which had lost all other meaning.

Mother and Father stood beside my bed. Out of her summer bathing suit and in a ski jacket, Eileen walked in with her mother. They all fed me. They talked. Sometimes I heard their voices coming from another room; sometimes the fans above my head killed all other sound.

"The fans kill my hearing," I said to Dr. Burton. "I don't need them anymore."

"I'll turn them off," he said. Then I could hear children's voices in the distance, the clatter of dishes on trays, and above these his loud scolding voice, complaining about the bed, the sheets and my chest. When he left, the fans went on again. The sullen figure of a monster strode up and down the hall outside my room; the lights went out and when they came on again a big spray of gladiolus and chrysanthemum grew out of the mirror on my dresser.

One morning I saw the sunlight in my room, the flowers in a vase, the ceiling empty of fans and an old hunched man outside my door. The nurse placed a basin on the bed. "Well, you're alive," she said. "You can wash up."

She carried in my breakfast tray. "Eat," she commanded, and left me to watch the steam rising out of the mass of porridge in its bowl.

Dr. Burton came, looked at my untouched tray, took it out, and brought me another. He began to feed me. Over and over he shook me back to consciousness. "You'll be going home," he said.

"When?"

"Any day now."

"When can I go to school?"

"Soon," he said.

After another week he said I could go home. I'd been in bed for three weeks, one at home and two in the hospital. My chest was burned and scabbed from the mustard plasters the nurses had applied. The skin on my arms and face was peeling; my hair was falling out. When I looked into the mirror from which the bouquet of flowers had grown, I saw a being I could not recognize. I touched my face; the mirror being touched hers.

Father carried me out of the hospital and down to the car. He placed me on the back seat and covered me with quilts. I fell asleep, but as we drove into our yard I woke up again. "I can walk," I said.

The wind blew sharp needles of snow into my face. I felt their sting in my chest. I held on to Father's hand. "We're going up the stairs now," he said.

"Yes, and through the porch."

He opened the kitchen door. I saw my bed at the far end of the bedroom, the white pillows and the rose-covered quilt. They merged into one haze. When I woke up the fans were back in the ceiling. Day after day the delirium returned. Yet, time had its boundaries. I was recovering, for I could eat now and even remember what I'd eaten earlier in the day.

In another week I was able to stand. The daily chores were everywhere around me, but I could do nothing. I tried to study again, to read, to write and to recall what I'd done before. I remembered nothing; the print blurred before my eyes, and my hand shook. Even worse, I had no middle range of feeling to draw upon; I either laughed or wept—wept because Father brought me a new pair of boots, wept because Mother cooked special foods for me, and laughed because I was too weak to keep anything straight.

Around me life went on with its usual rhythms. Father went to work, and Elizabeth and Edward to Revier School. They had a new teacher now, a Miss Calligaro, who wanted to know about Finnish customs. "She says it's important for us to remember them," said Edward, "but nobody knows what they are." He built a model of a catapult which would throw the rocks from our field to Lake Superior, three miles away.

"Is that supposed to be Finnish?" Mother asked.

"She won't know the difference," said Edward.

Elizabeth collected Finnish recipes, wrote down a list of Finnish family names, and then a list of given names, both with English meanings. She wrote a long story about Grandmother bringing her spinning wheel all taken apart and packed at the bottom of her trunk. "We haven't done anything else this fall," she said. "Just Finnish customs!"

I remembered my first year at Revier School, when we did nothing but read, dramatize and draw the Little Red Hen. I became sad again, for I had wasted a whole long year and now I was wasting another.

"Patience," Mother said. "Patience," repeating the word in the hope that I wouldn't forget that too. She was as cheerful as only she could be when "God had given her a special gift." Carl was already well, and in time I too would be.

Everyone had been helpful, Mother said, and sometimes even too helpful. One Tuesday morning Eileen had rushed in. "I came straight from the hospital," she exclaimed breathlessly. "She isn't dead, Mrs. Morgan! I saw her with my own eyes. So don't believe anything you hear."

Mother had heard nothing in the past half hour. Father had come back from the hospital to tell her that I was still among the living. Then he had gone to work, and she'd begun the weekly washing, for she had been delayed by Monday's rain. Every woman in Revier was washing clothes, so that the chance of Mother's hearing false reports, good or bad, was negligible. Eileen was certain, however, that bad news travels fast, and that she ought to be ahead of it.

Later Mother remembered that on Saturday she and Father had met deaf Sanna Lahti, who was at the hospital to see her husband. She'd inquired how I was, and Mother said that I was "at death's door." That was enough. By the time Sanna got home, I was well on the way to my burial.

On Monday morning my classmates collected money for my funeral flowers, and in the afternoon the florist began calling the mortuaries. Since he couldn't find me, he waited until morning to call the principal's office.

"Why doesn't anyone tell me anything?" asked Mr. O'Connell, and sent his secretary to fetch Eileen from her history class.

"She's not dead, because someone would have told me," said Eileen, "but I want to see for myself." She convinced Mr. O'Connell that she had to report the "true facts" to the family, so he drove her to the hospital and then to the farm.

Later, when he was back in his office, he called the florist, who had prepared the funeral bouquet and was waiting to hear where to send it.

Thus for a week I saw my own funeral flowers growing out of a dresser mirror. Eileen said that it was all very sad and inappropriate. "Suppose," she said, "Mary had realized that the flowers were for her funeral. She might have died of shock!"

"How can you tell the difference?" asked Carl. "One bunch of flowers is just like another. Besides, the guy took off the 'Deepest Sympathy' ribbon and even sent a card saying 'Get Well.' What more do you want?"

"That's the least he could do. Poor Mary!"

"Poor me!" Carl said. "I didn't get anything. And while you were chasing all over town to find out if Mary was alive, I had to fight the War of 1812 in history class."

"I didn't want to shock you," said Eileen. "Anyway, I'm sorry about the flowers, Mary. I hope you didn't notice anything."

I hadn't. No one had. Flowers are flowers. Only Eileen fussed.

One night the fever and the delirium returned. I was back in my dark hospital room and on my treacherous glass slab. Every sound was gone; I tried to breathe, but my lungs wouldn't expand. I tried to call Dr. Burton to tell him that I was sick again, but my voice was gone. Beside me, Oliver was crying.

Mother woke me up then. "Are you feeling ill, Mary?" She had lighted the small bedside lamp. Oliver was sound asleep.

"I want to get up." Mother helped me out of bed and we walked to the kitchen. We sat at the table.

The sky was turning red above the treeline beyond Montfer. I could see the dark mass of the barn and the shed. Closer to the house, the cooler box with a cap of snow blended into the basswood near it.

Mother rose to add wood to the fire; she made the coffee and cooked the oatmeal. "Would you like some maple syrup on your cereal?"

"Yes."

We sat at the table with our bowls of porridge and cups of coffee, both steaming into the morning air. Mother's long braids hung over the front of her nightgown. She seemed young to me and as lovely as she had been years before when the wedding photograph had caught the innocence of her youth.

"You're so pretty, Mother," I said.

"Not anymore. Goodness, I'm old already, Mary."

"Did I have a birthday yet?"

"Yes. A week ago. Your sixteenth. We listened to the election returns and you said you wanted Thomas to win."

"Did I? I don't remember it." I tried to think of some absurdity which would stop the watering in my eyes, but I could think of nothing.

"You're going to be well," Mother said. "From now on you won't forget a thing."

The whole eastern sky was rose and orange now. Morning had come. The barn stood free of the mass of trees behind it; the cooler box and the basswood were separate.

Everyone was getting up. The cows, horses, chickens, ducks and rabbits would have to be fed, the cows milked, and then all the milk cans and buckets washed. Later Mother would make a big breakfast for the family, but now everyone would have a cup of coffee before going out.

Mother asked me to slice the bread for her and I did; I got down the cups too. They were such easy chores but I couldn't finish them. The room began to turn about and Mother brought me to bed. I woke up when Eileen and Rachel, bursting with energy, hands cold to the touch, red-cheeked and laughing, came to stand at my bedside.

They had a surprise for me, for they had gone around collecting, they said, and now Eileen spread the coins and bills on my quilt. "There you are. Thirty-four dollars and a twelve-dollar check from Mr. O'Connell for past work and the work you'd have done if you had been in school."

Rachel began stuffing the money back into the brown envelope. "Now you can buy a new woolen snowsuit and heavy sweaters."

Eileen and Carl began to argue about how the people who had contributed ought to be thanked. An ad in the newspaper? Personal notes? Announce it over the radio? That's not proper. Why not, if it saves money? They got the Sears' and Ward's catalogues. Look for the sweaters first. Look for the snowsuit. Don't worry, Mary. We'll help. You're not supposed to, Elizabeth. You're family.

I thanked the girls. They had been kind; their mothers had been kind. Mrs. Salmi had prayed for me; Mrs. Larson had fed me. But now the girls' faces blurred into the distance; their voices mingled. How would I ever understand anything?

It was evening when I woke up. My fever was gone and I felt a change and, for the first time in weeks, an extraordinary sense of well-being. I saw the mantle lamp shed its soft glow over the kitchen, the shadowy figures of Edward and Elizabeth at the table, Mother in the rocker, Father reading in his chair, Big Hank in his, and Grandmother sitting in her accustomed place at the spinning wheel.

When I walked into the kitchen, Father moved his chair. At once I saw the easel standing in front of his shoemaking machine. "It's all yours, Mary," he said.

The wood had been sanded to a velvety smoothness and then varnished, and the ledge scooped out to hold tubes of paint and brushes. They were there, fresh and new. Father got up to show me how to fold the easel for storage behind his machine. He was shyly proud of his work, the scraping, sanding and varnishing. He had used oak for the legs and back, and ironwood for the ledge, he said. "It was such a nice dry piece, when I split it the hollow was there, almost ready. That was a good tree."

I remembered it standing tall in our meadow until the storm broke the trunk. Father had saved the wood and used it for handles and stirring spoons which would last a lifetime. And now the easel, lovelier than anything we owned. "It'll last forever," I said, and realized suddenly how long the weeks had been for him and Mother. Long enough to build this thing of beauty and far longer and harder than mine had been.

"You spent hours of your time, Father."

"It was worth it," he answered quietly, as though he had made an offering and his wish had been granted.

Early in fall, I might have mentioned that Miss Bates wanted her students to have easels, and Father had remembered it though I had forgotten. In the hope that Miss Bates could teach me how to draw, I had chosen art as an elective and had joined her class of fifteen students, but I still couldn't draw well enough to please myself.

I learned to paint, however, and the next summer, when Father would come home from his surveying job, he'd look at my canvas and nod. "That's a good sky," or "I like the shadow on the tree there," he'd say. Then he'd show my picture to Mr. Wiita or Mr. Ojala. They'd compare my colors to the ones outside. They wanted reality and when they didn't see it they said there was something wrong. Father said I was putting down what I saw, that's all. For two hours a day, I felt like an artist.

Mother said nothing made Father happier than my using the easel. She didn't care what I painted, as long as I was brushing paint on canvas. "You're bound to learn something. And now the sky is so clear, you can really see everything."

But the air wasn't clear. The strong breezes whipped the dust around and turned the colors muddy. Even the hills, usually bright with their varying shades of green, were as drab as in late August, before the frost brought back the reds and yellows. The fresh hues of spring weren't anywhere. How could I paint what I couldn't see? "The colors aren't right this year," I said to Mother.

"Then paint what you see."

And because I liked the smell of oil and turpentine and the sight of clean pigments in the tubes almost as much as I liked pads of paper, sharpened pencils and words forming patterns of sound, I used the easel Father had built for me. Then I found words to describe the feeling that I had wanted the shapes, the lights and shadows to evoke, and let the somber tones remain.

A few days before I went back to school, I walked to the Salmis'. The snow had long since covered the ground, rounded the bushes and capped the rock fences. The river had frozen except for a narrow stream in the center, black against white. I went over the railroad tracks, glistening in the sun, and then past our mailbox.

Mr. Salmi was resting; Mrs. Salmi was making their afternoon coffee. We talked in a whisper. "God hears our prayers, Mary."

The sun came in and touched the table with gold, and yet the whole house seemed dingier than I remembered it. The walls, always painted orange, had turned brown; the enameled floor had dulled and had begun to crack and chip. Everything bore the sign of age—everything except the clock, which chimed as cheerfully as ever. Three times. Revived by the sound, the calico cat came out of the woodbox and sat down to watch the pendulum move in and out of the sun's glow.

Mr. Salmi joined us at the table. "I don't know what will happen to us, Mary. We're getting old."

"The Lord will take care of us," said Mrs. Salmi.

We drank our coffee, ate our sugar-coated molasses cookies. Then I went out into the brisk afternoon, past the small barn and Mr. Salmi's blacksmith shop, its windows boarded up and the door padlocked. "Everything comes to an end," Grandmother had said about her own numbered days. Growing old long before he was due, Mr. Salmi had prospects no better. He was too old to work on road construction. Too old to work in his shop. Too old for these times.

I thought of school and study, that other world which bore no resemblance to Revier, and wanted to go back more than I ever had. But when I finally got there, it wasn't what I thought it would be. The noise, the confusion, the buzzers and the milling crowd of students in the halls—everything was magnified a hundredfold. I complained to Mr. O'Connell and he let me do an hour's filing. Then he said I'd soon become used to the place again. "They're full of energy," he said of the students, and sent me to my scheduled study hall.

Full of energy and full of complaints. All my classmates seemed to want was an escape from another quiz, another theme, another hour's delving into the facts of history. All I wanted was to lose myself in study once more. In English class, Miss Hanson was lecturing on Elizabethan England, the home territory of every English course at Hadley. Before I left, we had read *The Merchant of Venice.* While I was gone, Miss Hanson had guided the class from Chaucer to the Romantic poets and had returned to Shakespeare again.

"Why do we have to read the works of dead poets?" someone asked.

"If you don't learn to appreciate the best," Miss Hanson said, "you won't be ready for life's great experiences."

"What's a great experience?"

"You'll know when you have one," she answered, and went on with her lecture.

I tried to listen and to concentrate; all I could hear was a steady babble. Within a week, I became accustomed to the distractions, however, and began working regularly for Mr. O'Connell. The tasks were easy enough—filing, delivering mail and notices to the classrooms, and pasting stamps on letters, but since I now worked during my one free hour and half the noon hour, I had little time for study except at home in the evenings and on weekends. Over the Christmas holidays, I would finish the assignments which had accumulated in my seven-week absence.

After a long vacation, our classmates always said, "We had a ball," though they didn't say what they'd done. They were trying to live according to the idea that this was the best time of their lives, and not one moment of it could be allowed to pass without diversion. Thus the initial days of classes were always the worst. "They can't settle down," some of the teachers would say, and their students didn't. At any rate, not in study hall, where even a minor disturbance could provide the maximum enjoyment if the right teacher was in charge. Miss Jones was right. Bedlam was order wherever she was.

Now, let loose from our first class of the year, we filed into the auditorium for study hall. Usually Miss Reidel, my math teacher, was in charge. She wasn't this time. Miss Jones was. Tall, long-necked Albertina Jones, who taught typing, shorthand and book-keeping to girls only. She couldn't manage boys, and couldn't now. They were everywhere. "Pee-ople! Pee-ople," she piped. To no avail.

Then Mr. O'Reilly, jowls quivering, strode down the center aisle. Turning to the left and the right, he picked out those he assumed to be the most guilty. "Malowski, Johnson, Bernardino, Coxey, Schneider, into my office." No one moved. "At once," he bellowed. The boys picked up their books and papers and walked out.

Mr. O'Reilly waited until Miss Reidel came in to resume her duties. "Good day," she said calmly, and peace fell upon the barbarian horde.

No one ever questioned Miss Reidel. She was five feet tall and weighed less than a hundred pounds, but her pronouncements were as unassailable as the table of logarithms. They implied order and predictability, reason and decorum. How else could one understand a universe bound in one way or another by mathematical principles? How else, indeed? No one dared speculate.

Nor was there much speculation in Mr. Gardener's biology nor in Mr. Kendall's physics. Freely falling bodies and the reproductive organs of chickens might suggest something to a fevered young mind, but no one dared pursue the thought. Otherwise one could serve time in the hall, where one was ready prey for Mr. O'Reilly, who periodically stalked up and down to gather the less willing scholars into his office, there to instill in them the proper love of learning.

While Mr. O'Reilly bellowed, his subordinate, Mr. O'Connell, attempted to comprehend the vagaries of the young. We liked him and even worried about him, for he was exceedingly thin. He was lame in one leg and wore the hurt from it on his thin, sad face. "Now tell me, why did you want to do that?" he'd ask a student who'd committed some minor infraction which did not merit the attention of Mr. O'Reilly. The look of puzzlement and injury on Mr. O'Connell's face was worse than anything one could expect from his superior.

"The guy is so damned kind, you feel like an ass telling him that you made trouble for the hell of it," one student said.

He taught several courses in English too. Not very well, for he expected very little of his pupils, but he gave them something which, despite their shallowness, they valued. He made them feel older than they were, and more comprehending and protective. But comprehending of what and protective of whom? Mr. O'Connell himself? Their teachers? Their parents?

The students told a story about him. When he was young, he and his family had driven out into the country for a picnic. On the way back, a train hit their car. His wife had died, his two children had died, and only he had survived, though his leg was broken and his insides never the same again. Before that, Mr. O'Reilly didn't run the show. Afterward he did. There was the tragedy, not just for Mr. O'Connell but for Hadley too, and all the young. "If only Mr. O'Connell had more power!" the students said. But he didn't, and thus he remained the feeble conscience of Hadley High School.

Miss Carlotta Hanson had another role. She was the chief of protocol. Had George V of England decided to pay a visit, she would have known what to do and wouldn't have worried at all. The reason for her confidence went back to her father, a mining company executive who had built the mansion on Fourth Avenue.

Even before he brought his wife to Hadley, he had stuffed the place with about as much silver, crystal, china, linens and Oriental rugs as any house can hold. In due time, the Hansons had a daughter, Carlotta, who enjoyed the splendor of the home until she was eleven.

Then the question arose: What do you do with a daughter who'll inherit a house with everything in it and money besides? You send her to a boarding school in Boston and after that to a finishing school. After she was finished, she didn't have anything to do. She was bored; she traveled all over the world, but even that didn't cure her boredom. Finally she decided to go to the university. She wasn't satisfied with one degree; she earned two.

By this time the Depression had come to Hadley. Mr. Hanson died of grief, people said, though even the wealthy can die of disease. In any case, Carlotta came back to her mother and to the mansion with all the silver, crystal, china, linens and Oriental rugs, which were none the worse for wear. The only trouble was that Carlotta wasn't beautiful anymore. She was stoop-shouldered and heavy-footed. She probably had never been a beauty, but all the finishing in Boston and studying at the university had made her unmarriageable, at least in Hadley. That is how Carlotta Hanson came to Hadley High School and, once there, established herself as possessor of the latest knowledge in matters of etiquette.

"One can do anything properly if one allows enough time for preparation," she often said. Thus, if the girls in eleventh grade wanted a prom, then they had best begin planning sometime after the February thaw. "The warm weather provides such an incentive," she said. If nature didn't oblige and February threatened to go thawless into March, Miss Hanson intervened. She called a meeting of the junior class.

During the prom the year before this, fifty dollars' worth of canned tuna fish, pork and beans, corned beef hash and Spam was stolen from the cafeteria, now turned into a cloakroom. The junior class could not afford such a loss this year, Miss Hanson said, and therefore, if I were willing, the class would pay me a dollar to watch the coats, the tuna fish, pork and beans, and whatever else was portable in the cafeteria. I said that I'd be willing to do so, but I thought two dollars would be better, since my brother would have to bring me into town and fetch me again. She agreed.

211

The weather was perfect for the prom, as Miss Hanson had said it would be. One always hoped for the best. The women teachers came in long gauzy gowns and rustling taffetas. Mr. O'Reilly, belly large, escorted Miss Fleming in her pale green tight-waisted gown. How could she dance with him? At arm's length probably. Miss Reidel came alone, in a long black dress. Apparently she needed no one, even at a prom; perhaps she was in mourning; maybe she was on police duty. The young girls, still awkward in their heels, held their strange beauty parlor hairstyles high, as if they feared pitching forward. They wore white, pink and baby blue gowns with corsages like medals of virgin popularity pinned on virgin breasts.

"Isn't it just lovely?" asked Miss Hanson.

"Well, I wish they wouldn't wear heels," complained Miss Brock, sardonic, sour Miss Brock, a Ph.D. in English who couldn't find a job anywhere but at Hadley High School. "They wobble like ducks!" She shook her head.

"All the same, it is a milestone in their lives," said Miss Hanson.

"Oh, God," replied Miss Brock, and went off, paired with the football coach, who was safely married.

Carl and Eileen graduated; Carl was second in his class and Eileen held some neutral middle ground. "He ought to have been first," she said. "Revier would be famous then."

"Who cares about Revier being famous?" asked Carl.

"Well, I do. It's our hometown!"

They all came to our house—Reino, Rachel, Eileen, Toivo and Eino. Elizabeth and Eino had finished their stay at Revier School. He had grown to Toivo's height and carried a pocket comb but forgot to use it. "We're free at last, Elizabeth! We'll be in Hadley next year." He thought a moment. "Maybe I'll be a teacher too."

"You'll have to study harder, Eino," Grandmother said.

And when John returned, successful in his second year of study, she asked Carl at once, "You're going to the university, aren't you?"

"Yes, Grandmother."

"There's nothing here for a bright young man."

There wasn't much for anyone, for nothing grew and nothing prospered. The rains went everywhere around, but they didn't come to Revier. Grandmother's last trust in the land, which had yielded us our food, was gone. Not all of the Montfer emptied daily onto our fields could have kept our crops alive.

All the remorse of years past crowded her. All the decisions she had made had been the wrong ones. How could she have been so foolish? In buying Alex's land and in paying Otto's debt, she had bound Father to a lifetime of fruitless labor. When she saw his pride in the success of his sons and listened to his hopes for their future, she recognized that he had never wanted to be on our small square of earth, however carefully and wisely he had tilled and managed it. His wish to have his sons gone had to deny the worth of his own effort.

When he stood on the stair and looked out over our dying fields, she'd say, "The dear man, his whole life wasted here."

"Here?" asked Mother. "Where else would we be? We're lucky to have this."

Maybe Father saw the waste. He had to. Forty cents for a hundred pounds of potatoes. Twenty cents an hour for a man's hard labor. Ten cents an hour. A nickel. Or a total loss. "Well, it's a good life if you don't weaken," he'd say. "One makes the best of it. Right?"

Poor Father. The world going to hell and no way to stop it.

Eileen came to bid her cheerful farewell. She was going to be a nurse—that pretty girl, who had brought the one giddy season of our lives into being. "Stay well," she said, and kissed us all and left.

All that summer Grandmother talked of the future of "her sons." That's what they were. Had she not cared for them from the day of their birth? God help them. And when the boys packed their bags and their silvery laundry cases, she sat and watched them. "Your grandfather would have enjoyed this," she said. *"Two grandsons going away to school!"*

But they hadn't been gone a week before she began to fret. "Who knows if I'll even live until they come back." She wandered about in the woodlot, chopped wood and then slept whole afternoons.

Nothing gave her pleasure save her plants and the opening buds they bore, and even they reminded her of the grave. When the Christmas cactus began to bloom, she said she would never again see it in flower.

Had John and Carl been able to come home, her spirits might

have revived for the holidays, but they couldn't take the time. Both of them had jobs and a backlog of studying. If they did well on their examinations, they could apply for scholarships.

"It won't be Christmas without them," said Grandmother.

"We're still here, Grandma," said Edward. "We can make as much noise as they do."

"Yes, you're here, thank goodness."

But we weren't enough. She wanted the whole family together, so nothing amused her. She was sad the whole week of Christmas.

Perhaps it was the sound of Grandmother's bell hanging in its lofty place near the top of our tree that reminded Mother of the other wilderness house, surrounded by pines and smelling of Christmas the year round. Maybe she thought that in speaking of that enchanted place she could divert Grandmother's attention from the present which depressed her to a past more comforting. Whatever it was, Mother became absorbed in a description of aunts and uncles, cousins, kind friends and kind neighbors.

Grandmother must have heard in the echoes of Mother's voice a harking back to a world that never was. Her reply was brisk. "People were no better then than now, and life was a lot harder. I'll never forget trying to protect Otto and Alex from the drunken rages of their father. Every time I saw poor Otto limping across our fields, I thought of that devilish man."

"But, he was always good to me and to our little family," said Mother. "He was a handsome man too, and good to my bedridden father."

"Only because he didn't dare to come into our house when he was drunk. I'd have been satisfied if he was a decent man in his own home. Well, he's dead now, and God forgive him."

Two mothers looking at their world with separate vision. We had needed them both in our growing years. The reality and the enchantment had blended and become one. Grandmother's eyes hadn't faded much and Mother's had sharpened a bit with age. I had always wavered between their worlds.

And as for the neighbors, Grandmother went on, they had been faithful. They had helped her a lot after Grandfather died, but she had paid them. They hadn't worked for nothing.

The remembrance of her independence nudged Grandmother back to the living present. She got out her collection of yarn. She looked through the box of mittens. Everyone needed a pair. She began knitting the new and repairing the old. "These are the best years of our lives, Louise," she said. "Here with the children growing and becoming adults one after the other."

Now in the evenings she'd sit with us at the table, and as we did our homework she urged Edward to study so that he too could go to the university.

"I will, Grandma," said Edward. "That catapult I made didn't work so well. Maybe I'll be a doctor."

That pleased Grandmother. A doctor? Well, certainly if he wanted to be one, he could.

And when Easter came and it was time for Elizabeth to be confirmed, Grandmother wanted to see the rite. She had missed three and wasn't about to miss another. God willing, she'd go to Edward's, but who could say? Two years was a long time.

Elizabeth in her white dress and white shoes, catechism in one hand and her white bag in the other. All ready to become a Christian adult. Quiet, knowing what she wanted and determined to get it. Adult enough. She needed no rite to bestow this upon her.

Grandmother put on her churchgoing poplin and the silk scarf to cover her shining white hair. She stuffed a pretty handkerchief into her sleeve. "Well, I'm all set."

They stayed the whole day and when they returned Grandmother was as lively as she had been in the morning. "You should have seen her, Mary. Our Elizabeth speaking up clearer than all the rest."

Who was it who had said that I had kept Elizabeth voiceless for years? Never let her talk? Long ago. One of the boys—Paul or Toivo or John or Carl. I couldn't remember.

"How was it, Liz?"

"I liked it. Eino missed half the questions, but he passed anyhow."

"What else?"

"Same as yours otherwise."

Grandmother looked for a sudden remarkable change in Elizabeth. "Let me look at you now." She peered at Elizabeth. "Well, you're still our Elizabeth. Somehow you girls don't change much."

In those early months of springtime before the snow had gone, Grandmother wanted to teach Elizabeth and me how to spin. Who would teach us if she didn't? Mother had never learned the skill, though she had had plenty of time when she was young. She hadn't been able to sit still long enough.

When we were little, we had been fascinated by the spinning wheel and had tangled the yarn so often that Mother established the rule: Don't touch Grandmother's spinning wheel. We hadn't. We hadn't touched the cards or the wool either, except when Grandmother had allowed us to help by picking up a roll of wool and handing it to her.

She had known how to spin before she was twelve, and here we were, adults, who hadn't even begun to learn. Had we been living in Finland when she was a young girl, we would have been considered too inept to make good wives for ordinary men.

We did our best, Elizabeth and I, but my yarn was clotted and stringy; Elizabeth's wasn't twisted enough but at least it was even throughout. I made mine into mittens for Oliver. They were so tightly knit that when I washed them, they stood up by themselves. Elizabeth made a small scarf—very small, we decided. Grandmother was disappointed in our handiwork, but we had learned a lot. We would have to practice five years and even then we wouldn't be able to make a yarn as fine as hers. "That's a good thing to know too, Grandmother," I said.

"In my day, that wouldn't have gotten you far!"

As the days lengthened and the snow began to waste away, we sensed an impatience in Grandmother. When was the Montfer going to flood? She walked down the road and past the sauna to see if the ice had begun to break up. It hadn't. Then one night we heard the crash of one huge sheet of ice against another. Over and over. In a day, our fields had turned to one sea glistening in the sun, all fences and borders sunken and out of sight. Had the water licked the corners of our house, Grandmother's pleasure in seeing the spring tide would not have been diminished, but having seen it, she wanted it gone and the fields dry.

She studied the packets of seeds Father had ordered for her and sorted the labeled envelopes holding the harvest of fall. She wanted lily bulbs of all kinds and strawberry plants—ever-bearing ones. But the wind blew cold from the north and the ground stayed damp. Grandmother became uneasy. "We haven't had one day of warm weather," she said, "and it's getting so late."

"We could visit my cousins in Marengo," Mother said. They had invited us to come many times over and we hadn't gone. Why not go now when no one was busy?

"That'd be a nice change," said Grandmother, and began to wait for Sunday. It came, the first balmy day of the year, a day so clean and clear that we could see the blue mounds beyond the raspberry hills. Everyone wanted to get out and be gone; only Grandmother dallied. She chopped kindling and brought it in; she brought milk to the cats; she brought her plants out to air. She came in. "Louise, I've made up my mind. It's just too fine a day to waste in idle talk."

"We'll all stay home," said Mother. "We'll go next week instead."

"Next week?" asked Father. "It'll be six months before I have time to go anywhere."

"I'm sure Toivo and Eino will help us with planting."

"I'll still have too much to do," said Father. He had on his white shirt and his tie, and stood hat in hand.

Big Hank was dressed in new overalls, a bright chambray shirt and a summer jacket. All week long, he had looked forward to reviving old friendships dormant since the days he escaped seeding and harvest at our house. For years he hadn't gone anywhere. He had grown stiff with arthritis and, unless one of us was along, hadn't dared to venture far. He too stood hat in hand, pink-cheeked from shaving, smiling and ready.

I looked at him and Father, at Oliver in his matched shirt and pants, Elizabeth in her new spring dress, and Edward in his blue blazer. I told Mother that we'd have a day of misery if she didn't put on her good dress, get into the car and go. I'd stay home with Grandmother, because I had a lot of studying to do and didn't want to go either.

In ten minutes, Mother was dressed, and they all piled into the Model A. Standing on the stair, our skirts billowing in the wind, we watched Father turn the car around. He blew the horn, and as they rode away, we waved at their departing car. "You'd think they're going to California," said Grandmother. "I couldn't stand listening to Marianna and Julianna remembering how silly they were."

"Were they that silly?"

"They were young and giddy. The way you were that one summer."

I remembered. Pretty Eileen and her kissing lists and everyone enjoying the idea of being brave in hard times.

Years ago, Mother's cousins Julianna and Marianna, with their carload of children, used to visit us. The husbands had always been out working somewhere. Since there weren't any men about to change the course of the conversations, Mother and her cousins were free to relive their youthful escapades. On those long afternoons, Grandmother had always remained aloof and I had wondered what she thought. Now for some time, only the cousins' daughters Julia and Violet had come, more to entertain John and Carl than to talk to the rest of us.

I changed into overalls and Grandmother and I walked to the garden nearest to the house. We tilled the rose bed and spread the pansies. We worked for an hour, but then Grandmother's back began to hurt.

Since it was nearly noon, we went inside. I fired the stove, got some fresh water from the pump and heated some left-over soup. Grandmother watched me. "I'm not even hungry," she said, but as we sat down to eat, her appetite seemed to pick up.

She began to talk about her father. He had been a church official and because he kept records of all the rites, he had known the family histories of all the people in the village. "He was a learned man and would have wanted us children to study, but there were so many of us we had to start working. I was only twelve when I first left home."

She was silent, lost in musing. Then as though she were talking to herself, she said, "I still wish that my father had taught me to write. I could have written to my brothers and sisters how life was here in America."

"Didn't Mother write for you?"

"Yes. First Grandfather and then your mother when she grew old enough. But it's not the same, Mary."

And I thought of all the things she might have written to her sisters and brothers had she been able, and the words she'd have chosen to describe the unadorned and unglossed world she saw. Mother's phrasing must have sung to heaven and left Grandmother mute.

Sometimes I thought I shared her spare world. "People used to say that I'm like you."

"Yes, I remember, and I didn't think it was right. I always wanted you to be yourself, Mary." Still, she seemed happier again and at peace with herself. "The years have gone by so fast, it's no wonder I get tired." She looked at the wall clock.

"Why don't you rest awhile?"

"And what will you do?"

"I have a lot of studying to do, Grandmother."

"In that case, I may as well take a little nap."

The clock ticked away, the steam hissed in the teakettle, and the wood crackled in the kitchen stove. There couldn't have been a more peaceful time—perfect for doing nothing at all. But I had pages of math and physics to do, *Hamlet* to read, and if I had an hour left, I'd finish my library book.

In midafternoon, I looked in on Grandmother. She was sleeping soundly. She slept until five o'clock, when the rest of the family returned. They had had an exciting time. Because the Marengo River had flooded one bridge, they'd had to find another. By the time they arrived at Julianna's, she had the table ready and more food prepared than they could have eaten in a week. Afterward they had all gone to Marianna's.

We were cheerful, drawn together at the end of a successful day. Even Big Hank was happy. In family after family, he had found nothing but disorder. The children were badly behaved and didn't know a thing, and the parents were no better. "I told them how things are run at the Morgans' and how the boys are going to the university. That really set them back!"

"I bet it did," said Edward. "Did they ask you to come again?"

"No. They didn't, but I wouldn't go if they had."

For weeks after, Grandmother was in good humor. When school let out and the boys returned to tell her that she hadn't changed and hadn't grown old, she smiled, sat in the kitchen and watched them empty their suitcases, stuffed with dirty clothes for us to wash; with beakers and test tubes smelling of acid; with books, papers and huge gray bulging loose-leaf notebooks. In one moment, everything was scattered over the floor. Looking at the clutter, Grandmother said it was like Christmas years ago.

Suddenly into the muddle of that summer morning, the car backfired furiously, rattling the dishes on the table. John and Carl looked at each other. Edward was driving the car into the garage, and in so doing, established his claim before the older boys could say, "You're too young to be driving anything." In a moment he was back, coughed a few times to get his voice to a lower pitch and said, "We always keep the car in the garage, don't we, Grandma?"

"We certainly do, Edward."

Despite her pleasure in having everyone around her once more and her assurances that she was well, we could see that she was weaker than she had been. All her efforts to plant her flowers had come to nothing; most of the seedlings waited in their pots and boxes; the colorful packets of seeds and the dozen plain envelopes still sat on top of the dresser. I offered to help her and for several days we went out into her garden, I to transplant and seed and she to stand and watch.

I was ready to set the bulbs into the ground when Grandmother said she was too weary to stay outside. I thought I could do the planting alone, but she was insistent. "No, Mary. You're tired too. If you want to put the bulbs in later, they'll still come up." She began to walk to the house and then stopped. "Could you help me a little?" I ran to her and took her arm. "I'm so tired, Mary. I think my days of work are over." I got her into the house; Mother and I prepared her for bed and then let her rest.

The next morning, Grandmother was feverish. She was unable to eat, and though she could sit up long enough for us to wash her, change her bed and her gown, she had no wish to stay up any longer. She slept the whole day. In the evening when Dr. Burton came to see her, she refused to open her eyes. He examined her. She had some congestion in her lungs, but that wasn't as serious as her lassitude. She needed to sit up and she needed fluids.

After he left us, we asked her if she understood and she nodded her head. We brought her tea; she took a few sips and then would take no more. "I want to sleep," she whispered so softly we could hardly hear her. Within moments, she was in a deep and peaceful slumber. We did everything we could to make her comfortable, but she didn't respond to our love and our care.

She began to fail quickly one afternoon, and seven days after she told me her work was over, she died. It was the day of the leaf house.

We gathered around her bedside. Mother wept. The rest of us

kept our grief within us, as Grandmother would have had us do. I held on to Oliver's hand.

Two days later, we met at St. Paul's. The minister had arranged a ceremony devoid of our sadness. He recited a short history of Grandmother's life and a ten-minute sermon on the dignity of life and the necessity of "going home." Then the sound of the organ filled the church. Had we not seen Grandmother's gray coffin before us, we would have thought the occasion a concert of Bach, Beethoven and Dvořák.

The church bells rang. We went out into the hot sunshine, climbed into the cars standing at the curb, and followed the hearse to the cemetery. There we watched the gray box drop down into the earth, which our grandmother had known and loved as long as any of us could remember.

12

FOR WEEKS, I SAW GRANDMOTHER'S SOLID FORM moving about wherever I looked—in the woodlot, in the shadows of the trees behind the house, and among the flowers. At night, I saw her walking along the paths in our yard, and willed her back into my life. I cared faithfully for her garden, saw it bloom as never before and felt her pride in it.

Mother spoke of Grandmother as if she were with us still, though we saw the silent spinning wheel and her unoccupied chair. After John and Carl went back to Madison, the house was emptier than it had ever been; nothing seemed to fill the vacant corners of our lives. Oliver felt the absences most of all and didn't want to be alone anywhere.

Loving though I intended to be, I was no longer Oliver's favorite. He preferred Elizabeth, who was quiet and gentle and willing to read to him by the hour. When he grew tired of listening, he'd say plaintively, "I want my Edward." Edward expected nothing of him. They'd spend hours exploring the woodlot and return with a baby rabbit, a squirrel, a frog or a bird, always some creature for Oliver to feed and love. Sometimes on weekends when I had an afternoon of freedom, I'd sew a pair of trousers or a jacket for him. He hated the fitting and resented being called in from his play. "I not stand. Play first." Then when I had finished the garment, he'd say, "I say I not like."

"It's nice on you, Ollie," I'd coax.

"Not nice, Maymay, and you not nice, Maymay."

And yet when he was tired or hurt, he would come to me. "Little Mother," he'd murmur softly, "you very nice." Then I could hold him and rock him as I always had.

School began for us. Revier School for Edward and Hadley High School for Elizabeth and me. As we walked to the school bus on those fall mornings, I began to see that Grandmother's death had had a far more lasting effect on Elizabeth than on Edward or me, though she had never sought Grandmother's counsel as I had; she had wanted Mother's. Now her feelings came out in unexpected ways. "I think Grandmother was foolish for moving out here."

"It's so pretty at this time of year," I said. It was, with the dew glistening on the green meadows and the leaves beginning to turn color. To me it was the most beautiful sight on earth.

"Godforsaken, Mary. I hate it!"

And one afternoon when we were walking home, she looked at the Lahti place—the prettiest in Revier. I could see nothing wrong with it, though the buildings were small. "Do you realize, Mary, that that house is the best in Revier? Every other house is worse —not even decent, and everyone works his head off!"

"But if we hadn't known this, we would never know how hard it was for people long ago."

"I heard enough about it from Grandmother," she said, "and I don't want to hear it from you too. I could've done without the knowledge in the first place."

"Maybe we both feel bad about Grandmother."

"Oh, hell," she answered, and didn't say another word all the way home.

There was no way I could reach her. She would talk when she was ready, but I thought of her and our changed lives and I realized that it wasn't Grandmother's death by itself that bothered Elizabeth. It was the isolation that I'd become used to long since and accepted as a part of myself.

More lively than we, John and Carl had always attracted the young people just as Edward brought in the children. Grandmother, who had been revered for her remarkable stamina, had had a host of friends and distant relatives. Sunday after Sunday, they had come to declare her unaltered and to keep Elizabeth and me at the dishpan for hours on end. "We've washed a million dishes," we had said of our summers' endeavors.

"Loneliness is far worse than doing dishes," Mother had told us, but we hadn't believed her.

It wasn't until the Days of Arrivals and Departures that we understood what she had meant. We had lost much those years, though we hadn't talked of it often. I remember looking down the road and thinking: What if I saw Otto and Mandy driving in? And suddenly the past would come back. The bags of stinging sauna soap, the Times of the Great Anger, with Otto hanging up new wallpaper and Alex taking forever to mix his paints. The long sauna nights. The white-stocking cousins, with their pretty clothes and patent leather shoes. It was at such times that Elizabeth and I would take a walk through the silent woods, where no one would intrude upon our remembering. Then for a while, we were too busy trying to be grown up to look back together.

There was that one remarkable year—Elizabeth's eleventh and my thirteenth—when, for the first time, she, Reino, Rachel and I were invited to the same parties as John and Carl. Everyone who wasn't a drunkard was at these crowded Saturday night get-togethers in the homes of friends. One half of the living room was always cleared of furniture, carpets and plants, so the older people could dance cheek to cheek, and we younger ones could watch dreamy-eyed. Sometimes we all joined in a game while the phonograph scratched through "The Blue Danube Waltz." Around ten o'clock we always had cake and all-yours with tea and milk. Soon after, the party was over.

Handsome in their dark jackets and white scarves, John and Carl brought their girls home. Rachel, Reino, Elizabeth and I walked by ourselves, worried about timber wolves and wildcats, and wondered what people would say if we never got home at all. To make sure we did, we sang at the top of our lungs. When we got to our mailbox we parted, and Elizabeth and I, walking through the eerie pasture, remembered again the days of our childhood.

All that seemed so long ago. Elizabeth was in her second year at Hadley High School and we were paired as we had always been. We walked to and from the bus together, sat next to each other on the bus, and ate our lunch together every day. I realized how much I had missed her in the first two years, for I still had no other close friends.

She was doing well. Many of the slights which had disturbed me didn't touch her. Miss Hanson was a good teacher; Mr. O'Reilly simply heavy-handed.

"There's more to it, Elizabeth."

"I don't have to listen, do I?" She didn't. Now that we were able to buy a few new clothes with the money I earned in Mr. O'Connell's office, she was confident about her appearance. "I'm as good as they are, and a lot smarter than some."

It was Edward who had the fewest worries. "Life could be a lot tougher," he'd tell Elizabeth and me. He was especially pleased with himself these days because he was firing the furnace for Mr. Wiita and earning a dollar a week. "I'm working my way through," he'd say, as he stuffed a dollar bill into his Kresge wallet.

Edward was now the eldest son, Mother's right arm or left arm —she still hadn't decided which her sons were. This sudden promotion loosened his tongue and freed him. "Now I can practice driving the car."

"Only in Revier," said Father.

"All right, but for the whole summer I couldn't even look at the key. Next summer I'm going to have a duplicate made."

He began to fill the vacated areas, moved upstairs and brought home his friends to show them his new "hideaway." He stayed out after dark and said, "You didn't even know I had friends, did you, Mary?"

"Of course I did. We've fed them often enough."

"But you didn't see them."

"I saw them, Edward." But maybe I hadn't. They had simply been much younger children who could be sent out to play or sent home. They could be told to keep quiet, to stop bickering and to stop being silly. Now they were taller than I, gangly boys soon ready for adulthood. They couldn't be sent home to their mothers; they'd go home when they felt they ought to go, but not before.

"I just sneaked up on you, Mary!" said Edward.

He would soon be thirteen. He wouldn't have to prove his adulthood by going to parties. He could keep track of the car keys instead.

"Come on, Ollie," Edward said. "Let's go sledding." He bundled up Oliver and took him outside to feel the first snow of winter.

"We have such good boys," said Mother wistfully, as if Elizabeth and I were more troublesome.

"I don't know where we strayed, Mary," said Elizabeth.

Mother looked at us and laughed. "Don't be silly, girls. I count my lucky stars every day."

Within the family, this shifting of position from younger to older affected the boys more than it did Elizabeth and me. We held the middle ground year after year. We never got the key. I always assumed Father wanted the boys to have the first chance.

John and Carl tried to teach me to drive, but they thought I was too inattentive and that Reino would be more patient with me. For a long time he said he didn't want to, but when Carl began preparing to go to the university, Reino had to look around for someone to take his place. Arthur and his mother had moved to Woodland. He had a steady girl and wasn't interested in coming out to the country anymore. Reino had to settle for Elizabeth and me.

Of the two of us, he preferred Elizabeth. She was quieter, he said, and didn't argue all the time. Then he complained that I acted too old, that I'd rather sit at home than go anywhere, and that all I cared about was stuffing my head. Nothing else.

Yet in exchange for help on his book reports he agreed to let me sit at the wheel of the Salmi car, and as we rattled up and down Revier Road, he'd tell me about all the things I did wrong. Ground the gears, drove too fast and braked too hard. After that, I brought the pedal down slow and easy. But once when I saw Mr. Wiita's Chevy coming down the hill, I went off the road and over the frozen ditch into the Lahtis' field, made a circle and drove back. Reino had hidden his head under his jacket. "Jesus!" he said as he came out. "I thought you were going straight into the barn wall. Now I know why you don't get the key at your house."

"What did you want me to do? Hit the old man? He had the whole road." Mr. Wiita always did. Right down the middle as he peered above, below and through the spokes of the steering wheel. All one could ever see was his white bobbing head.

That was enough driving for me. After running off the road once, I didn't want to risk wrecking the Salmis' car again. Besides, I had more schoolwork than ever before, and I wanted some time for teaching Oliver.

He had mastered the alphabet, but he hadn't been able to see the letters. Now that he had new glasses, he could learn to read. Because he was having trouble adjusting to the lenses, I waited a week. Then I took him aside. "We're going to read, Oliver," I said. I made an A an inch high and traced the letter with his finger. "This is an A." He recited the whole alphabet. "Can't you see it?"

"That paper, Maymay?" He had his face so near the letter that he had to see something. "Paper?" he asked.

"Yes, it's paper, Ollie." It was obvious that he couldn't see.

The next day during the noon hour, I walked down Iron Street, past the taverns blinking, "Girls, Girls, Girls," and into Woodland. It was a clear brisk day with all the rooftops covered with snow and the smoke rising straight into a deep blue sky.

As I walked up the stairs to Dr. Burton's office, I was certain he would give me permission to bring Oliver to the university hospital. We'd take the train and we'd ride to Madison, and John and Carl would meet us at the station. I could miss a month of school and it wouldn't matter. Or two months. A whole year. I'd find a job there if I had to.

The office was empty when I went in. The ashtrays were clean, and the magazines on the rack. Dr. Burton would soon return. I tried to read but I couldn't. I thought of Oliver and of falling with him that day when the leaf house was rustling its last.

Dr. Burton came in. I sat opposite him in the small office I knew so well from past visits there. Narrow. Neat. An efficient place. He had saved my life.

"Have you talked to your parents, Mary?"

"They'd let me bring him there if you agreed."

"If I had thought it would help, I'd have sent him years ago."

I looked out the window and saw the steeple of St. Paul's against the winter sky.

"He has a brain tumor, Mary. All the test reports and x-rays are already at the university hospital. I've talked to the surgeons and they can do nothing."

"I fell with him once, doctor. Long ago when he was a baby."

"It's not from that, Mary. It's a malignancy he has. Those growths he has on his chest and his leg—they're the same kind and he had them at birth. I wish I could say I can help. I have children of my own."

227

"But he can't see anything, Dr. Burton."

"I know that, Mary. He's going blind. He's never had vision in the one eye."

I looked at the steeple, that symbol of Christian hope everlasting. A promise. "When he's older, couldn't he be cured?"

"Perhaps."

I sat a long time. Dr. Burton was silent too. I couldn't look at him.

"He's loved in your family, Mary. Let's let him be as he is."

I left. I stopped at Kresge's and bought a red visor cap for Oliver and, in the raw afternoon wind, I walked down the Woodland streets to Hadley and to the high school.

That evening when I gave Oliver his cap, he was delighted. He wore it every day and at bedtime he had to have the cap on his head. Later, when I checked to see if he was covered, I saw the visor pointing to the ceiling.

On Saturday morning, I got up early so I could be alone with Mother and tell her I had gone to see Dr. Burton. I asked her if she knew that Oliver had a brain tumor. She and Father did. They would have told us, but the doctor had thought we might shield Oliver too much and not let him go about freely. He had to learn to take care of himself and learn to be useful so he'd feel needed. Maybe someday there'd be a cure and we could take him to the university hospital.

"Should I tell Edward and Elizabeth?"

"If you want to, but our knowing doesn't change him, Mary. He's still the same little boy and we love him."

So I didn't tell them. They'd find out soon enough. But I wanted to talk to Father, and later in the day when he had to take a load of potatoes to the Woodland Hotel, I rode along. We had little to sell. After the bins in our cellar had been filled, there were only a few dozen bushels left over. The yield had been cut down to a tenth of what it might have been if the flooding and the drought hadn't ruined the Northfield. "So it goes," said Father as we drove into the late afternoon.

Father was more talkative than he had been in a long time. He too had wanted to take Oliver to Madison, but when the final diagnosis came back, he gave up on the idea. Yet, there was hope, because doctors made new discoveries every day. "He's such a bright little boy, Mary. It's hard to believe, isn't it?"

"I can't get used to it."

"Well, whatever happens at home, I want you to go to the university. If you go, Elizabeth will and then Edward. When I was a young man in Freeport, I took some night school courses in English and history. Every evening when I came back to my boardinghouse, I got all dressed up in my good suit, and as I walked off, books under my arm and my hat at an angle, I felt like a million dollars. I don't want any of you to miss that experience."

"I don't even know what I want to study."

"Well, I don't know if it matters much, Mary. You always learn something."

We delivered the potatoes and stopped for coffee. As we sat in the booth, our coffee steaming before us and the snow falling outside, he told me about his new job as a translator for the county agent. They'd go around taking soil samples, telling immigrants how to use their farms to best advantage, to cull their woodlots, lime their fields and grow alfalfa, which put nitrogen back into the soil. Though he had already been using some of the techniques, he was learning a few he hadn't thought about before.

Always something new. How else could he make a living? There wasn't enough building going on. He had one or two surveying jobs every six months. What could he do? Scramble about. "I'll try anything once," he'd say.

We went to the A & P. I looked for the staples and Father for his specials. He couldn't find any there so he went out and came back with the best sausages and the biggest oranges in town. When we got home, Mother said, "Sending you to shop, John, is like sending Oliver to a candy store."

Mother was always saving the egg money; Father was always spending the milk money. It was the weekly argument and the Saturday joke, as certain as the sauna and Mr. Wiita, Mr. Ojala and Eino.

The long days tired Elizabeth as they had tired me the first years at Hadley. But she didn't recover on weekends, and sometimes she stayed home for several days so she could sleep late in the mornings. Though she'd return to school, each time she seemed less able to keep up with me. One day we missed the bus and had to walk back. Her fever rose quickly; her joints swelled. By the time Dr. Burton arrived that evening, she was very ill. She had rheumatic fever.

She lay in bed for weeks. She was totally dependent on Mother, who had more work than ever when we were in school. Yet when I came home, Elizabeth was lying in a clean bed smelling of the outdoors. Her nightgown was fresh, her hair was combed and her round face pretty. "She's getting better," Mother would say cheerfully.

Always depressed when one of us was ill, Father came home with medications and special foods by the box or bushel. Perhaps he believed that the larger his offering, the sooner we would heal. Perhaps he blamed himself for our frailty and tried to make amends. When our ailments hung on, he became silent and withdrawn.

Mother, self-assured and confident, went on with her nursing duties. When I was very young, I used to imitate her. I'd put on a blue dusting cap I had won at a raffle, a cap crocheted into huge roses and lined with taffeta, a cap so large it would have fit our horse, Maud. I wore this grand headpiece whenever anyone was ill. I fetched water, sliced oranges and apples into the smallest of pieces, and rubbed foreheads with alcohol. Once I rubbed turpentine on Carl's burning head. As sick as he was, he leaped out of bed. "She's out to kill me!" he screamed. "Get her out of here." For the duration of his illness I was deprived of nursing duty.

I asked Elizabeth if she remembered that, because I thought it would cheer her, but it didn't. "That's long ago. Now you'd be a good nurse, Mary. Maybe if I don't get well, you could take care of me."

"You'll get well, Liz. And when you're through with Hadley, you can come to the university. We could room together." I had brought her some books from the library, and some cards and notes from her classmates. But even these didn't raise her spirits.

"I can't even think that far ahead," she said. She no longer felt any discomfort, but since she had to be on bed rest, she sensed no improvement. "For all I know, I'll be in bed forever."

Her ailment was serious—far more difficult than the dramatic illnesses I had suffered. Once the crisis had passed, I could struggle for recovery, but Elizabeth had no such advantage. The best she could do was nothing, and with each day of inactivity, she grew weaker and more despondent. If she could have sat in a chair, come to the table at mealtime and studied with us in the evening, she would have felt better. But she wasn't allowed to. Inactivity was the only cure.

I told Dr. Burton that the cure was far worse than the disease. I couldn't have tolerated lying down week after week. I'd have risked my life; I'd have stood up once the fever was past; I'd have defied the order that debilitated rather than healed.

"And on you it would probably work. But I know no other cure and I have to prescribe it. She's making a good recovery."

I felt helpless because I could do nothing for her. Even my good health, my being able to go to school and to work, were an affront. All I could do was talk, see the brighter side of her situation and look ahead. "The weather has been miserable, Liz," I said. "You haven't missed much." She just looked at me. "And you have to admit you're feeling better. That's the important thing."

"How do I know I won't get sick again?"

"You can't fight battles before they come," I said. And I talked of Madison again. If she got sick, she could go to the university hospital. Maybe we could even find an apartment. The possibilities were endless. We could share clothes and books; we could cook our meals. But I might as well have talked to the wall. There was no one on earth more adamantly miserable than Elizabeth and every moment of her misery made me want to do something to help her. "I'm sure we'll be able to find you a scholarship when you get out of Hadley."

"Where?" she asked, not even wishing to hope.

"Heavens, Elizabeth! Somewhere. Anywhere. We'll manage. We can't worry about that too."

I felt her desperation but I was as powerless as she. I went into the kitchen and saw Mother at the stove, then saw everything at once—Mother, Grandmother's spinning wheel, Father's stack of pamphlets, Oliver searching blindly for his toy truck, the dust on the floor and the afternoon's dishes in the washpan and again Mother's face, rosy from the heat of the stove—and I turned and clung to Mother as I had as a child.

"She'll get well, Mary."

But I wept anyway and, remembering our losses, mourned as I

hadn't before and felt even more bereft. Calm at last, I said, "You don't need a weeping daughter just now."

As she had years before when grieving came as lightly as laughter, Mother wiped my tears on her apron. "We all need to weep sometimes."

But I knew that I had gone out to watch the last glow of the departing sun and found the lone star shining bright, the moment of grief would have passed. I began to do the dishes, cleared the table and set it for supper. I remembered that small token of my caring—the red visor cap I had bought for Oliver.

The next day, I took time off at the noon hour, walked to the florist in Woodland and bought a yellow rose and stored it in my locker. By late afternoon, the petals had wilted, but when I got home and placed the stem in water, they grew firm. "There, Liz," I said as I brought her the flower.

"Mary, how pretty it is!" For days, the life of the rose preoccupied her, but then the petals fell off and we waited again.

Soon after Thanksgiving, Elizabeth was allowed to sit up and finally to move around the house. At Christmastime, when John and Carl were home, all their friends stopped in to visit. Our house was livelier and noisier than it had been for months. Everyone simply assumed that Elizabeth was well since she was up; John and Carl were attentive to her and amused her with their stories. And without even realizing it, she became self-assured and cheerful once more.

Before John and Carl left again, they looked at my portraits and landscapes. "Even the dog has pop eyes," said John. And Carl wondered what my art teacher thought of my work.

"She thinks I have talent," I said.

"Doesn't she see very well?" asked Carl.

I said I didn't know if she could or couldn't or if she knew what talent was when she saw it. Every living thing I drew was lonely; my elongated, emaciated creatures were the lost souls of mankind; my plodding, flat-footed creatures revealed a dumb determination to go somewhere. Unfortunately, the emotion wasn't there by design; it was there because I couldn't draw any better. And I couldn't learn, though I was interested in art and wanted to know more about it before I gave up altogether.

John and Carl thought I was too frivolous about my future. Why couldn't I choose a field of study and prepare myself for it? Elizabeth and Anna wanted to be teachers; Eileen and Rachel were going to be nurses. Only I wanted to waste time.

How could studying anything be a waste of time? There was so much to learn that I'd never know enough. If I dabbled around awhile, I would discover what I liked most. Maybe I liked literature best, but how would I know if I didn't find out about other fields?

Miss Brock had given me a list of books to read so that I could pass the attainment test in English literature if I ever got to the university. She didn't think I should study art. Why not art history, which had been her minor for her doctorate? She gave me several of her own books. Every teacher I had wanted me to specialize in something dear to himself.

More and more, I withdrew into my own world of books. I did the work that had to be done at home and thought about my reading. It was endless.

As we were walking home from the bus one Friday afternoon, Elizabeth asked me if I could take some time off to fix up the house on the weekend. All of Grandmother's belongings were still in place, even the spinning wheel. "I wonder if Mother would let me have it. I'd keep it in the attic."

"And when we have an apartment, you could bring your wheel."

We gave Grandmother's bed to the Niemis, who had moved into Arthur's place soon after Grandmother died. They had children of all ages and never enough beds. In return they helped us bring the oleander tree to St. Paul's. After we had rearranged all the furniture, Father came home. "Where did Grandmother's spinning wheel go?" he asked, as soon as he walked in.

I realized at once how thoughtless we had been. We ought to have waited until he could be with us, but we hadn't. We had gone ahead as if Grandmother meant nothing to him, though he had loved her as much as we. To him she had been a faithful mother. Then he noticed that the oleander tree was gone too. And the bed. "Well, I suppose it had to be done," he said, and went outside.

The snow was melting from the hills and hillocks; Revier Road was bare again, like a fresh cut through the mottled land, all its promise dormant still. It was a Friday evening; Elizabeth and Edward had taken the car to pick up Eino and then visit the Niemis.

Oliver was asleep on his cot and Big Hank upstairs dreaming his anarchist dreams. Mother, Father and I sat together for a cup of tea, I at one side of the table, the two of them at the other. They had both aged in the last year; Mother's hair was turning gray; Father's beard had already turned silvery. He had his hands on the table, his right hand in his left as if he were sheltering it.

They were telling me stories about us as children—stories I had heard many times. How John had said he wanted to be a minister; how mischievous Carl had been. And how when Father bought his first car, only I had dared to ride with him. We had gone around and around the field until Matt Kaari had come running across the field to pull the brake. I saw his eyes grow moist, and like a child, he wiped them with the back of his hand.

And Elizabeth had always said she was Father's girl and would never go to anyone else, not even to Mother, when Father was in the house. But Edward had gone to anyone. He had been the littlest and the happiest; he had been able to stand under a chair, he was so small. Then when Father had given me a sack of nails, I had hammered every nail into the stairs and they were there still. As I listened to them, I realized they were talking to each other more than to me. They sat together as they had in their wedding photograph. They had leaned forward to look into a future they could not know; now they were looking back at what it had been, with us there sharing it. I got up to put on my coat. "I'll be back soon," I told them. They went on talking.

The Montfer had risen and then fallen just below the banks. The air was cold and the wet ground had frozen on the surface and crackled underneath my feet. I heard the wild geese over my head. Perhaps they could see where they were going on their northward path, for the half moon was high and the stars out. I walked to the mailbox, saw the shadows of the Salmi place and, beyond, the lights from the Larsons'. I heard a train hooting far back behind the trees and I ran across the tracks as I had a hundred times before to watch the cars rattle over our road. I saw the dim light from Aksu's cabin; the yellow glow flickered through the trees.

Soon I would leave; I would make my home wherever I went. Not here, though I loved every rock and hill and fencebound field. And when I returned, I would no longer belong to this land; I would be a guest. That's how it would have to be, unless I wanted to be bound to this place forever.

Spring came to Hadley at last and with it, the purple, white and lavender lilacs. They were everywhere, and had they not been, Hadley High School would not have had a graduation ceremony, or at least not one as grand, for the lilac was the school flower and was as necessary to the rites as we were. No one could escape, just as no one could escape becoming an adult if one's parents were Lutheran. One became an adult, and four years later one was blessed again. Graduation was an even holier ceremony, however, for the seniors had to be blessed by three holy men—a Lutheran minister, a Catholic priest and a Jewish rabbi. We would have invited a Muslim, a Hindu and a Buddhist if there were any in town, but there weren't. Thus, if this year's ceremony was to be better than last year's, the students had to settle for secular trappings. They did.

Though half of the parents were on relief, and another quarter wished that they were, the young thought only about the glory of graduating in the proper style. They wanted class rings, engraved invitations, a dinner and a formal dance. The girls wanted a tea; they wanted two formal gowns—one for the dinner and dance, and one for the evening of the final ceremony. And who could possibly graduate without a cap and gown of Hadley gray? No one, said Mr. O'Reilly. Those came early. We had to get used to wearing them.

I didn't even tell Mother and Father about the foolishness. I didn't order a ring; I didn't order the invitations. And I didn't get the formal gowns. I bought a short navy blue shirtwaist dress. That would have to do for all occasions. "You'll certainly feel odd," said Miss Hanson, senior class mentor and instigator as well.

We sang the school song; we practiced marching, we practiced walking across the stage in the assembly hall, and we practiced accepting the diploma from the hand of Mr. O'Reilly. We wasted whole weeks. Still, when the final day came, when we gathered in the evening just as the sun was setting and began marching two by two under branches of blooming lilac held by the junior class, the girls began to weep. Never again would they pass through the doors of Hadley High. They'd go out to the great world waiting for them. We walked around the building twice, then through the hallowed doors and into the assembly hall. A few of us marked for special mention filed onto the stage and seated ourselves with the holy men, who were already there and sitting on the metal folding chairs.

After the shifting and weighing of academic achievements, I was first in our class of a hundred and forty-four. Anna, my classmate at Revier, was next. "In terms of grades," Mr. O'Reilly told me. Other achievements could have been measured, but the tradition of considering only numerical grades was strong at Hadley. In the past, the arithmetical game had indeed worked to the advantage of his school. Now, for the first time in history, the game had failed. Had he known earlier, he would have advised the scholarship committee to sift once again. He had not known, however, and now the two of us from Revier were on top of the heap, as if Hadley High School could send nothing better into the world but two white-haired Finnish girls with accents like those of country maids. What would the people of Hadley say?

I don't know what they said or even what I said. I had practiced my speech, yelled it from one end of our nearly empty hayloft to the other, and when I finished, the drunks were gone, the girls were gone, every tavern was a workshop for the unemployed and every day the school bus came bundling down Revier Road. Now I repeated the performance on the stage of Hadley High School.

Father stood at the back of the assembly hall. He clasped his hands above his head in a signal of congratulation. The fat June bugs flew in through the windows; the lilacs sent their heady fragrance to the roof of heaven, and I, the best that Hadley High School could send out into the jobless world, sat down and heard nothing else for the rest of the evening.

As we drove home, Mother and Father said that they were proud of me. I was the smallest of all, and yet I stood on the stage as if I owned it. They could tell that I had written my own speech. It was the best, even if the taverns and the girls would stay, and even if a school bus never came down our road. That wasn't important, but that I'd said what I wanted to say was, and I'd certainly said it loudly enough. Of course, Mr. O'Reilly had forgotten to mention my scholarship. Still, I had the honor, Father said.

It was a small award—fifty-four dollars at the bursar's office at the university in Madison. If I didn't go there in September, I'd lose half; if I didn't go in January, I lost all. The honor would remain, however.

You should give the scholarship to some other student who had already made plans to go, Mr. O'Reilly urged. Since I wouldn't go, it was selfish to hold on to the fee waiver.

Why wouldn't I go? My brothers had.

I was too frail, Mr. O'Reilly said. Besides, country girls just didn't go to universities, that's all. They became maids. It was easier for them.

Then I'd be a maid with a scholarship.

Mr. O'Reilly said that I was even more stubborn than my brothers.

I agreed. I was much more stubborn. If I never left Hadley, I would still keep my scholarship.

He said that I'd never get anywhere in life.

I never saw him again. A few years later he married the county nurse who had looked down our throats every year. They had two children who didn't turn out well, people said. They were probably no worse than others might have been had they had Mr. O'Reilly for a father, to stare them down, to set them straight and to urge them to buy lilies for their young souls. To Mr. O'Reilly's dismay, they never left Hadley, but remained there as reminders that children are always ungrateful wretches.

The Monday after school was out I found a job. For three dollars a week I was to help a young mother who'd just had a baby and had two toddlers besides. There wasn't much to do other than to keep the freezing unit in the old refrigerator full of Popsicles, hold the baby, prevent the toddlers from climbing into the toilet bowl, and dust the small dingy house, scarcely less cluttered than our own. The mother talked, chain smoked, drank one cup of black coffee after another, and assured me every day that I was a good worker. What I could have done to be a bad worker I didn't know. I was prompt. I came in with Father each morning, and he picked me up at the end of his workday, five days a week for a month. Then my brief career as a nursemaid was over. The family could no longer afford to keep me.

For the first time, my brothers didn't return for the summer. They had found jobs in Madison. "The days are long and hot," Carl wrote, "but we're getting richer and wiser by the day. We may not need to borrow money this fall."

237

"I hope they're eating enough, poor dears," said Mother.

I was at home again; I washed, cleaned, cooked and read the want ads, which had nothing for me. But to make up for the lack of job offerings, the society page stretched to two, then three and finally to four pages in order to record all the weddings with gowns, veils and trains dragging behind. My classmates were there, standing as brides or bridesmaids, grooms or groomsmen. What would the couples do now? Read the two inches of want ads just as I did, go on relief, eat surplus beans and grapefruit and pray? Pray for a miracle to end what might be a pregnancy, pray for a childless marriage and for a place to live. Pray for everything.

At least I was free. All I needed was a ride to Milwaukee or Chicago, where I could find a job. But no one was going there except by train and I didn't have enough money for a ticket. Eventually someone would go by car; someone always did. I waited. Knowing that in time there would be a last day of familiar routine, I bought a suitcase at Kresge's and gathered my meager belongings.

At the end of July one of the older Niemi boys came back from his job in Milwaukee. After his week of vacation, he would be returning and I could ride with him. I could stay with his married sister until I found a job. His sister had two children and could use a little help, he said, so room and board wouldn't cost me anything. And Mother knew his sister and her husband. She was sure I would be safe with them.

Three more days. I still had to weed Grandmother's garden, blooming now even lovelier than it had the summer before. Mother came to help me. We pruned and watered the plants. "I won't be able to keep this up, Mary," she said. "I'll have so much to do."

"I wouldn't even try, Mother. You can't do everything." We kept busy at our work. Otto's rose bush was in full bloom now. Grandmother would have been delighted with it. I could cut a few blossoms and bring them to her grave, but she would not have done that. "Cut them just to have them die in the sun?" she'd have asked.

"I always hated to see the boys go," Mother said. "But you, Mary—I just never let myself even think of it."

"It's hard, Mother. But let's not cry."

"I won't, Mary. I know it would bother you." We sat down to rest in the grass near the flower beds. "We wish we could give you the money to go to the university right away."

"I couldn't take it, Mother. You have enough ahead." I sought her hand, rough and hard to the touch. "You've done so much for me."

"I don't know about that. You grew up so fast and wanted to be such a help. Sometimes I wonder if you had a childhood at all."

"I always thought I did."

"There's one thing I've wanted to say now that you're grown and leaving us. If you marry someday, go where your husband wants to go."

"I decided that long ago, Mother."

She had tears in her eyes. "I'm so glad. It didn't seem right to talk about it when Grandmother was alive."

I didn't want her to regret her decisions now. "It was the best of lives for us children."

"And for me too, Mary." We walked back toward the house, already becoming alien. I saw the drying board of the siding, the forward lean of the porch, and then the whole place becoming smaller as if it were disappearing into the distance. Soon it would be suppertime; then evening; then the Saturday of cleaning and sauna.

"You don't need to hang everything on the line," Elizabeth said the next day.

But I did. Every blanket, every bedspread and pillow. "It'll be easier for you and Mother next Saturday," I said. I washed the windows, moved the beds and scrubbed the floors.

"It's your last day, Mary," said Elizabeth, protesting. "At least we could enjoy it. I just hope no one comes to sauna, just this once." And only Toivo came, not to sauna, but to say good-bye. When he left, she sighed in relief. "Now we can enjoy the evening."

Father didn't read his newspaper; he sat in his chair, his hands together again. "You can always come back, Mary, if things don't work out," he said. He was trying to find something to say on this, our last evening together. "The home will always be here."

"I know, Father," I said. "It's been a good home too."

"Well, Mother and I tried hard."

I wanted to say something kind so he would know that I would always miss him and Mother, but that would make him sad too. "I'll never forget the Christmases, the Fourths and the Times of the Great Anger. They'll cheer me up when I get homesick," I told him.

He laughed. "Those were happy times," he said.

After he had gone to bed, Mother said, "He feels bad too, Mary. The house will be so empty." She stroked my hair. I held her hand for a while and then she too said good night. Elizabeth, Edward and I talked for a long time. Someday we'd all be together at the university and then perhaps Mother, Father and Oliver could come to see us there and we could show them everything—all the big university buildings and the state capitol.

Veikko, the Niemi boy, came early. Mother had made us a big sack of lunch and Father had filled two bushel baskets of vegetables for Veikko's sister. It was time to go. I shook hands with Big Hank, who didn't come outside. Everyone else did. "Thank you, Father," I said as I held him for a moment.

"Do you have enough money?" he asked.

"I have lots," I said. "Mother, thanks." A brief hug and a handshake. "Bye, Liz, Edward." And then, because Oliver was so sad, I gave him a kiss on the cheek, but he wiped away my kiss.

Veikko and I rode away into summer morning.

I had three dollars and I knew it wasn't enough, but I couldn't accept money from Mother and Father. Not when I was leaving them with all the work. And I would manage somehow, though it would be hard. I would have room and board, and I'd walk instead of riding the bus. That's what I thought. And I did walk, but I had to use the buses too.

At the end of the second week, in Milwaukee I had a dollar left. I had spent two dollars, wasted two weeks and worn out a pair of shoes to discover that Mr. O'Reilly had had more sense than I. Just as he had said, I was qualified for nothing but housework. Even worse, since I was from the country, I had to be a "country maid, lacking training but willing to learn." My employer, Mrs. Field, would do the teaching.

The training was largely a matter of stating the prohibitions in a way which made them appear universal to all households in which maids were employed. A maid could not use the front entrance; she could not sit in any part of the house other than the kitchen and her own room; she could not receive telephone calls nor call anyone; she could not speak to guests unless they addressed her first; she could not eat before the family had eaten, nor before the dogs had been fed and walked; she could not correct the children or the dogs. She could not use her full name—only her first, followed by "the maid."

Thus I became Mary-the-maid. I had Thursday afternoons and alternating Sunday afternoons free. Otherwise my total effort was to enhance the comfort of the Fields—Mr. and Mrs. Adam P. Field, son David, age six, daughter Diana, age two, cocker spaniel, age three, and collie, age four. I could talk to the children, the dogs, order milk, butter and eggs from the milkman, and order baked goods from the baker. I could say, "Yes, ma'am," to Mrs. Field, "Yes, sir," to Mr. Field.

I had no past after I was hired; I had no home; I had no family of my own. I was reborn. Henceforth there was only a future, which Mrs. Field said would be a fine one after she was done with her training. If I had problems, I was to speak to her. If I had questions, I was to ask her in the morning before she became involved in her day's many important projects. They, the Fields, were now my family. As a member of it, I had room, board, a blue uniform for morning wear and a white uniform for afternoon wear, and ten dollars a week allowance. In return, I was to keep the fourteen-room house clean, cook the meals, wash and iron the clothes, polish the silver, watch the children and walk the dogs.

My workday began at seven in the morning and ended at nine in the evening. Days blended into each other, weeks into other weeks. The world I could see from the window stopped at the fence with the row of honeysuckle. Beyond was the blind wall of another house, the tops of trees and a patch of road.

Sometimes I saw the purple hills of home, the gray house and barn, the echoing wall of trees behind them, and the meadows following one another for a mile into the distant woodland; heard the sounds of the river, the ax and the saw; smelled the drying, frost-bitten land and the opened ground. The vision came so suddenly, so unbidden into that snug and proper house that for a moment I was back where I began.

Was I lonely? Homesick? Sad? Was the work load too heavy?

I didn't ask myself. I waited for Thursday mornings, when Mrs. Field called me to the den and gave me my ten-dollar bill, which I carried upstairs into my room and placed in an envelope with the other ten-dollar bills I'd saved. After lunch, I changed into my own clothes, walked to the streetcar stop, rode in the clanging car past the little shops, the big houses, then the smaller houses and worn apartment houses, a hospital and a park, the grand apartments, and then Lake Michigan, past the railroad station and down Wisconsin Avenue.

I got off the streetcar at the stop opposite Gimbel's. I walked for blocks up the shop-lined street. Then I crossed and walked down the other side until I was back at the entrance of Gimbel's. Every Thursday, rain or sun, wind or calm, I traced my steps and gradually became Mary Morgan, free to walk with everyone else, and free to breathe the same air. Then I walked inside to study the wares on one floor after another.

When the store closed at five-thirty I crossed the street to Walgreen's Drugstore. I sat at the lunch counter and ordered a bowl of soup and two packets of saltines. I ate slowly, counted the pieces of pie and cake under the glass cover, and watched the mixer turn milk, ice cream and malt powder into foaming liquid, listened to the waiters and waitresses shouting above the noise of mixers, crashing dishes and the traffic outside. I felt as much at home there as I could anywhere.

Finally the bowl was empty and the crackers gone. I had to leave. Sometimes I let one streetcar go by and waited for the next one to take me back through the darkened town, to the quiet streets of the suburb. At the end of the line my free day was over. I got off and walked the half mile to the Fields' back door.

On my Sundays off, I never lost my maidhood. I had three hours, from three to six in the afternoon. Usually I stayed in my room, but now and then I walked to the drugstore in the shopping area where I boarded the streetcar on Thursdays. The pampered young of the neighborhood gathered there at the drugstore soda fountain. They giggled and gossiped over their Cokes and malteds, held hands and looked into each other's eyes as if they had just discovered the wonder of eyes and hands, once and forever. Perhaps they really had, for they were still too giddy to have discovered anything else. Yet they were lovely to look upon, as sleek and handsome as well-fed idle stock put out to graze.

I bought whatever small items I needed—toothpaste, envelopes, paper or stamps—and left again as Mary-the-maid.

"Who's she?" one might ask, as I'd heard them ask about other young girls who worked in the homes.

"She's the Fields' maid. I think I've seen her walking the dogs."

The curiosity about household help was always there, for we lived a separate and secret existence. What did we do on Thursdays, for instance? Where did we go? Not that it mattered really, because whatever we did, it had to be dull. Or was it?

By December I had a hundred dollars in my envelope. Not much, but enough, and if I worked another month I'd have thirty dollars more. I waited, and then when all the Salvation Army bells were ringing up and down Wisconsin Avenue, all the trees were lighted, and Christmas was everywhere, I gave notice. I'd leave on the first of January.

"You can't be serious, Mary," said Mrs. Field.

"I'm quite serious, Mrs. Field. I'm going to the university."

"You! Mary, you don't understand. One doesn't just go."

"I have already enrolled. I have a scholarship there."

Mrs. Field became angry. "You didn't tell me."

"You didn't ask me, Mrs. Field."

She told me that I was foolish, that I'd fail, that I was throwing away an opportunity to learn how to live among better people, and that if I changed my mind I could stay.

"I can't change my mind."

Within a few days I lost my maidness. Mr. Field said he'd walk the dogs because he needed the exercise. Mrs. Field thought I was too thin and ought to eat more. She hadn't realized that I ate so little, she said. Yet they were puzzled. They tried to be friendly and wanted me to believe that they felt I was an equal or would be someday perhaps, if I had the chance to live "among better people."

One day Mrs. Field introduced me to her friend, who had attended the University of Wisconsin, and told her that I was going too. How very exciting! I would certainly find it a delightful place. Mrs. Field said she had gone to Vassar, but hadn't finished because life was altogether too interesting and fascinating then. Her friend hadn't finished either. "I don't know any girls who did," her friend said. "We just went to parties and football games."

Perhaps they were telling me that I wouldn't finish either, that

243

I'd be back again, no better off than I was now. More likely, however, they thought of nothing but their own frivolous girl-hood, which had after all proved useful since they had found the boys they married.

On New Year's Day I packed my bag, and Mrs. Field called a cab. I put on my coat and waited in the vestibule. Mrs. Field sat in the den a few feet away. When the cab drove up, she came out. "The cab is here, Mary."

"I saw it," I said.

She stood at the door and out of habit ran her finger along the frame of the hall mirror. Had I dusted it? I couldn't remember.

"You will write to us, won't you?" she said, offering her small, slender hand, as soft as a child's.

"I can't promise, Mrs. Field."

I went out into the cold clear day and we drove off. Christmas had left behind its lights and tinsel to sparkle and glitter in the New Year streets, deserted now as if everyone were asleep. We drove past the silent houses and the lake, as smooth as Mrs. Field's hall mirror frozen into its frame.

There it was—the red train station with its clock tower. I paid my fare and picked up my suitcase. "Happy New Year," I said to the cabby, but he was driving away from the curb and didn't hear me. I walked into the station—a palace of marble floors and stair-cases, of bookstands and newsstands, flower stalls, restaurants and cafés. Outside, the train was waiting. I bought my ticket and climbed on.

And then as I rode through the snow-covered fields, I thought of Revier as I had left it and as it would always be, the Montfer glistening in the sun, the yellow grain bending in the morning breeze, and the leaf house growing green in the woodlot. In this static place, the people I had known since childhood move about like marionettes in an endless show. Mrs. Salmi reads her Bible. The Watkins' man, one eye blue and the other brown, recites his wares—lemon pudding, vanilla pudding, chocolate pudding, white pepper, black pepper, cinnamon, nutmeg, allspice, liniment, oil of peppermint, carbolic salve, camphor salve, and extracts of all kinds. Mother always buys one item, whether she needs it or not.

Every evening the old men come to sit, to drink their coffee and to tell their tales. And the young men come to work for a week, stay another, ask Father for the key and he tells them to bring it back by midnight. The children come and go and leave behind half-emptied cups and a trail of crumbs.

Even now, though the houses and barns are gone, the fields lost to the forest, and the seasons speak only to themselves, the bonds stretch and hold me, and the shadow figures call as if they were alive.